DEAD MEN DO TELL TALES

A 1933 Archeological Expedition
into Abyssinia

by Byron de Prorok

With biographical notes
by Michael Tarabulski

THE NARRATIVE PRESS
HISTORICAL ADVENTURE AND EXPLORATION

Dedicated to Father A. Delattre of the White Fathers of Carthage, Professor Francis W. Kelsey of the University of Michigan, Edward Stoever of Princeton University, Prince E. de Waldeck, Professor Henry Washington of the Carnegie institute, Major F. Shorey of McGill University, Professor G. Guidi of the Tripolitan Museum, Professor Stephan Gesell of the French Academy, C. Chapuis of the French Foreign Legion, and my other Arab and Ethiopian companions of the long Desert Trails who are no more.

BYRON DE PROROK, F.R.G.S.

The Narrative Press
P.O. Box 2487, Santa Barbara, California 93120 U.S.A.
Telephone: (800) 315-9005 Web: www.narrativepress.com

ISBN 1-58976-245-2 (Paperback)

Produced in the United States of America

TABLE OF CONTENTS

Editor's Introduction. 1
Foreword. 3
1 A Dream Begins. 6
2 First Days in the Field 14
3 The Mummies. 24
4 The Singing Sands 31
5 We Visit Fayum 38
6 The Mystery Man of Ethiopia 45
7 The Hippo Feast 58
8 The Bili Cult. 67
9 Along the River of Gold. 76
10 The Mad Sultan 84
11 Wild Bees and Bush Fires 97
12 Plagues and Pests 109
13 Dajjazmac Mariam Gives Us a Dinner. 119
14 A Nice Assortment of Horrors 125
15 An Audience with Haile Selassie 135
16 Slaves En Route to the Red Sea 141
17 The Man in the Iron Cage. 146
18 Rendezvous in the Desert. 158
19 The Caravan of the Living Dead 165
20 The Young Pretender of Ethiopia. 174
21 A Society Wedding in Tajurrah 189
22 Last Stories from the Tombs 199
Afterward 215

EDITOR'S INTRODUCTION

Dead Men Do Tell Tales, originally published in 1942, is de Prorok's fourth and final book. In its first chapter, Byron reveals more about his past than he has in his first three books. His poignant description of life at boarding school hints at what George Orwell would develop so masterfully in his 1947 piece "Such, Such Were the Joys." There is poignancy, too, and a seeming awareness of greater things in his later description of victims of genital mutilation and slavery whom he encounters in Ethiopia. He also touches on wider political matters; the war brewing in Ethiopia in 1934 had broadened to include much more of the world by 1942.

Alas, as with his own story, Byron steps up to the edge of something profound, contemplates the abyss and – and then dashes off to report something sensational, salacious, or merely inconsequential. He leaves us with many unanswered questions. Like the pussy cat in the nursery rhyme, he visits royalty (in this case Haile Selassie) and reports only on the mouse beneath the throne. Lurid descriptions of the sex lives of mice, or "savages," or the eating habits of cats, or Ethiopians, make for fascinating reading but do little to help us understand what was happening in this part of the world at this time.

Not that professional archeologists expected much from Byron. An editorial note in the early pages of the March 1934 issue of *Antiquity* had this to say about his Ethiopian expedition plans, lumping them with similar pseudoscientific exploits to give...

...readers and the general public some idea of the difficulties encountered by the professional archaeologist and others concerned with the advancement and diffusion of real knowledge. These difficulties are not minimized by the laws

of libel which operate in favor of the crank, the charlatan and the common swindler.

[In] the sands of the Libyan desert and 'the unexplored Upper Nile and Abyssinia.' Here or hereabouts 'one of the largest scientific expeditions of recent years led by Count de Prorok' hopes to find 'the body of Alexander the Great and King Solomon's mines.' Later on such minor items as the 'Royal Tombs in the Mountain of the Dead,' the 'lost oasis of Zerzera' (sic) and the 'famous emerald mines of Cleopatra' will be roped in. 'Lost African civilization will also be sought, linking up the theory that the North Africans and the Mayans of America both originated from the lost continent of Atlantis.' But it is always as well to have a second string to even the best linked theory, and further we are told that 'Prorok expects to find another Atlantean migration in this research' in Abyssinia.

The account from which we quote, published in The Egyptian Gazette ('about 14 December 1933'), concludes by stating that 'the expedition is being undertaken under the auspices of the International Anthropological Institutes of the British, French, Italian, Egyptian and Ethiopian Governments:' and that 'in addition to Count Byron de Prorok, F.R.G.S, the party includes certain persons named The expression 'International Anthropological Institutes' has no meaning; but if it is meant to include (as it obviously is) the Royal Anthropological Institute of Great Britain and Ireland, we are informed that the statement is incorrect. We also understand that Count de Prorok is not a fellow of the Royal Geographical Society.

That notwithstanding, *Dead Men Do Tell Tales* was well reviewed by the popular press, in 1942, and several times reprinted. It was the most widely and easily available of Byron's books before the Narrative Press undertook to reprint them all.

Michael Tarabulski
Moscow, Idaho
July, 2003

FOREWORD

"NO MORE WORLDS TO CONQUER!" That has been the disconsolate cry ever since the covered wagon vanished from the plains of Western America and the din of cannonading faded after the First World War. From Pole to Pole and wherever the path of the Equator led adventurous Man, the earth suddenly became laced with modern inventions particularly appertaining to communication and transportation, and there seemed to be no undiscovered or unpeopled lands remaining. Frontiers in the Western Hemisphere became a myth, and new territory nonexistent. Man had so circumscribed the globe, including the much-heralded Seven Seas, that the universal cry of "Nothing new under the sun," passed unchallenged.

But it was all a mistake. Thoughtful people know today that no continent is ever conquered. The old idea that "might is right" has come back to roost among us, whether Civilization likes it or not. Any area of land or water on the globe may be conquered anew when and if an abler and stronger group than the one hitherto enjoying possession happens along. So there have always been new worlds to conquer, and there always will be.

It was so with many parts of East Africa: notably the Somalilands, South Sudan, Ethiopia, and the lands bordering on the Red Sea. For thousands of years Time had stood still in these strange lands, unaffected by Man's progress in the fields of mechanical and scientific discovery, communication and transportation, invention, and the development of medical and surgical care. Even in remote and mysterious Tibet the influence of civilization, although resisted with fanatical vigor, was more definitely felt.

Then came a turn of events. Explorers penetrated to the uttermost recesses of Ethiopia, Somaliland, and the South Sudan, and in the course of their high adventures disclosed the fact that the natural resources of these countries were extensive and were going to waste in what may have been rightly described as the most backward and forbidding land in the world – this, despite the valiant efforts of a few enlightened rulers who, acquiring educations in Europe, returned to save their people and found they could save themselves only with the greatest of difficulty.

Byron de Prorok writes of all that in this volume, lifting the curtain on a tragic scene which at once conveys invaluable lessons to the outside world – lessons which we greatly need, for among the many things that this World War, in which we are now engaged with all our heart and strength, proves, is the indisputable fact that we have not managed our affairs with more faith and probity than did Haile Selassie, the now restored Emperor of Ethiopia. It is well to reflect upon his character as a man and ruler.

A word on the name of the country referred to: Byron de Prorok follows customary usage in employing the names Ethiopia and Abyssinia interchangeably in his book, as I have done in these prefatory remarks. Either name is correct.

No man turns out to be an important adventurer or explorer who is not born with a passion in his heart and a determination in his soul to dig back into the past to find out, regardless of possible rewards, where we begin, whither we are drifting, and what is best to do about it. I know Byron de Prorok's ability in his designated field and his understanding. His heart is in his work. He is constantly sacrificing pleasure and comfort to contribute substantially to exploration and archeology. My acquaintance with him and my familiarity with his work and achievements are of no brief tenure. So deeply rooted is his passion for solving riddles of the past, through archeological research, scientific study, and the faithful recording of his experience, that I often wonder how he can keep to his task. He is youthful, as we reckon today the sands that pass through the glass, and yet he turns away from the comforts of life in modern cities, to hammer, blast, dig, and perspire in some out-of-the-way place which can offer not the slightest attraction to the average man. His traveling is not deluxe.

This intrepid adventurer, scientist, and archeologist reports the facts, and the world is interested in what he reveals. For twenty-one years Byron de Prorok, recognized archeologist and author of several valuable books on the subject of his labors and discoveries, has visited remote parts of the world to which the finger of History seems to point. He has been digging up art treasures and relics of ancient civilizations, and has written new versions of old theories that have attempted to bridge over the centuries between the world that was and the world that is. His achievements amount to a distinct contribution to the history of the world as it is today, and credit will be accorded on that basis.

Attached to the expeditions which de Prorok has led, have been many eminent mineralogists, geologists, and ethnologists, whose findings have augmented the general value of the reports and publications of the explorer and leader. The author of Dead Men Do Tell Tales does not believe that a story of sheer adventure is all that the reading public expects, once an expedition has finished a given task. He very properly takes the view that it is important to the world to know whether new riches, in the form of natural resources, previously undiscovered, will henceforth add to the world's store of wealth. Politics and economics thus take their place alongside hieroglyphics in a well-balanced volume, which those who keep abreast of the times will read with interest and profit.

RAYMOND C. SCHINDLER
The Adventurers' Club
New York City

CHAPTER 1

A DREAM BEGINS

While we were digging with pick and shovel on the sites of ancient Carthage and of Utica, in the Valley of the Nile, at the oasis of Jupiter Ammon in Libya, and among the vast remains of buried cities in Yucatan and the Sahara, my dream of an expedition into Abyssinia formed and grew.

I collected ancient maps of the caravan trails leading through the Sahara and Egypt to King Solomon's Mines, and from the Blue Nile to the Red Sea. There were few facts and many legends and tales of the one great country left in Africa, not yet under the control of Europeans. Abyssinia had never in the four thousand years of her history been conquered; nor, in spite of the recent Italian occupation, has she been now.

As every newspaper reader now knows, Haile Selassie has the longest genealogy in the world. Before the time of Christ, the Queen of Sheba bore King Solomon a son. The Negus is the direct descendant of that heir, and Emperor of a country which has been free and independent since the beginning of time. Abyssinia's civilization is one of the oldest in the world; 10 per cent of her population is concerned directly or indirectly with the Church – the Coptic form of Christianity.

I heard fantastic tales of wealth in ivory, in gold, in jewels, and in vast undeveloped oil fields. Oil was said to seep from the ground in so pure a state that it could be burned in lamps without being refined. There were stories of dangers from savage tribes and jungle animals, rumors of cannibals. The more I learned, the greater the lure and the hope of exploring this great land.

The beginning of that dream of exploration came through my finding a penny. Realizing that dream brought suffering, loneliness, and racking hunger. Never a clear pattern, it evolved in a tortuous chain of starts and jolting stops, of hope and despair, of tragedy and laughter, of academic encouragement and financial crashes. It meant nights without sleep, sometimes because of work that had to be finished, or done secretly, sometimes because it was too dry or too wet, too hot or too cold, or because of aching hunger and, occasionally, danger. A large part of it was labor, digging with a pick and shovel.

In 1909, when I was eleven, my English grandmother decided that French life was decadent. Though I was living happily at home and going to an excellent Jesuit day school in Paris, she made up her mind that I ought to have an English education. She was a determined woman who refused to learn Polish when she lived in Poland, Hungarian when she lived in Hungary, and French when she lived in France. English was the language *she* knew; therefore, everyone ought to speak her language. With her, determination meant action, and action meant a one-way road – whichever way she was going. She was a matriarch who permitted no noes; my parents were not even allowed a protest.

I was still eleven when I was enrolled in an English school, Pretoria House, near Folkestone. That was the first time I was transplanted from the country and family I knew and loved. From the charm and colorful gayety of a Parisian home, I was sentenced to a harsh, drab environment, for me not unlike a prison.

Lecturing recently in a boys' school near New York, I felt sorry for an Italian lad there. I, too, had been a foreigner in my first English school, though I was partly English; and I remembered the hazing and punishment I had to take from students and teachers.

Pretoria House was a school for young gentlemen, a prison where on weekdays one wore ugly gray uniforms, too tight around the neck, with Eton collars and top hats on Sundays. You had sixpence a week for spending money, but you had to put half of it in the collection plate on the Sabbath. The food was nourishing but without variety, porridge and milk, hot or cold joints, creamed vegetables that looked like library paste, and tasted worse. Small for my age, and the newest foreigner in the school, I had to fight time after time. A broken nose was no sooner healed than I had three ribs smashed. I hated the place.

Actually I was too young and too small to box, but Sergeant O'Keefe came to the school one day each week to teach the older boys the manly art of self-defense. He was a warm-hearted Irishman with a quick temper, and he was stationed at a military post near us. I asked the Sergeant to teach me how to fight; he put in a word for me with the masters, and laughingly they agreed to let me try to work with him. I came just above his waist. He called me "Bantam 'Arf Pint,'" but he forgot my size once when I jumped and struck him on the nose. He lost his temper, struck back, and knocked me out. Since my turn to box came last in the afternoon and we boxed in the cellar of one of the houses, no one ever knew about that blow. I learned to avoid hitting the Sergeant on the nose; every time I did he lost his temper, but he did harden me and make me tough.

My admiration for boxing and for O'Keefe grew; and on my first holiday in London I found a book, the first volume I ever bought for myself, *The Life of James L. Jeffries*. Jeffries was the world champion, or had been, and attributed his success to the crouched position from which he fought. This method was unorthodox and un-English, the Sergeant told me, but he did not discourage my using it when I had to fight a larger boy after hours and out of bounds. He still called me "Bantam 'Arf Pint,'" but I knew he was proud of the way I'd learned to fight and win.

Success made me leader of a small group of boys, perhaps it made me a little cocky. We organized a strike – a hunger strike against the tiresome sameness of the food. For that, I was reprimanded and given a whipping in front of the other students. I tried to start a revolt against putting half of each week's sixpence allowance into the chapel collection. Again I was caned.

We were sent off in pairs or foursomes to take long walks in the country. I rebelled at that, and persuaded the head master to let me and another boy explore the Roman ruins of Caesar's Camp, not far from school. There I found "The Penny." It wasn't an American cent or an English penny, but an old bronze, Roman coin. From that time on, four of us excavated those old ruins in all our exercise periods.

Then Sir Ernest Shackleton came to the school to give a talk. Someone told him of my finding that Roman coin and of our working with picks and shovels in the ruins. That led to my meeting him before his lecture. He told me of the difficulties he was having to raise funds for his voyage and expedition in search of the South Pole.

I offered to try to raise the money for one sled and team of dogs; then I asked him how much it would cost. "Seventy pounds," he answered – three hundred and fifty dollars. That was discouraging, but I had offered; and I had learned to fight and win. It couldn't be done on the threepence we had left over after our weekly chapel "offering." I knew my family wouldn't give me that much: I'd have to get permission, and write to the boys' parents – and my handwriting was bad, my composition worse. With ninety boys in the school, a letter would have to go to each parent asking for a pound. I'd have to tell them what for and why. With the help of the English teacher and nearly a pound, I managed to write the letters and pay for the stationery and the postage.

I waited for two days. Between classes I would run to the letter boxes to see if there were any mail for me. The third day the answers began to dribble in, but not all of them contained checks. Some of the people wanted more details about Shackleton and his expedition, which meant more letter writing and more postage. At the end of five weeks sixty pounds had come in; I wrote my grandmother and asked her for the other ten. She had been one of the first to send me a pound; so I told her all about it. I wanted to get the full amount off to Sir Ernest Shackleton, and could I please borrow fifty dollars. She sent me the money, but added that it represented two things – her birthday present in advance, and my holiday trip to France to visit my mother and father. Gratuitously she added that it was fine for me to learn the priceless value of self-sacrifice – of doing without so that I could give to others.

One of the possessions of which I am proudest is a piece of that sled which Shackleton sent me afterwards; it is wood from the dog-sled that got farthest south, nearest the South Pole, in his unsuccessful quest. I always kept it in my room at school and college, and took it with me as a mascot on the expeditions which I later organized. It was left behind for the first time in France in 1939 when I was ill, and I can only hope that it has not been burned for firewood, smashed by bombs, or maliciously destroyed in the months that have passed.

Once the money was sent to Shackleton, I had too much time and a strong urge to do something. This led to further trouble. Our increased interest in geography and in the news of the expedition was not enough. Two of us ran away to see the Davis Cup tennis matches; one of the teachers who was there, too, caught us and took us back to school. Again I was caned.

Beyond a high wall at one end of the school grounds was a girls' school. With stones tied to letters, and with sling shots, some of us managed to write and hear from the girls in the adjoining grounds. After this had been going on for some time, I suggested tunneling under the wall. We swore a group of boys to strictest secrecy, and set to work. Day after day we scratched and dug. If a teacher came near where we were digging, one of the boys would start asking questions, or lead him in the other direction, or manage to warn us. That was fine so far as Pretoria House went, but when a hole appeared in the yard next door, we were caught.

The girls' head mistress came to see our head master. Together they searched my box while I was in class; all the letters I had received from a girl in the school next door were there. I was called from class to the head master's office. There I was offered no choice; my previous offenses had been too many. I was not suspended for thirty or sixty days. "For the good of the school," I departed abruptly from Pretoria House, "By Request."

On my way up to London I worried a little over what my grandmother might say and do, but dismissed it with the thought that she was going to visit my parents in the south of France, and that probably I could persuade her to take me along. I hated the school anyway, except for tennis and boxing and Sergeant O'Keefe.

But my grandmother was surprisingly unamenable. She sent me to my room without supper that night, and the next morning began hearing my lessons herself. She couldn't tell about my French since she had refused to learn the language; she passed over my geography without comment, but my arithmetic, reading, grammar, and writing were awful. She told me that with uncompromising truthfulness, elaboration, and at length. I was sent to my room to study, and was told not to leave the house. This was certainly not the right time to suggest going with her to the Riviera.

What the head master at Pretoria House wrote her, I never knew; she made no attempt to get me reinstated, but she lost no time in looking for another school. When I thought she was in a soft and forgiving mood, I suggested going with her to France, but she sniffed and humphed so vociferously that it seemed better not to pursue the matter. She worked with me on my lessons three hours in the morning and two in the afternoon, and study or not, I had to stay in my room except for an hour's walk each day.

Within two weeks she had me in another school, a worse prison than the last one. This was no school for young aristocrats; it was for the sons of working men who had decided on careers for their boys. The discipline was severe; there may have been some boys there who were rated as incorrigible. The rising bell rang at six-thirty every morning, and "lights out" rang at seven-thirty in the evening. To be caught moving or even whispering after that hour meant a caning. The food was terrible; breakfast consisted of stale bread and lukewarm porridge covered with blue milk.

Again, the so-called gymnasium was in the cellar, but there was an athletic field and track outside, and tennis courts. My ability to fight won me friends quickly, and my hours were full of sports, geography, and classes. I never did learn to play cricket well, but running, rugby, swimming, and tennis came easily. We didn't learn very much at that school, but we did build strong and healthy bodies, in spite of the bad food.

Every letter from my grandmother complained of my laziness, and urged me to study. She was not satisfied with the low marks I earned in a school where work was easy, but she insisted on my remaining there for three years until the head master assured her that I was not the incorrigible she had believed.

Then came Margate and, later, Laleham College, still secondary schools; in both of them my marks were low, and my athletic progress excellent. I got into trouble regularly, but because of my running and swimming I missed being suspended. Finally, Grandmother agreed to send me to Switzerland to a school of high academic rating – its graduates were accredited to Oxford without entrance examinations. That interest, which had been born with my finding a penny and had led me to raise the money for a sled and dogs for Shackleton's expedition, was still my first. I never even considered any other life or profession than that of an explorer. I heard that Professor Edouard Naville, who was an outstanding Egyptologist and archeologist of the time, was teaching at the University of Geneva.

To get into that university to work with him gave me my first real urge to study. The Château de Lancy graduated its boys for the universities, but like many schools it had a small number who would not or could not study. In the school were sons of men of title, boys with titles of their own, men from all over the world. There was an Egyptian Prince, the son of a Sultan, and a young English Lord, but whether these were of the group who did or did not study, I don't remember. I only know that I did; for the first time in my life my marks were high.

On a visit to England I said that I should like to stay on in Switzerland, and go to the University of Geneva. "Oxford!" my grandmother said sternly, as if there were no other place; but she was getting older and less fiery than she had been. My mother didn't approve either, but she cooperated; and when the time came, I entered Geneva to study archeology and Egyptology under Professor Naville.

Those were happy years of studying under an inspired teacher; then the first World War came. For a time things went on as before, then they began to change, and finally our courses were interrupted. The University became a bureau of exchange for prisoners of war; and those students of varied nationalities who were still there, acted as clerks and correspondents. Before the end of the war, due to ill health I apprenticed myself to an archeologist whom Professor Naville recommended, the great Professor Giacomo Boni in Rome. My first real work began with excavations in the Palatine Hill there under Professor Boni's direction. In the Forum and in Pompeii we worked, with pick and shovel and our hands. While we were excavating in Rome, searching for historical pieces, an old Roman drain caved in carrying the street with it. Fortunately, no one was killed, but from then on we had to have a permit to dig, and had to have our excavations shored up and approved by engineers before we could proceed.

It was while I was working in Rome that I met one of the White Fathers at the Vatican; he told me about the buried ruins of the cursed city, Carthage. I met him several times, and each time that I talked to him my interest grew. I wrote my family that I wanted to go there, but they opposed the idea. I wrote again: the answer was a very positive *no*. But I had to go; something within me compelled it. I could not sleep, or work, or eat. There was something in Carthage that drew me. Though I was not of age, I decided to risk parental discipline and go. In reply to that, my family wrote to say they were stopping my small allowance. That letter found me working in Carthage.

CHAPTER 2

FIRST DAYS IN THE FIELD

Carthage was not as I had seen it in my dreams; it was lonely, dirty, and depressing. First I had studied with Professor Naville who had the University behind him. Professor Boni had the support of several societies and the Italian Government – both of them surrounded archeology with glamour. Professor Renault, though he was a noted archeologist, had no financial backing whatsoever. For years he had worked in the most abject poverty, often entirely alone. His belief in the importance and value of buried Carthage, and his fanatical love for history drove him on.

There was no glamour there. I had always lived in comfort; Professor Renault's home, which he let me share with him, was actually an old Roman cistern. It was cold and damp, and in addition there were snakes and rats, scorpions and bats, inside and out. There were not even primitive conveniences; we ate sketchy meals and slept on hard cots. The place was isolated and desolate; not speaking Arabic, there was no one with whom I could talk except the professor and, occasionally, one of the White Fathers.

Money had never interested me – probably because there had always been enough. Now pipe tobacco and food were all that I could buy. There was no place to go, and nothing to do but work in Carthage. For a time my pride was too great to let me tell the Professor that my allowance had been stopped; it was too great, too, to let me tell my mother of my disappointment. When I wrote to her, I told her of our work, and nothing of how we were living.

We worked from daylight until the heat became insufferable, then we slept or rested for two hours and returned to labor till it grew too dark to see. Day after day in the broiling sun we dug with pickaxes and shovels, and carted the dirt away with wheelbarrows. Wind and storms and sun had pounded the earth so hard that every shovelful had to be loosened with a pickaxe. We had started digging on a mound which, the Professor's calculations indicated, might cover an important ruin. Each day we moved a ton or a ton and a half of earth, and uncovered – more hard-packed debris.

In spite of his years, Professor Renault worked as hard as Ali, Hassan, and I did. Only when it grew too dark did we stop for supper; then, frequently, the Professor would talk for an hour, and to those hours I owe a great deal. At last one night I told him that my family had cut off my allowance. He only shrugged, but after a few minutes he suggested that we try living on the Arab diet. Rugged, hardy, and extremely frugal, the Arabs have great endurance. We found that we needed twice their daily ration of tea, black bread, and dates; and we added goat's milk when we could get it.

Usually, when we visited the White Fathers, we copied their parchment maps of Carthage, but one night we studied maps of Utica, the Libyan Desert, and the caravan trails that led south to the British Sudan and then east to the Blue Nile, across Abyssinia and Eritrea to the Red Sea. Those caravan trails were at least four thousand years old; and they still offered an explorer more promise than any other place I knew.

Using the names Ethiopia and Abyssinia interchangeably, one of the White Fathers outlined its history briefly from King Solomon's time to the present. It is once more the oldest independent kingdom in the world, and the only nation in Africa which has kept its own individuality. Its borders have been little changed in four thousand years; and it has practiced the Coptic form of Christianity for eighteen hundred years.

Dimly I heard the White Father speak of Carthage's ghostly, ghastly past. When he changed the subject to our present surroundings, my mind kept on with thoughts of the Queen of Sheba and the great wealth of Ethiopia's resources and history. "Carthage," I heard him say, "was founded as a colony by business-minded Phoenicians in 850 BC in an attempt to corner Mediterranean trade and markets. Five hundred years later that colony had become so rich and powerful that it roused envy and fear in Rome."

Every schoolboy knows that this started the Punic Wars. With the fall of Hannibal, Carthage was destroyed. Palaces, great temples, and magnificent gardens were desolated foot by foot and stone by stone till there was nothing left except debris. And on that site the Romans placed a curse.

It seems fantastic that this barren desolation covering a buried city had to do with heroic Hannibal, Hamilcar, Salammbô, St. Louis, and St. Cyprian. Augustine and Cato had little apparent connection with our shoveling tons of earth, but our later excavations proved that they did. I looked at Professor Renault; tired and old, he had fallen asleep in the warm, dimly lighted room. One of the Fathers smiled and shook his head to keep me from waking him.

But visitors must leave at ten. Severe self-discipline of the monastery puts this as the limit. We walked back through the moonlit magic of an African night to the damp cistern which for us was home. Day followed day without a change or break; dig, shovel, and wheel – work, work, and more work – rest, dig, shovel, wheel – we became robots.

Mail came irregularly, so the delayed news of the death of my father was a shock. I had not even known that he was ill. The news of his illness and his death came at the same time, and with it letters from my mother and from lawyers. My father had not disinherited me; there was a bequest. Though I was saddened by his death, I visualized all the things that money could do for the Professor and our work: new equipment, workmen to help, easier living for both of us – perhaps even a moving picture camera for the necessary photographs.

But Professor Renault was a stoic. He insisted that we go on living almost as simply as we had; workmen – yes, two to speed things – and expensive motion pictures might help to interest people in ancient history and our excavations. He would take nothing for himself, but there was a new light in his eyes and a lift in his step which had not been there before. He had never spoken of discouragement, but hope served to give him youth. With hope came fresh energy – we unearthed fragments and sections of long-buried Carthage, more important than any we had found before.

One day two Tunisian antique dealers appeared and offered to sell us some very old parchment maps of caravan trails from the Mediterranean "to King Solomon's fabulous mines," or so they claimed. The Professor glanced at them, shook his head, and went back to digging. But I could not stop studying those maps – they showed a route up the Nile to Khartoum, then eastward. King Solomon's mines are mentioned in the Bible and many times in history; their wealth and mystery has made them the inspiration for works of fiction. These maps were not duplicates of any the White Fathers owned; so I bought them and have never regretted that extravagance.

The importance of our finds in Carthage leaked out and brought visitors and newspaper men, who in turn sent more sightseers. The reporters played up my youth and the serious work I was doing with Professor Renault. That eventually led to my being given a two-year scholarship by the Archeological Institute of America, to lecture all over the United States. To the Norton Memorial Chair of Archeology, I took the first moving pictures ever made of our excavations. This led to other lectures, and helped me get contributions to further our work in Carthage – for by this time my first inheritance had been spent.

Professor Renault did not live to see his life work completed, but it was so well on its way that he was happy. What he did was so important that it attracted the attention of English, French, and American archeological societies, and of museums and individuals. This attention made possible further excavations there, and led to explorations and expeditions in Utica, Siwa, with its Temple of Jupiter Ammon, and to Cleopatra's palace on the shores of the Mediterranean where she spent the last happy hours of her life with Antony. But the various grants and contributions never provided for my exploring Abyssinia.

In *The Golden Bough* Frazer says: "We shall learn from buried cities, and from savages of the desert and jungle, the facts of the history of humanity – the ascent from savagery to civilization." That is the aim of archeology. Abyssinia with its ancient civilization, its jungles and its slaves, had been neglected.

Expeditions demand the gathering of contributions, planning, organizing, and months or even years of hard work under conditions of isolation and deprivation. Twenty museums in the world have rare historical objects which we dug out during our explorations. But Ethiopia remained untouched – a land of vivid promise and remote reality.

More than ever I wanted to trace the old caravan trails of the Sahara and across Ethiopia. They had been used by slave traders for many centuries; they were still being used secretly for the same purpose. Historians and archeologists owe much to slavery. Unknown and unsung, those forgotten slaves were the real builders of the cities and the tombs. Those works of art in architecture serve as a source for ancient history; they were built, stone on stone, by unknown hands whose work has been credited to the Pharaohs, to Carthaginian Suffetts, and to Roman Emperors.

The source of gold for ornaments and jewelry found in the many tombs was believed to be in Ethiopia. Along the slave trails that crossed the British Sudan, Ethiopia, Somaliland, and Eritrea was the promise of vital history – the story of slavery itself and of the life of ancient peoples from the beginning of civilization.

People seem surprised when they hear that slavery still exists, but it does; there are millions of slaves today in spite of all the efforts enlightened and humanitarian nations have made. The horrors of ancient Egypt, Greece, and Rome continue, and I have seen them in Abyssinia, Arabia, the Belgian Congo, and Italian ' Tripoli.

One year while in Paris on my way to a lecture engagement in London, I had met the head of the Ethiopian Legation, His Excellency Teckla Hawariate. When he learned of my dream of some day exploring Abyssinia, he invited me to the Legation to see his collection of documents and maps. These made me want to go there more than ever. Then a small inheritance from a distant relative helped make such an expedition possible. But it still seemed improbable and far away.

Highly educated and deeply patriotic, Teckla Hawariate took an interest in my project. "My August Master will be greatly-interested in your undertaking to bring to light the origin and magnificence of his illustrious ancestors," he told me. He explained things which the Ethiopians were anxious to learn – one being the exact location of oil. Then he sent an eight-hundred-word telegram to the Emperor, Haile Selassie, explaining the project in detail, and asking for his approval and for the necessary passports and permits.

The Emperor replied after some delay with characteristic caution: "He was favorably disposed to our idea and would be willing to send the permits and passports once the expedition was organized."

Teckla Hawariate was genuinely helpful. He suggested that the expedition be given as little publicity as possible: local chiefs and sultans in a country as wild as Ethiopia did not always see eye to eye with the Emperor – especially those farthest from Addis Ababa. Even the vague possibility of making this long planned expedition gave me new hope. Then the Trocadero Museum in Paris offered me a small amount of money and agreed to send an ethnographical expert with us. The International Anthropological Institute made me a similar promise, subject to getting organized.

But there was still another hazard. England had always before refused to grant any permit to cross the British Sudan from Khartoum to the Abyssinian border. To my complete surprise, a visit to the Foreign Office in London provided me, due to the courtesy of the British Ambassador in Paris, Lord Tyrell, with those permits without delay or argument. The Foreign Office even contributed a small amount, and agreed to send an English surveyor and mapmaker along. With the help of further contributions from individuals and museums and all of my own small inheritance, the expedition could now be organized.

I returned to Paris and spent hours in the offices of the Ethiopian Legation, copying maps and learning all that I could about the country. The Legation did not minimize the dangers. Part of the journey was across barren desert. We would encounter jungle, climb to elevations of nearly ten thousand feet, and finally descend to cross Somaliland or Eritrea, or both, to reach the Red Sea.

Trusting to the promise of the Emperor, I left for Alexandria to begin my work. I decided to start from Alexandria by truck, go on to Cairo, and then up the Nile to Khartoum. From there we could cross the British Sudan to Kurmuk and Rosieres and thus enter Abyssinia. We could get our outfit and supplies in Khartoum and our mules in Kurmuk. Teckla Hawariate assured me that not only would the passports and permits be sent, but also that the Negus would send an escort to meet us somewhere inside the borders of Abyssinia. Trucks, personnel, and the material and supplies we were doubtful of finding in Khartoum, we hired or purchased. The Egyptian and Italian governments furnished permits. Everything was in order and we were ready to start, but the passports from Haile Selassie did not arrive. The scientific men were to join our party in Cairo. On expressions of regret for the delay and assurances that the permits would be forwarded by the Ethiopian Legation in Paris, we started.

Captain Norman Hillier, "The New Lawrence of Libya," started with us. He was an Englishman who had pioneered in the Libyan desert, and who had been with me on a number of other expeditions. Our fleet of eight trucks created a sensation as we loaded them in front of the Grand Hotel in Alexandria: tents and camping gear, guns and ammunition, food and supplies, medical stores and moving-picture equipment. There were flags of the United States, Great Britain, France, and the Explorers' and the Adventurers' Clubs. The newspaper men turned out in force, but unfortunately where they failed to get authentic information, they relied on fertile imaginations. It was not until later that we learned of the fantastic stories that had been printed – not until we got into difficulties because of them.

At last, in all the excitement of the crowd we had attracted, the signal was given, our trucks roared, and we started through the crowded streets of Alexandria. That night we camped at the lovely oasis of Mersa Mattruh.

Of all the places in the desert where imagination creates satisfying dreams, Mersa Mattruh cannot be surpassed. Reflected in opalescent, turquoise-blue lagoons, you see the sad remains of Cleopatra's once magnificent summer palace, which was excavated in 1929-30. You can almost see the purple-sailed galleys go floating past with the figures of the immortal lovers together on their shaded decks. And then with dusk there comes the shadowed promise of the desert night; slowly the stars spring out, like brilliant, nearby lamps, and it is light again. There is a mysterious warmth of feeling that seems to draw you close and make you a part of the heart and pulse of the desert.

Mersa Mattruh was an ancient port of Ammonia to which the Greeks brought their finest wares – armor, shields of Achilles, and works of art – to barter for the gold from Ethiopia. From there they crossed the Libyan Desert, sometimes in ox-drawn chariots, to consult the famous Oracle of the Temple of Jupiter Ammon. A large part of their gold was given to the priests there in exchange for prophecies. In the endless caravans came slaves and gold and ivory and precious stones.

Today in Mersa Mattruh the Levantine merchants fill their bazaars with spurious antiques which they sell as objects dating from the time of Alexander the Great. It was amusing to listen to their oily and persuasive words about the beauty and authenticity of scarabs, coins, and statuettes. We knew they came from factories in Alexandria or, maybe, Birmingham, but we purchased a quantity of them, nevertheless.

The next morning we were on our way with dawn, straight into the desert wastes. Along the way were stones and inscriptions which had seen plumed elephants go swaying by, and creaking oxcarts carrying the treasures to the temple. Here it was that Alexander had passed with his army of servitors to be assured by the Oracle (for a stupendous sum) that he was of divine origin.

Travelling at thirty miles an hour, it seemed incredible that Alexander, Hannibal, and the Pharaohs had slowly traversed these immense distances and this utter desolation in the same intense heat. Yet their artists had carved pictures on the rocks; one carving showed a procession of elephants and another Roman chariots drawn by oxen. That there are no pictures of camels there, is one proof that these animals did not reach Africa until the Mohammedan invasion in the sixth century, AD.

On the third day we came upon one of the most beautiful landscapes that I know. Eyes tired from facing glare and eddying heat looked down and saw the lost and forgotten kingdom of the Ammonians. A chain of emerald-blue lakes shimmered in the sun; reflected in blue mirrored waters were snow-white villages built along the shores. In the midst of semi-tropical vegetation stood the ruins of a city with its temple – a sight which never fails to make my heart beat faster. And on the silent desert air there floated the song of the Siwans, as they gathered their rich harvest of dates.

The cars moved slowly down from the heights through the canyons to the lakes below. Captain Hillier led the way to the camp site he had selected on the side of Jebel Muta – the melancholy Mountain of the Dead – which I had seen from the air some years before. After paying visits to the local authorities, I asked if any new prehistoric rock drawings had come to light since my last visit. The *Omda,* Governor of Siwa, obligingly summoned the chiefs of the district for the next morning.

"Have you seen any devil-writing on the rocks?" he asked them then.

There was a long silence. Finally, one old chieftain scratched his head, made some gesture to ward off evil and the Devil, and stared at me. Men who risked their lives for the sake of "devil-writing" were mysterious, and mad. "I know where the Devil's pen has been at work," he declared solemnly. "I saw his messages in the 'Land of the Devil' while I was hunting for lost camels."

He went with us in one of the cars to act as guide. When we reached a rocky, mountainous spot, he touched my arm; then he seemed to waver as to whether he ought to tell me or not. There was a simple remedy for that – baksheesh. With money in his hand he led us to the summit of a naked mountain. There we saw a whole gallery of pictures drawn by historic and prehistoric man. These drawings on stone were symbols of the old Sahara cults: serpents, the solar disk of Ammon Ra, the triangle of Tanit, and lions – perhaps the Lions of Judah. And on the very peak was the sacrificial stone; no doubt that priests had practiced human sacrifice there in distant days.

Browne got busy with the cameras; these rock drawings of the past had never before been photographed. The sacrificial stone was similar to those of the Hoggar Mountains in the Atlas chain two thousand miles away. Further on we found drawings of ships with sails and oarsmen like those in the Museum of Cairo. This supported my theory that once upon a time a branch of the Nile flowed through the Libyan desert, and supplied wealth and a water trade route for the Ammonians.

Back at camp, we found that word had arrived from Cairo that two of the scientists who were to go with us had been delayed. Far more serious was the news that the passports and permits to cross Ethiopia had not yet come from Haile Selassie.

CHAPTER 3

THE MUMMIES

There seemed to be nothing to do but wait, and the Jebel Muta gave promise of a wealth of anthropological material. The International Anthropological Institute in Paris had asked me to collect all the mummies and skeletons possible, for the Institute wished to make a comparative study of the peoples of the ancient empires we were to cross, from some of which they had no specimens.

Alone, one night just before sunset, I climbed the Mountain of the Dead. The rocks looked golden in the setting sun against the vivid, multicolored background of that Libyan plateau. Thousands of tombs had been hewn out of the stone mountain; from a distance it looked like a many-terraced modern apartment house.

Centuries of sand storms and sharp changes in temperature had broken the stones so that some of the tombs were open to the sky. When I reached the summit and looked down, the place looked like a charnel house. Skulls, bones, and mummy wrappings lay everywhere, in utter confusion. The jackals and hyenas had dragged the mummies from the tombs, and the dried tendons and parchment-like flesh showed signs of the animals' sharp teeth.

I turned, entered one of the deep tombs there near the summit, and turned on my flashlight. As I stepped to the back, I had a sudden, sickening feeling. The stone floor surged and swayed like "rubber ice." Before I could step back, the floor sagged, crumbled, and let go. I felt myself falling . . . then I stopped . . . and then I was falling again. The weight of the debris struck the floor of the underlying tomb, smashed through, and landed on the second floor below.

That, too, surged and swayed for seconds, but it held. I had to put my handkerchief over my face in order to breathe, the air was so thick with mummy dust and sand. When the dust had cleared, I found that I was not seriously hurt, but that I was looking up at the sky as if I were at the bottom of a well two stories down. The acrid, pungent, biting, mummy dust was choking, even when I breathed through the handkerchief. My head had hit a sandstone ledge and was bleeding; my knees, elbows, and knuckles were bruised and raw. I tried to yell, but the mummy dust was in my nose and throat; all I could do was croak.

In my fall my electric flashlight had disappeared. I tried to find a match. My foot slipped, and I fell and crashed through and into a wooden mummy case. Another cloud of the peppery mummy dust engulfed me. When I did manage to light a match, I saw a dozen mummies lying on stone benches on either side of the tomb. I was surrounded by broken pieces of sarcophagi that had been smashed by the falling stones. They were beautifully painted, and covered with hieroglyphics of scientific value. The plaster walls of the tomb had been painted. I was evidently in the tomb of a farmer of some means, for the pictures depicted agricultural scenes. But there was no sign of a door.

I tried piling up the coffins in an effort to climb out. Every time I climbed on one it collapsed, and the poisonous dust would rise again. The dust made me sick at my stomach. Every time I moved, the floor trembled, and I was afraid of falling deeper into the tombs below. Finally by the aid of a match I found my flashlight, turned it on – and it worked. I set it so the light would shine up through the aperture above. Then I fainted. Mummy dust and my fall had been too much for me.

When I recovered consciousness, I could hear shouts. A rope was dangling in front of me, and then someone slid down beside me. As he descended – dislodged by his descent – a skull came tumbling down and struck me an aching blow on the head. The next thing I knew a rope under my arms was choking me, and I was swaying dizzily as I was pulled up and out. Captain Hillier had descended into the tomb to get me. It was after midnight; I had been down there for seven hours.

Sometimes it takes weeks of tunneling to locate a rock tomb which has gone unmolested through the ages. Often one encounters outer, false tombs planned by canny priests centuries before, the better to hide their sacred dead. But here at the Jebel Muta we had no such problem. We found that a block of sandstone served for the ceiling of one tomb and the floor of another at the same time. The mummified bodies must have been lowered from above, the carefully fitted stone slab placed over the tomb and then plastered. We discovered that the stone which had given way with me had been put in place at least four thousand years before. A cut, forty feet deep, had been made into the side of the hill, and the tombs had been chiseled from the solid rock.

As the members of a family died, they were mummified and put in temporary holding vaults. Not until the last member of the family died, were they put in their private sepulchre together. Then the tomb was sealed. The ceiling of such a tomb, made of sandstone, often weighed a ton, but over the centuries it crumbled and disintegrated.

A family was buried together in order that its members might remain together in the next world. (But never did we find in such a group one whom we could identify as a mother-in-law.) Individuals were identified by the paintings on the walls over them, and by the objects which were placed beside them.

Above one mummy the picture of a soldier had been painted in red, and showed him with a square, black beard. Prostrate at his feet was the body of another warrior wearing three plumes. The plumed figure had been a Nasamon, a member of the Libyans who repeatedly raided Egypt about 1500 BC. Experts who worked with me in Carthage had identified them as such in 1931. And Herodotus speaks of this race, individualized by their three, brightly-colored plumes in his *Kingdoms of the Sahara,* written about 550 BC.

History shows that when nations acquired great wealth, luxury, and leisure they became decadent; because of rich living, the people preferred hiring mercenaries, rather than going to war themselves. This was true of Carthage, Egypt, Greece, and Rome. The soldier whose mummy we examined had probably been a mercenary in pay of the ancient Ammonians.

Beside him lay a small, round shield made of specially treated leather, and studded with nails. The head of his spear was of tempered bronze. His dagger was similar in type to the knife the natives near and around the Red Sea still use. For his arms, to be worn above the elbow, there were two massive, tempered-bronze bracelets with great bumps on them. The Tuaregs still wear similar biceps bracelets, and they wear them for the same grim purpose for which they were used in ancient times; they get a man's head under their arms, and with all the tremendous leverage they can exert, crush his skull against these rough bracelets until it cracks.

We found a tomb which held the mummy of an Ammonian fisherman who had evidently been poor, for there were only two bronze fishhooks near him, and one mummified fish. The hooks and fish identified him, and were supposed to furnish him with an occupation en route to and in the next world. His teeth showed that he had been very old when he died. Though we sprayed his mummy with the antiseptic solution which is supposed to preserve and harden clothing, hair, skin, and bones, he fell into dust the moment we touched him.

In another tomb we found a young couple lying side by side. When we unwound the mummy cloths, we saw that the skulls of both had been broken, and one of the girl's arms and both the man's legs had been fractured. How had they met their end? The paintings on the stucco above them showed a chariot, and beside the man were leather gauntlets such as the charioteers wore; perhaps they had had a traffic accident. The roads leading down from the heights to the oasis of Jupiter Ammon were steep and precipitous, and without a rail or guard.

The skins of both these two mummies were dark as though they had been deeply sunburned. Perhaps they had honeymooned along the emerald lagoons of Ammonia and had met with tragedy on their way home. Near the girl were jewels which included part of an emerald necklace, comparable in size and workmanship to those found in Cleopatra's summer palace. There were other objects which might have been wedding gifts. In these mummies the brains had been removed and replaced with an unusual preservative: it contained aloes, cloves, myrrh, cassia, and cinnamon. Two of the ingredients defied analysis. The mummifying process preserved the features and often even the soft texture of the skin.

The trunks of their bodies were filled with some aromatic, bituminous composition which included rock salt. Not only were the bodies preserved, but even the mummy cloths had been treated to make them last for centuries. The soles of the feet of these two were still elastic and soft to the touch, as if they were alive. The woman had a film of wax over her face, neck, shoulders, hands, and feet. This was often done to female mummies; then makeup was applied to give them a healthy, natural coloring. The nails of both hands and feet were manicured and colored. (The most perfect example of this lost art is in the Guimet Museum in Paris, that beautiful specimen being the noted and justly famous Thais.)

Scientists have estimated that there are more than seven hundred million mummies in Egypt alone, and that only a few of them have been discovered. There, in the Mountain of the Dead, thousands lay buried. We opened several tombs which housed the bodies of courtesans. Their lives were pictured in all too graphic a manner on the walls, in paintings similar to some of the pictures to be seen in Pompeii. The detailed drawings of those colored designs were clear although they had been made more than three thousand years before.

In the tomb of an antique dealer we found one bracelet which was hundreds of years old when the dealer died in 1445 BC. Professor Breccia, of the Museum of Alexandria, believed that this bracelet had belonged to the Queen of the King of Zer – about 4366 BC; so it was more than six thousand years old when we found it. Two intertwined serpents made of pure gold were roughly inlaid with turquoises.

In the tombs were implements and other objects to indicate the occupation and pursuits of the individual, as well as any of his avocations or special interests. It was usual, also, to leave a supply of food and wine for their journey to the next world.

We found a lady of fashion of thirteen hundred years before the coming of Christ who had had her hair bobbed, dyed a vivid red, and permanently waved; that wave and dye had endured more than three thousand years. When one of the noted coiffeurs of Paris examined her, he told me that her hair originally had been black. There were stone vaporizers and atomizers for her perfumes beside her. There were, also, nail scissors, bronze mirrors, combs, tweezers for plucking her eyebrows, and decorated bronze razors. Near her lay her favorite dancing girl – a mummy wearing golden cymbals and bells decorated with etched pictures of the dance. Beside her lay an ivory vanity case which contained alabaster bottles and jars. In these were seven shades of rouge and lipstick, and kohl to shadow and lengthen the eyes. Those lipsticks and pots of rouge were still moist and usable after thousands of years.

A lawyer had been entombed with rolls of papyrus, the subject matter of which had to do with taxation. He might even have been an income-tax expert. He must have been unpopular or very thrifty; instead of food and drink being present, the pictures of these essentials had been painted on the wall. In several of the tombs the footprints of the slaves who had closed them centuries before were still clear in the sand on the floor.

One man had been a great epicure (or gourmet or gourmand, as it may have been). Beside him lay mummified legs of mutton, loins of beef, ducks, geese, and trussed wild fowl. There were a variety of spices and great amphora which had contained wines. The stucco walls were decorated with his favorite recipes and menus; and kitchen and tableware were by his side. He was the only really fat mummy I have ever seen.

By the time we had photographed, preserved, catalogued, and arranged all these mummies, our camp looked like the dissecting room of a medical school. Our collapsible tables were covered with skulls and skeletons (and spare parts) which had to be packed in specially made, padded boxes along with the mummies.

The Governor of Siwa was so afraid that we might discover valuable objects in our work that he became a nuisance. But he left us alone for a few days while he celebrated his fifty-ninth wedding – not an anniversary, but another wedding. He already had so many wives that he had catalogued them according to age, beauty, and utility. The first group included those who were young and beautiful; the second group included those who were still lovely but were required to do the light work of the household; the third group did the scrubbing, cleaning, and cooking. A woman ripens early and matures quickly in that country; before she is thirty, she is an old, old woman.

The Governor had a revolving harem; when a girl reached the age of eleven or twelve she automatically became a member of the household. One day, when I was in the car with the *Omda* some distance from Siwa, a child ran out and called him "Papa." The Governor scratched his head, looked at the boy, then looked at me, and said: "Probably." At seventy he married a girl of nine, and we had a chance to photograph the wedding procession. He had already married a girl from each of the wealthy and important families within a radius of two hundred miles. "For political reasons," he said. This girl was so loaded with necklaces and beads that you could scarcely see her in the parade of gifts and dowry which accompanied her to her new home.

CHAPTER 4

THE SINGING SANDS

Rather than go to Cairo to wait, we decided to stay where we were for a few days and search for the legendary "oasis of the Blacks," Zenzura, and collect some more mummies at Siwa. Supposedly this was a colony of Ancient Ethiopia, which could supply some of the historical information for which we were looking. We never found it, nor have other later explorers who have tried to locate it from airplanes.

But we did solve the riddle of the Singing Dunes. This is a phenomenon of the desert to be found in various places in the Sahara; the Arabs call these dunes "Accursed Mountains," and believe the cries which come from them to be the voices of spirits who warn of accident or death. They will never willingly camp near a spot where "the sands sing."

At sunset and dawn the sands make this eerie, mournful sound which rises and falls like an evil chant. It is uncanny and weird and alarming. Most Arabs, though they are born traders, have never had the opportunity to learn to read or write; so it is not surprising that they are superstitious. The cause of these strange unearthly cries is the abrupt change of temperatures at night and in the morning: a quick drop in heat cracks and cools the sand over a good-sized area. Millions of particles of sand shifting and cracking make this weird chant, "the howling of ghosts and ghouls."

One day, after collecting flints and fossils, we returned to our camp in the most extensive sand dunes in the world. The heat and glare of the day were over; the nerve-racking winds had died; the spirit of peace reigned everywhere. Sand drifts like snow, and before us was a vast sea of it which was radiantly alive in the setting sun. It wore a sheen of many changing colors, vivid silver and pale gold, vermilion and black-cherry red, pale violet and shadowed purple, which seemed to extend to meet the diamond-studded velvet canopy of the Sahara night. Till the sun dropped, there was no sound, but when the dunes began to sing, one heard the startled cries of alarm from the Siwans.

While we were smoking our pipes after dinner, Hillier reminded me of an incident that had happened several years before when I was exploring in the Libyan Desert. At that time we were camped well inside the Anglo-Egyptian border; the British Commander of the Western Desert Patrols at Mersa Mattruh had warned us not to go near Djarabub because of the fighting there between the Italians and the fanatic Senussi.

Sitting then, as we were now, a strange new sound had come to us out of the desert night. It seemed to die and zoom again out in the vast darkness. It came nearer, and it was no phenomenon of the desert.

"Gor blime me!" My black Sudanese boy who had been brought up in Khartoum, much as was Kim in India, recognized the trucks. "They be bloody Eyetalians – that's what they are."

He was right. It was an Italian desert convoy of a dozen light-armored cars. They drew up abruptly when they saw our tents and cars in the lee of a great sand dune. They were as surprised to find us in this forsaken spot as we had been to hear and see them. They were in British territory, and they knew it. The change of expression on the young lieutenant's face, when he found that we were not a British Desert Patrol, was so ludicrous that it gave him away. If we had been, it might have led to an international incident, and to his being put on the carpet.

He drew himself up smartly, "Lieutenant Cimmeruta, third section, Royal Italian Libyan Desert Patrol. We are looking for a band of Senussi traitors who escaped in this direction."

I introduced myself and Hillier, and explained that we were the Franco-American Archeological Expedition to Libya – hunting for fossils and traces of prehistoric man.

In the glare of the headlights Cimmeruta was handsome; his immaculate uniform made a sharp contrast with his sun-bronzed face. When we invited him to stay for supper, he decided to interrupt the "hunt" for the night. Over macaroni and chianti we became friends.

"You didn't see those escaping Senussi?" he asked. "This is Egyptian territory," Hillier answered dryly. "We haven't seen them, but if we had, there would be nothing you could do about it."

"Really, Signor?" But he knew as well as Hillier and I that he was some distance away from the Italian border. As is often true on explorations, we had been without news from the outside world for some time, so we were surprised to learn that the Italians had captured the fanatic Senussi center, the Djarabub Oasis. Probably this patrol had been sent south to occupy the oasis of Siwa; our being where we were happily prevented that.

Whether he reported the incident to his superior officers or not, I never knew, but only Djarabub was taken by Italy, and never Siwa. This was one of several incidents which showed me what the Italian tactics were. Later, in the British Sudan, a Fascist patrol penetrated south of Dwenat on some vague excuse; and another time Italians were "discovered" at Wal-wal, one hundred and fifty kilometers inside Ethiopian territory. This was before the Italian occupation, and the commander of that company proved to be my plausible and charming friend, Cimmeruta, promoted to the rank of captain. This incident became the *casus belli* of the Italo-Ethiopian struggle.

In the first instance the Italian Desert Patrol might really have been lost. As an archeologist I myself had crossed geographical lines several times with little thought for boundaries and special government permits. And I had been accused and suspected so many times unjustly that it seemed only fair to give the other man the benefit of the doubt.

Scientific expeditions are frequently suspected by government officials of searching for oil for one of the great corporations, or using exploration as a pretext for accomplishing the annexation of territory. Directing the excavations at Carthage, sponsored by the French Government, the Archaeological Society of Washington, D. C., and the Universities of Michigan and Rochester, I was accused of searching for oil; and another time some newspaper started the rumor that we were intriguing to free Tunisia from France.

Siwa, when first I knew it, was called "the Sodom and Gomorrah of the Sahara," and the great licentious festival of Sidi Suleyman was an orgiastic fete. Over the years it had been turned into an almost puritanical place, on the surface; there were rumors that the morals were, under cover, no better than they had been. With the drinking of *lubki,* palm wine, the sacrifice of sheep and goats, the bestial orgies in the groves of Astarte, and the public exhibitions of diverse sexual practices, Siwa was once rated as the most obscene place in the world. It grew and developed into a modern, well-ordered city under the late King Fuad of Egypt.

King Fuad visited Fayum in 1928 to inaugurate the new road through the desert from Cairo to this wealthy oasis. The excavations of the University of Michigan expedition were not far away, and the King expressed a desire to talk with me about Saharan exploration. Previously he had come to hear one of my lectures before the Royal Egyptian Geographical Society in Cairo, and had begun to take an interest in archeology. Now he seemed dubious about the beauties of the desert landscape.

"What can you see in it?" he asked me. "To me nothing could be more melancholy than this expanse of sand and rocks." He gestured toward the rock-strewn dunes and the desolate view.

"But has Your Majesty seen that gem of your dominions, the oasis of Jupiter Ammon at Siwa? It is like something out of the Arabian Nights."

"No," he answered.

When I finished telling him about Siwa, he said, "If it is half as beautiful as you say, I must certainly go there. Perhaps you will help me spend a week there – say next year?"

The following year he did visit that oasis. Accompanied by eight hundred attendants, he traveled through the desert over a magnificent new road which he had ordered built by thousands of Siwans. Along this road were comfortable rest houses with every modern convenience. As Alexander the Great had done, King Fuad made his pilgrimage to the temple of Jupiter Ammon.

That royal visit marked the decline of one of the most romantic spots in Africa. Since then the historic Fountain of the Sun, which was described by Herodotus in 550 BC, has become an everyday, controlled water supply; surrounded by utilitarian masonry and used for irrigation, its ancient picturesqueness has been ruined. Once it was a crystal spring which bubbled from the rocks and overflowed to form an emerald pool; reflected in it were palms and pomegranates, masses of flowers, and the moss-covered ruins of Egyptian, Greek, and Ammonian architecture. Now it is merely a walled-in cistern.

The Egyptians have ruthlessly spoiled many of their natural and historic beauty spots. Even the Pyramids are supposed to show to better advantage under enormous electric searchlights than under the magic of the moon.

But on this visit to Siwa on our way to Ethiopia, a strange thing happened. We had been greeted cordially, and everything had been done to help us. But suddenly every member of our expedition seemed to be under suspicion, and each was inexplicably being shadowed. At camp we found men lurking behind the cars, snooping in the kitchen, tampering with our luggage. The reason for this we learned only on the morning we left; an adjutant appeared, and I was ordered – and not asked – to call upon the Governor.

When I entered his office, the Governor's attitude was anything but friendly. On his desk lay a pile of telegrams. The first question he put to me indicated that he regarded me as some kind of criminal.

"Now tell me the truth! What is your real object in coming to Siwa?"

"Archeology, Your Excellency, as it was on my last visit here. We are here, my fellow scientists and I, to make what you might call a supplementary investigation on the site of ancient treasures–"

"Treasures!" He emphasized the word when he interrupted me. "What do you mean to imply by that word?"

"Archeological and historical treasures, Your Excellency. We have been photographing and copying ancient inscriptions and pictures, and studying a few mummies."

"That does not interest me," he broke in testily. "I want to know how much gold you have discovered?"

"Gold?" I still did not understand what he was trying to find out.

"Yes, I said gold, and I mean gold. My police have reported that at night you and your companions disappear into the Mountain of the Dead and return with cases and objects made of gold."

"We have been in the tombs, Your Excellency, but your men are misinformed. We have been filming hieroglyphics, and we have removed no treasures of any sort – only mummies."

"When do you leave?"

"Immediately."

"Now I begin to understand." The Governor leaned over and struck a gong.

When a policeman entered, the Governor talked to him in so low a tone that I could not hear. The officer listened, saluted, and hurried away. When His Excellency looked at me again, he was even less cordial, and he dismissed me with frigid politeness. With the finding of the great wealth in the tomb of Tut-Ankh-Amen, all Egypt had become treasure conscious, but I still didn't see how this could affect us.

When I left the Governor's mansion, I was permitted to get in my car and drive off without being detained or followed. I overtook the caravan, and that evening we reached Captain Hillier's rest house at Mersa Mattruh at sunset. No sooner had we stopped in the courtyard than we were surrounded by a small army of Egyptian police. When we demanded an explanation, we learned that, "Under special orders from the Governor of Siwa and headquarters in Cairo," all our baggage must be examined.

Neither Hillier nor myself could understand this, but it was useless to protest or make any opposition in the face of an official order. Those Egyptian policemen laboriously lifted out all the boxes and other luggage from the cars, piled them in the courtyard, and proceeded to examine their contents with the most scrupulous care.

The first comic episode came when the police discovered the fake antiques we had purchased from the Levantines. They pounced on these oxidized bronzes, scarabs, and imitation-gold earrings – sold to us as ornaments which Cleopatra herself had worn. They found little else that interested them, but their Chief insisted on looking into the cars, lifting off the seats and even the hoods. They opened our moving picture camera, too, and spoiled one reel of film. When they opened a gasoline can, a straw-wrapped mummy head fell out and smashed. Their shocked surprise gave us another laugh. The fake antiques were repacked and taken to Cairo for examination, but still we did not learn the reason for all this fuss.

That night, Hillier came rushing into the dining-room while we were still at table, with an armful of newspapers. "The Key!" he said, and laughed. Here were papers from Cairo and Alexandria, dated some days earlier; the headlines gave us the cue as to why we were being searched.

Prorok Expedition Leaves for Jupiter Ammon
Alexander the Great's Tomb Located!
Discovery of Vast Treasure

One of the articles explained that it was logical for scientific archeologists who had already made a preliminary investigation to conclude that, "Beneath the ruined temple there, beneath the village, there exist subterranean passages and tombs wherein lies Alexander the Great." It concluded with the idea that so great a man would naturally be surrounded with ornaments of great value.

Of course, the stuff that had been taken to Cairo to be examined was returned, and we were permitted to pack and leave, with profuse apologies for the delay.

CHAPTER 5

WE VISIT FAYUM

When we reached Cairo, there were still no passports. Again we telegraphed to Addis Ababa and to the Ethiopian Legation in Paris. We chartered the yacht "Seti I" for the journey up the Nile, so that we could study the old caravan trails from a number of strategic points, and thus still save time. Paris assured us that the passports would be forthcoming, but by this time I had begun to suspect an attitude which later proved to be characteristic: Ethiopian procrastination is something with which you must always contend. Teckla Hawariate had not minimized the dangers we had to face even with passports; without them, the risks would be still greater. It was with a feeling of great uneasiness that I determined to go on. I was not afraid for myself, but my responsibility for the other members of the party was a serious matter.

Just before sailing we gave a farewell party on the yacht; two hundred guests came aboard, some of them uninvited. The newspaper photographers and reporters found their way up the gangplank, but, fortunately, this time in their stories they stuck to facts, so we did not repeat our Alexandrian unpleasantness. We were anchored in the shade of palm trees of the palace of the Prince and Princess Lotfallah, in a setting reminiscent of the Arabian Nights. The old palace had been the residence of the Empress Eugenie when she had come to open the Suez Canal. At a luncheon given for us in the palace, all the service on the table was of gold – soup tureens, platters, plates, and spoons. It was similar to the famous, massive plate of the Sobieskis of Poland, which, the last time that I heard of it, was still preserved in the Chateau de Montrésor in Touraine.

The morning after the party we began our voyage up the Nile. Our first stop was a camp at the oasis of Fayum, about a day's journey south from Cairo. This is a model archeological camp, founded by the University of Michigan. Once I had worked there for seven months, entirely cut off from the outside world, but happy to dig up historical data with a pick and shovel.

Because several of the men with us on the yacht had had museum and university training but had never been in the field on an expedition, we stopped to show them how this one operated. In 1928, with more than a thousand sites to choose from, Professor Kelsey of the University of Michigan had selected Fayum. At that time it was only a sandy waste covering the ruins of a city of about eighty thousand people, which dated from early Roman days.

The first step on any archeological expedition is to get permission from the government of the country or countries to explore and excavate. Negotiations with the Department of Antiquities of Egypt took three weeks. The permit to excavate at Fayum was granted on condition that enough money be deposited to insure that the work should continue for three years; that none of the objects uncovered should leave the country without permission; that all such objects should be photographed, catalogued, and reconstructed or restored where possible; that all scientific data which our experts supplied should be printed and published; and that we should employ a Department of Antiquities inspector on the site.

Fifty thousand dollars was the minimum required, and that is relatively a small amount for such an undertaking. One question that people at my lectures often ask is: "Where does the money come from?" Expeditions and excavations are financed by philanthropic individuals, institutions, foundations, museums, universities, and governments. Sometimes a university or museum will not only supply a part of the funds but also will send an expert in some special line of archeology.

It was not necessary to organize a staff for Fayum, for they were coming from the Excavations at Carthage as a group. Such a staff is made up of experts, including a physician, surveyor, camp director, photographer, architect, and an epigraphist to decipher the ancient writings.

The purpose of archeology is to learn the history, habits, progress, and scientific growth of peoples from their literature, religion, art, music, and everyday life. We try to learn a people's pursuits, pleasures, accomplishments, and progress through their dams and irrigation projects, through their architecture – such as the pyramids – through their mode of government, including taxation, and their zest for war and colonization.

First a camp had to be built at Fayum – eventually it grew to be a town of six hundred people. Bricks, mud, and beams had to be gathered from the ancient abandoned city. An artesian well had to be drilled and tested. Kitchens, quarters, and storage rooms had to be erected; then came rooms for the scientists, a laboratory for sorting and treating the antiquities, rooms for such equipment as microscopes, rooms for cleaning devices and materials, for coins and jewelry, rooms for spraying and preserving fabrics and pottery and, most important, papyrus. The value of the papyrus found on this project than covered the cost of the whole excavation.

Camera-men have to have darkrooms on an expedition. The room for pottery means building hundreds of feet of shelves. Dishes, oil lamps, cooking utensils, and decorated pottery supply many of the keys to the past. Pottery is particularly important, for it shows what the people made and used, and gives clues to the countries with which they traded.

It took less than a month to get that camp going. Chanting lines of Arabs moved back and forth with full or empty baskets on their heads, as we uncovered the buried city. In a few months, more than twenty-five thousand objects had been collected from the buried past. One of our group could supervise a gang of from thirty to fifty men.

Arabs are notably light-fingered, so each basketful of sand had to be watched as it was shoveled in, carried, and dumped. We established a bonus system by means of which any Arab who found an object of value was rewarded. Most Arabs have never learned to read and write, but they are born traders with an uncanny sense of values. They could tell the value of gold from its weight, and they seemed to sense the value of anything they handled, even the papyrus. And in addition to this, we had to make arrangements to buy back, from antique dealers to whom they might be sold, objects stolen from these excavations.

Fayum had been a large city in its time; there were many large and small houses. Why it had been abandoned we never learned; there were no signs of siege or war, and we could only guess that it was because of pestilence or excessive taxation. It had simply been deserted with everything intact.

We found household records, carpenter's tools, forges, and looms with the fabrics still in them, their colors still bright. In every house there were idols – the household gods. In the outer walls of the city we found a few bronze arrowheads, probably mementos of an occasional attack from the desert. Many of the bows, arrows, slings, projectiles, and shields were in perfect condition. There were so many baskets and carpets of Haifa grass, interwoven with palm leaves, papyrus and fabric, that we kept only the better specimens. Their colors were well-preserved, and the designs showed astral emblems, mystic symbols, and priests in front of altars burning incense.

A little distance from the city we excavated an ancient "undertaking parlor." In it were coffins made of cedar and sycamore that must have been brought from great distances, probably from Lebanon. The coffins were ornately painted.

Behind one brick in a house kitchen we found a collection of coins some thrifty housewife had concealed. The kitchen stoves were of stone and pottery, not unlike the pot-bellied iron stoves found in rural American railroad stations today. In every house we found incense.

On one piece of papyrus we deciphered a complaint written centuries before. The writer had complained that he was being taxed for his own funeral before his death had occurred. Our excavations uncovered bronzes made of six different metals, wigs and ceremonial beards, real and counterfeit money. The residue left in the bottom of some amphora showed that they had contained beer and wine.

Many of the objects went to the museum in Cairo; others were sold or exchanged and went to other institutions, museums, and collectors. But the papyrus proved to be more valuable than any of the many objects found in Fayum.

Sometimes at night the epigraphists would put papyrus under glass and translate for us; for them this seemed as simple as reading English. It was like hearing someone read from the files of old, old newspapers.

The office-bedroom of one house furnished a collection of papyrus which later thrilled archeologists all over the world. This excavated room was equipped with a bed complete with coverings, and chairs, table, and an inkstand with a number of unused quills; there were empty wine bottles, and the manuscripts of some long dead writer.

Because of its contents this villa was named "The House of the Scribe." The writer had been a Roman soldier two thousand years before, and the series of letters written by the Greco-Egyptian were to his mother, probably the last occupant of the house. Like so many other boys, he had run away from home to join the army. Never had I seen more vivid documents.

He told his mother about joining up, about his departure from Alexandria, of his life on a war galley. In Rome he was astonished by its grandeur, and made naïve comparisons between the city and his own simple, Egyptian birthplace. He wrote of games in the arena and life in the Forum in the simple terms a soldier of today might use in writing home. One letter concluded by saying: "And do not be worried, dearest mother, for I am in a wonderful place. Give my love to my brothers and sisters, and tell my friends in the village that I saw the Emperor himself in the Amphitheater." (Later, this and other letters were published by the University of Michigan in its "Humanistic Series," edited by Professor Kelsey.)

After several days at Fayum, we continued on up the Nile, making stops for side expeditions. Along the caravan trail which follows the river, we found old Roman milestones, as clear and informative as the signs, arrows, and route numbers along modern highways. They gave the directions for finding rest houses, water holes, bridges, and fortresses.

At Aswan, about a thousand miles south of Cairo, we heard stories of the cruelty and barbarism of the Shankallas in Western

Ethiopia. These tales, plus the fact that our passports had never come, made several of the party decide to turn back.

Without these men we crossed the great Nubian Desert to study the ruins at Meroe, a city which was probably the capital of a rich and powerful Ethiopia that had existed over four thousand years before. Roman Legions had followed this same route; so, too, had the Persian Army when it had made attempts at different times to conquer the country. The magnificence of the ruins in Meroe gave visible proof of the wealth and power of the ancient, Ethiopian builders. In his book on Nubia and Abyssinia, the Reverend Michael Russel wrote:

There is reason to believe that a sanctuary, dedicated to Jupiter under the character of Ammon, stood in the peninsula of Meroe near Shendy, the principal seat of the Ethiopians. Near the town of Moscho there is still a position known by the name of Campusis Aerarium – the treasury of Campyses. It is admitted that the Roman Legions advanced as far as Napata, considerably further to the south.

Modern Merawe now stands on the site of ancient Meroe, which all accounts unite in representing as without a rival among all the cities of Ethiopia. Meroe may have extended to Dongola on one side and to Shendy on the other in the days of her greatest glory.

To quote Russel again:

There are the remains of seven temples of which the largest is four-hundred-and-fifty feet long – almost equal to St. Paul's – and one-hundred-and-fifty-nine feet wide. The principal apartment is one-hundred-and-forty-seven by one-hundred-and-eleven feet. . . . Some of the materials are in so confused and shattered a position as to indicate that they had been broken down and skillfully repaired. In two of the other temples most of the chambers had been excavated from solid rock. This is a part of a lofty eminence called Gabel el Berkal, or the Holy Mountain, along the foot of which the monuments are erected. Here also are seventeen pyramids, while at el Bellal, seven miles further up the river, there is a more numerous and lofty range of these structures, none of which, however, rivals those of Memphis. The sculptures and ornaments bear marks of very different periods of art, some being extremely rude, and others nearly as perfect as any in the palaces of Egypt.

As we pushed on toward Khartoum, I became more and more uncertain of what I ought to do. Exploring Abyssinia was something for which I'd planned and hoped for years, yet did I have the right to risk the lives of other men? In Khartoum I would have to decide either to abandon the expedition, or to take the risk and enter the real Ethiopia by way of the fear-inspiring and barbarous Shankalla country; assuming, of course, that our passports had not arrived – and I had little hope now that they would.

CHAPTER 6

THE MYSTERY MAN OF ETHIOPIA

The American and British Ambassadors to France had given me letters of introduction to the Governor General of the Sudan, Sir Stewart Sykes. Those and the official permits to cross the closed area from Rosieres to Kurmuk – the first official permits granted – led to a private conversation with Sir Stewart. He was not very encouraging. He intimated that some of the international clouds on the political horizon were serious; and told me of the reports of raids and fights on the ill-defined frontiers – slave and ivory raiders were particularly active. But in spite of all this, I determined not to abandon the expedition, but to push on, passports or no passports.

When they learned of my decision, one more member of my party thought it best to drop out unless the passports came in time. I did not try to minimize the dangers we would have to face, or the risks we would be taking. Most of the men agreed to take the chance. Hillier seemed to think well of it, prejudiced perhaps by his love of danger, though I had known from the start that he would be unable to go all the way through with us.

Once the British learned we were determined to proceed, they did everything they could to help. The Governor General never questioned the fact that we were in search of archeological and ethnological information. When he discovered that he and I had attended the same school, Pretoria House, though at different times, he was even more helpful. He and Hamilton, the Civil Secretary, advised and guided me in a way that kept us from making mistakes, and expedited the organization of our caravan.

In Khartoum we had to buy supplies and hire mules and bearers. Facing such a wide variety of climates and lands – desert, jungle, high elevations and low – we had to carry with us an enormous quantity of stores; and there was no place to replenish our stocks until we reached Addis Ababa. Gathering our stores was not aided by the proprietor of the hotel at which we were staying. He was a Levantine, and he was only interested in diverting our dollars and pounds sterling into the pockets of his unscrupulous compatriots.

Mr. Coxen, editor of the *Sudan Daily Herald,* whom I met at a luncheon the Governor General gave for us, helped us by publishing an article about our expedition. As a result, I received an odd letter in which the writer said he had seen the article; he went on to say that he was interested in our project, had a great deal of valuable information about Ethiopia, and suggested that I meet him at a little-known café in a secluded part of Khartoum. Written in excellent English, the name of the writer was clearly of Italian origin – "T. P. Stromboli."

Within a very few minutes after I met him at the suggested appointment, he had won my complete confidence. The manner in which he introduced himself, his appearance, and his evident ⋅ experience inspired faith in the man. He was small, closely shaven, about forty-five, and had the clean-cut features of Napoleon. He was followed by a bodyguard of three colossal Ethiopians armed with shillelaghs. All the time we were talking, these three guards were on the alert, and threatened instant attack on anyone who might try to interrupt.

Stromboli told me that he was a native of Sicily and had left home to search for gold, first in Australia and then in Tibet. From India he had wandered to Abyssinia, where he had lived for years, and he claimed that he knew the country thoroughly. He said that he was a mining engineer and that he could speak and write Italian, French, English, Arabic, Swahili, and the official language of Ethiopia – Amharic; in addition, he knew at least half a dozen of the Abyssinian dialects.

He wanted to organize and manage the practical details of the expedition, and said that he had done this sort of organization many times before. If I would entrust him with making the purchases, the hiring of the mules and men, he knew he could save me not only unnecessary trouble and worry, but hundreds of pounds. "And may I add," he ended with a winning smile, "you are in possession of a new friend and fellow explorer who, I assure you, is ready to stand by your side to the death if need be." I had liked him on sight, so now we made our bargain, a bargain which at times I could not help but question, for it was so extremely just and generous toward me. And I never thought to ask him for credentials – they were engraved on his face, in his manner, in a certain subtle way he had of indicating that he was a man of strong personality and determined will. Here, I felt, was a man who could help me surmount the enormous difficulties I knew we were going to face.

"You have three hefty followers, Signor Stromboli," I said, after we had shaken hands on our bargain, and were having a final *Cinzano.*

"Yes." He smiled. "I call them the Three Black Musketeers. They are indispensable members of my staff. Running a business such as mine, one makes many enemies, especially among the Greeks and Levantines. I don't doubt that they've already tried to rob you."

After a moment he continued, "That landlord of yours is one of the band. We shall have to watch him and certain of the others. But there are some of them who buzz around like mosquitoes, and would suck my life-blood just as eagerly. I am supposed to be rich – and the ladies of Khartoum are enterprising – " He ended his speech with an infectious laugh, and rose.

"Then I'll see you at my hotel tomorrow morning," said I, and left, feeling as if an enormous weight had been lifted from my shoulders.

When I told the other members of the expedition about him, they slapped me on the back and congratulated me on my find, but when I spoke to the British military and diplomatic men who had shown an interest in our project, there was silence, grave faces, and that significant dropping of monocles from the eyes. These men exchanged glances, and maintained a silence which was ominous.

"What's wrong? Have I made a fool of myself?" I asked.

"My dear fellow, awfully sorry if I gave you the wrong impression," one young official replied as he adjusted his carefully polished eyeglass, and gazed at me with a bland smile. "You are to be congratulated on having come across this human dynamo. Wonderful man, Stromboli – named after the volcano in whose shadow he was born. Wish I had his linguistic and other knowledge; he possesses an extraordinary faculty for picking up money from time to time."

I was surprised at the amount this man seemed to know about Stromboli, but I did not interrupt.

"One day he appears to be without funds, then he disappears somewhere to the back of the beyond and returns, dramatically, with some huge amount to his credit. He hints at gold and diamonds and platinum tucked away in some outlandish corner of the treasure house of Africa. Wherever he gets it, the money does not stick to his fingers long. Off he goes, accompanied at times by some beautiful Haidee – to Paris, or Berlin, or London. He's a pauper again before he knows where he is, but always a potential millionaire. I wish I had a little of the wealth that has passed through his strong hands. Of course, my dear fellow, we need hardly tell you that you have to look out. In the case of any man who is a mixture of the Italian condottieri and Garibaldi, and Don Juan and Don Quixote, one has to be on one's guard."

All this was said half-seriously and half in the spirit of humor. So I returned to my hotel, resolved to keep my own counsel, and to rely on my own judgment.

Within myself I felt a strong faith, a positive knowledge that I could trust Stromboli completely. It was strangely as if we had bared our arms, made small cuts and exchanged red corpuscles in the mystic and symbolic rite of becoming "blood brothers." Why that feeling should have been so strong, I do not know, but during our many months together in the desert and the jungle, he never gave me any reason for regretting my decision. He was a great explorer, a connoisseur of human nature, a man of vast knowledge and indomitable bravery.

The next morning Stromboli arrived as he said he would, and we agreed on plans he outlined for the caravan. He had just left to get things started when something occurred which, I found later, would occur again and again. A bell-boy came to tell me that there was a lady in the lobby who wished to see me. When I went down, there was a beautiful woman, picturesquely dressed, but with a wild look in her eyes that put me on guard.

"I am looking for Signor Stromboli," she announced. "I understand that he is a friend of yours, and is staying here. Will you tell me when I can see him?"

"I'm sorry, Madame. I do know Signor Stromboli, but he is not here. I believe he is leaving Khartoum on a long journey."

"*Sacré nom d'un chien!*" she exclaimed. "I thought so. But I'll get him yet. *Merci et au revoir, Monsieur.*"

She turned abruptly, and as she did, I caught the glint of a revolver she was holding underneath her shawl. I recognized her as one of those "mosquitoes," out for blood and vengeance, about whom Stromboli had talked at our first meeting.

With the medical and other supplies from Alexandria, Cairo, and Khartoum, Stromboli went on to Kurmuk to get the mules, porters, provisions, and the Maria Theresa thalers for that trip of more than a thousand miles through a wilderness of jungle, desert, and high mountains. Thalers are the only accepted currency in most parts of Ethiopia; letters of credit, traveler's checks, English pounds, and American dollars have no value outside of Addis Ababa.

These silver coins weigh almost an ounce, and were worth fifty cents apiece at that time. They bear the motto and the coat of arms of the Empress Theresa of Austria, and the date 1780. Minted in Vienna, Nesbitt says of them: "The white Empress is still honored in a nation of blacks, though most of the Coptic Christians believe her silhouette to be that of the Virgin Mary."

We needed twelve thousand of these thalers, and two thousand of them are a full load for a mule – six mules were used for carrying them alone. Stromboli insisted, that we take quantities of the smaller coins, piasters and tamons. The natives were so ignorant of money values that in some sections these would buy as much or more than a thaler.

It was not until Stromboli had gone that the worst happened. Having decided to go through Ethiopia's savage fastness with or without passports, the British informed me that we should not be allowed to take either arms or ammunition without the permission of the Emperor himself. Till then I had worried more about our passports than our permits. The shock and surprise of that statement, and the finality with which it was made, left me stunned.

I wondered if Stromboli knew about this strictly-administered regulation; it was part of an international agreement between England and Ethiopia, so I was told. For a moment all my sympathies were on the side of the gun-runners, and I felt that this expedition was hoodooed. But again I determined to go on. There was a chance that Stromboli did know about this and had arranged to smuggle some guns through without telling me; if not, we would have to buy rifles and guns from the gun-runners. That was that.

En route to join Stromboli in Kurmuk, we went into the ethnologically interesting Tabi Hills. Ancient, aristocratic, and physically superior, the Shilloks have a mixture of Nubian and Ethiopian blood. Their rocky land, covered with dense forest, has one of the finest climates in the world.

Cut off from our civilization, their picturesque villages are full of laughing, happy Negroes. Stark naked, they are as unaware and unashamed as were Adam and Eve in the Garden of Eden. Many of these black Apollos were more than six feet, six inches tall; and their ebony Venuses were as unconscious of nudity as were their multitudinous children.

Through the courtesy of a British doctor stationed there, the Shilloks put on an athletic contest for our benefit. It was magnificent to see these giants wrestle, play their games, and race. They were like children having a party on the lawn. The doctor had been stationed there for so long that he could answer all my questions. Professionally he had very little to do because everyone was in such perfect health. The Shilloks, unlike many of the black races, believe in monogamy, but their birth rate is high. They are a moral people with self-discipline and self-rule largely determined by groups of individual families. They are so peaceful that they are permitted to use and own any kind of firearms except machine-guns. The fixed British policy of respecting the habits and customs of tribes and territories has worked particularly well in administering the affairs and protecting the rights of the Shilloks.

From the Tabi Hills we moved on to Kurmuk. Here Stromboli told me, without explaining how, that he had arranged for guns, and said that he would need another week to complete his preparations. Rosieres was the first town we reached in Ethiopia. From there to Addis Ababa we did not expect to find a single place in which to replenish our supplies, except for grain and fresh meat. We were also told that water was scarce on this thousand-mile trek. While I was waiting, Stromboli suggested that I would find "The River Folk" worth investigating.

About a hundred miles to the east of Kurmuk, near the Blue Nile, was a region which had never been archeologically and ethnologically explored. The escaped slaves from there were tall with square heads, receding brows, and narrow, slitted eyes; they looked like the silhouettes and sculptured figures I had seen on the ancient temples in Nubia and in the Land of Punt. The Sudanese refer to this territory as "The Forbidden Land"; it is cut off from the rest of Ethiopia by towering mountains and the almost impenetrable jungle of the Blue Nile.

We arranged with a Greek trader to take three of us and our porters to Bambode in his truck. At that outpost "Native Trustees" provided us with food, guns, mules, and gifts at unbelievably high prices. Then the trader led us to the edge of the jungle, and left us with these comforting words, "If you do not return in ten days I will tell Stromboli, and he can go in after you." He muttered something more about murder, kidnapping, and being held for ransom.

"What did you say?" I asked.

"Without your Abyssinian passports the Sultan Baburi may hold you for ransom, if he does not have you killed. If I came in after you, he might hold me too. He's as dangerous as the Mad Sultan Ghogoli in Beni Shangal. And whatever else you may do, don't try to help any escaping slaves."

He enlarged a little on the matter of escaping slaves whom we might encounter coming down the river on rafts or on our trail. "If you're caught helping slaves get to British territory, you will have your nose and ears cut off, and will be buried up to your neck in a hill of red ants. When red ants penetrate a man's brain you can hear his screams five miles away." He concluded with an oily smile.

That particular brand of Greek traders never take any risks which they can possibly avoid, but when and *if* you return, they are avid for all kinds of information. When we got back from that trip of exploration, they wanted to know if the natives were friendly, would we give them copies of the maps we had made, where were the placer mines, and what about the ivory, skins, and game. They even asked me about the possibilities of gun and slave-running. Those traders are a despicable lot, but at times indispensable. On the strength of the information they get from people who do take risks, they determine where and when to locate their safe and lucrative trading posts. Though they are known to act as informers when it is to their own advantage, they are wily enough to remain friendly with both government agents and the natives. Unless you have friends in government positions who might shut off their unethical and sometimes illegal trading, you cannot trust them.

From the edge of the jungle we had to fight our way in through shrubs and trees which had fishhook-like thorns that cut hands, tore clothes, and penetrated deep into the hard, bare feet of our porters. This made for slow going and for frequent stops. As we moved along, I couldn't help remembering a story the jolly District Commissioner had told me at Kurmuk. The Shankallas are able to train men to develop and use their sense of smell like bloodhounds. I knew this to be true, for I had used some of them to track down game.

The year before, handicapped by weights and chains, one hundred and forty-six slaves had attempted to escape from "The River People" in one body. These human bloodhounds were put on their trail, but the escaping slaves were expecting this. Like animals, they tried to keep their scent from blowing toward their pursuers. They hid in crocodile-infested waters, they crossed streams, they slept in snake-infested swamps. They suffered from hunger, from malaria, from cuts and bruises and wounds. They were at the mercy of jungle animals on one side, or their merciless pursuers on the other.

Thoughts of the tortures awaiting them if they were caught, strong constitutions, and determination – these carried most of them through to British territory and freedom, but they were in so pitiable a condition that several of them died soon after, and many of them were sick for weeks, or invalided for life.

We fought our way on through creepers as thick as a man's wrist, through a tangle of trees, through diabolical thorns, past bushes whose leaves stung like nettles. Our interpreter, Derissa, warned us to be especially careful not to touch one particular variety of plant – it had been known to cause death to white men. We moved on wearily in the intense heat; the humidity was so great that the air supported fine vegetable matter, almost like dense coal smoke, which irritated our throats and nostrils as the nettles did our hands. Sweating, scratched, and itching, we crossed the Blue Nile in dugouts and camped at the foot of an extinct volcano. It took more than an hour to attend to our wounds and scratches – in this humid, hot climate even a tiny cut can, in an unbelievably short time, cause blood poison, serious sickness, or death.

After two days of this exhausting walking, one man became so ill and ran so high a temperature that we had to halt for a day. One of the Negro scouts went on to investigate. Late in the day he came rushing back to say he had found a young girl, ill, perhaps dying, hiding under a great boulder on the river bank. In spite of the danger we knew we were taking, we got out our guns and went to rescue her.

Never have I seen a human being in so great a state of fear as that naked creature. Her features were those of a distinctly aristocratic Abyssinian, but soft and feminine; her eyes had the pleading pathos of a frightened animal. She was so completely exhausted that even a mixture of milk and brandy had a very slow effect. She was covered with cuts and scratches, some of them festering; and flies were swarming all over her naked body.

While we bathed her with antiseptics and bandaged her wounds, our Shillok scout went further along the trail to make sure that the human bloodhounds and her master were not following. Before he returned, she recovered sufficiently to discover that some of us were white. When she realized this, her face brightened and, for the first time, she looked intelligent. We kept her under the effect of opiates that night, she was so ill; and the next day we sent her with one of the porters to Fasogli, where she would be safe. Before she left she told us her almost unbelievable story.

When she started to talk an expression of such puzzlement and incredulity spread over our stoic interpreter's face that it alarmed me.

"Tell me what she said, Derissa," I demanded.

"Girl says – not a girl; she's a boy."

The rounded breasts, the features, the soft flesh – we had found her naked – how could we believe that this was a boy?

The girl went on talking for a few minutes, and this is her story as Derissa translated it there in the shade of the great Baobab trees, with birds and monkeys fluttering and chattering in the dense foliage overhead:

"I was born at Zemi, in the Goggam, on the first day of Genvot; because that is the birthday of the Virgin Mary, they named me Lidata in spite of the fact that I was a boy. I was brought up with another lad, a little older than I, Wolde; though we were slaves, my Abyssinian Master was kind, more like a father. He was Head Man in the village, and when I grew big enough, I was permitted to carry his umbrella, and sometimes his gun; so I was very happy.

"One day an Abyssinian nobleman visited my Master. They talked all night about *gibir* – taxes, taxes. I could see that my master was troubled; the visitor was angry and ugly. The next morning my Master called Wolde, who was twelve, and myself.

"'I want you and Wolde to go to Debra Marcos with the leader of the advance guard and take a letter to a friend of mine. You will stay there two days and then return with two new mules,' my Master said.

"Wolde and I were happy, for this was a mission of importance and trust. We never dreamed of that which was in store for us. My Godmother, Lidata Mariam, never told me in my dreams that there was danger of never again seeing my dear Master and my happy mountain home near the singing stream. We were proud to show our Master's friend our strength and endurance on the trail; and we were eager to see Debra Marcos, for that was the great city of the ancient Kings of Goggam. We skipped along, for to us this was a great event – our first journey.

"At the first village where we stopped, several young girls joined our caravan. At the next village more were added, and still more as we went along. But we were not allowed to play or bathe with them. We could not understand this, for at home we had always been allowed to swim and play children's games. Wolde was especially annoyed for he liked to play with girls, and had already had two or three affairs.

"I had tried to copy him, but had been too shy; and that shyness proved to be the curse of my life. When we reached Debra Marcos we were lodged in the house of a wealthy, but repulsive Governor. We delivered our Master's letter, and the next morning a guard took us out to see the wonderful city. Then we returned and waited patiently for the time to travel home. On our second night in the house of the Governor, his Chief Man visited us with an attendant. The Chief Man was a huge, fat eunuch who asked us many funny questions. Finally, he seized Wolde by the shoulders and stared hard at him.

"'Tell me, little bastard, the truth. Have you ever had intercourse with girls?'

"Wolde began to smile, then laugh; proud of his virility, he began to brag and tell stories of his conquests. He was nervous or maliciously eager to prove his precocious manhood to the eunuch. This made the eunuch angry and he pushed Wolde away from him.

"'Shut up, you little rat. I have been cheated.' He turned to me and felt my plump shoulders as you test a chicken for tenderness; he smiled loathsomely.

"'And you, my little friend; what have you to say? From the look of you I am sure you still retain your virginity. You do not belie your name; tender little dove thou art, Lidata.'

"Brought up to tell the truth, I did not know how to lie. I remember looking at the floor and saying 'I am not like Wolde.' If I had looked up I might have read my cruel fate in that evil eunuch's eyes. When I did manage to look at him he was leering at the harem attendant.

"That night my drink was strengthened with some potent drug. When I awoke I found that I was prostrate, my legs were tightly bound together; my hands were tied; the agony in my body was such I thought I could not live. It was as if a knife had been driven upward from between my legs into my heart, and left there to cause pain. Later I learned that this agony was caused by a piece of bamboo which had been thrust into me and not removed.

"I had been castrated to change my sex and personality to please some depraved voluptuary; the bamboo was left. . . . The Ras was half Abyssinian and half Arab, and he indulged in every form of depraved vice. His palace was the eunuch factory for the whole district.

"I was kept under drugs for days. When I awakened I was always in agony, and cried for Wolde and my former Master. When my wounds had almost healed, the bamboo shoot was removed. I had been changed from a boy into a living plaything to be sold or given to some hideous depraved new master. My hair had been permitted to grow and was dressed like a woman's. They fed me fattening foods and sweets and wines; they gave me a woman attendant who massaged me every day, and then scented and rouged me as if I were a courtesan."

This incredible victim of viciousness went on talking in his peculiarly light, feminine voice; occasionally he would stop and close his eyes – perhaps to remember, possibly to shut out some picture of torture. But he made no appeal for sympathy; it was a matter such as he might have told about some stranger.

"I was treated like a pampered girl, loaded with bracelets and necklaces, given jeweled combs to wear in my hair. Only when I wore them was I looked upon with favor. My waist became slender, my legs grew fat, my breasts developed. That was when I was presented to the harem."

Derissa interrupted him with some question. For moments our guest was silent, then he began to talk again:

"For months I lived there shamefully. I was the play-thing of the Ras, and he knew every vice; his soul was a cesspool of evil. At times he was like a savage beast playing with a lamb, or a cat playing with a mouse, brutally teasing it, hurting it, but never killing it. He was a lover of tortures and wanted you to watch them with him. I could never bring myself to pander to his caprices as did my other companions in wretchedness. The real girls there had neither courage nor character left; but for me there remained some little thread of masculinity. No matter how cruelly I was treated I could not forget that my ancestors had all been fighting slaves. My grandfather fought beside the Emperor Menelik at Adua, and died; and I too would gladly have given my life for my first Master, though selling me in lieu of taxes was for me a worse fate than death.

"One day when I was allowed to go to market with my serving woman I mixed with the crowd. I was determined to escape or kill myself; the tortures practiced on slaves who escape last too long to be endured – death is far easier. For weeks I hid in the jungle, living on berries and roots; I knew that if I followed the Blue Nile I would some day reach the British Sudan, and then my days of utter debasement would be over. Will they mock and laugh at me in the land of the *Ferengis*?"

CHAPTER 7

THE HIPPO FEAST

We were travelling in a country so dangerous that no really good maps of it had ever been made. Surveyors had tried to map it and had failed, or they had disappeared never to be seen or heard from again. Some of the tribes were said to be cannibals. Far from Addis Ababa, this section lived its own life entirely, a life which had not changed in three thousand years. It was full of cruelty – savage and ugly. The Sultan paid lip service to Haile Selassie, but was independent to the extent that he exercised the power of life and death. Unfortunately, death means very little to these savages, and torture seems to offer them delight. Two Jesuit missionaries had been killed and eaten there not very long before.

The trail we were following was almost impenetrable in some places, disappeared in others, but was marked by occasional stone monuments which were obviously phallic. I wondered about those dolmens. Did they mark the trail on to the Red Sea? And was there some connection between the ancients who erected and carved them, and those who built the chain of monoliths which stretches from Stonehenge in England across the Channel to Brittany, Spain, and then, thousands of miles across northern Africa? They were cyclopean, and similar to others I had found at Garama and Fezzan. Later an eminent fellow archaeologist dated them as belonging to the Mousterian Period of prehistoric man.

We made camp at the foot of Mount Kako – "the Mountain of the Evil Spirits" – and sent bearers ahead with gifts. Then we waited. We were not far from Dul, but our bearers did not return. Hours passed – two days. It was necessary to do something while we waited, so we explored the plateau. I hoped to find ancient tombs containing proofs of the period of the men who were buried there. Pictures cut into the rocks, charms, tokens, jewelry, and inscriptions give one new data, or furnish evidence for existing theories.

We had neither seen nor heard any of the savages, and were digging with pick and shovel in the blistering heat when someone touched my arm. Silhouetted against the edge of the jungle, there stood six, naked, black savages armed with long spears. They had come without making a sound; now they stood without speaking. Obviously unfriendly, they made no move to stop us or attack. When Derissa spoke to them, they stared, turned, and slithered into the dense jungle growth with the stealthiness of panthers. One moment they were on the edge of the jungle; the next, they were gone, and there was not even the tremor of a leaf to show the direction in which they were moving.

"Stop digging," Andalamu, our guide, warned, and his voice was husky with terror. "This is their sacred mountain, and they will do something if you continue."

But the opening we had made gave promise of being a cave or sepulchre – rich with archeological possibilities. Besides I was known as a mad man; and mad men are treated as holy men in most of the African wild country, as they were by the American Indians. The heat was terrific, the humidity high, the work hard. A foul gas like a thick fog issued from the hole we had made, and the stench was sickening.

We were digging into a deposit of guano – the accumulated excrement from thousands of bats – which was mixed with the putrefying bodies of their dead. That was a nitrogenous mass which would have delighted the heart of any gardener, but it meant long hours of extra, filthy labor for us. Hours later, when we had made a hole large enough to enter, a round object came bounding down from the rocks above us. We heard it coming, and knew it was not a rock from the way it bounded. We saw it land. It burst when it struck, but it was not a bomb – it was a large nest of infuriated African wasps.

They stung us on the arms and legs and face till we scrambled and ran like children. There could be no question – the natives who had seen us meant to stop our work. We had to return to camp to have the stings extracted and the wounds treated; such stings in that climate, like other minor abrasions, can cause a serious infection. When we reached camp, we learned that some of our mules had disappeared. The savages had stolen them. Without mules we were helpless. My only hope was to appeal to the native chief, but we did not know where he was nor how soon we could find him. Our problem was no longer one merely of digging and exploring; it was a question of getting our mules back so that we could go on across this territory – and of remaining alive. To wait was nerve-racking. The bearers we had sent ahead with gifts had not returned.

It was not till the late afternoon of the second day that we heard the distant beat of tom-toms. We then unpacked and displayed a variety of gifts which we hoped would please the chief and his men, and again we waited. The tom-toms sounded nearer. With our guns handy, we waited in the shade of the dolmens, our backs to them, trying to appear nonchalant.

At last the chief appeared out of the jungle at the head of his men. Tall, broad-shouldered, smooth-muscled, he carried a gold-headed stick – the insignia of his office as chief. Over his right shoulder he had thrown a lion skin. He walked straight toward us with great dignity, in spite of his nakedness. His warriors formed a circle around us.

The chief demanded an explanation of our presence and of our sacrilegious act of tampering with the tombs. Derissa tried to explain. As he talked, I noticed that the naked warriors were looking at the mirrors, beads, and the shiny electric flashlights we had laid out for them. Even the chief's gaze wandered to them occasionally, while Derissa explained our interest in history, and pointed to the presents as indicative of our peaceful and friendly intentions. The gifts roused the curiosity of the savages, but not one of them made any move toward them.

The chief still looked unfriendly, and I was afraid we were in for trouble, when Derissa came over and whispered to me, "Offer to shoot a hippopotamus for them."

When I nodded, he went back to the chief and stated that we wanted to go down to the river and shoot a hippo "in honor of a Great Chief and his people."

For moments the chief seemed to consider; at last he agreed. The crowd muttered and finally laughed their approval. The thought of a feast made them friendly at once; Shankailas are especially fond of hippo meat. Two warriors were delegated to go down to the river with us to select a likely spot. The chief and his warriors remained on the hill where they could see, and the people from the village watched from a lower level.

Along the river bank we found plenty of recent hippo tracks. Hippos climb out of the water late in the afternoon, follow a tunnel through the tall grass by the river's edge, and go up to pasture. They swarm along the rivers in this part of Africa, and each one has his private tunnel. When they leave the water, they rush like giant locomotives to the meadows. Should one of these huge beasts trespass on the tunnel of another, it means a battle to the death. It is equally dangerous for a man, or any other animal, to trespass on a hippo's private right-of-way. Where we were standing, there was a maze of these private tunnels.

We posted ourselves behind brush and boulders at a spot which commanded several of these runways from the river. It was late in the afternoon, the time when the hippo usually clambers out of the water to charge toward his feeding grounds.

"Wait until one opens his mouth before you shoot," Andalamu cautioned me. A moment later he whispered, "Look!"

There was a wake on the river such as might have formed at the stern of a boat. It was apparent that some enormous body was moving rapidly just under the surface of the water. Finally, a head appeared, a huge head with two eyes so tiny that they were out of all proportion to the face in which they appeared. The hippo saw me; like a flash he was under the water again. But he had not emerged long enough to take even one long, deep breath. He would have to come up for air again in a few seconds, or in a minute or two at most.

I moved to a point that was better concealed, and waited for him to rise. With my rifle raised and my finger on the trigger, I stood waiting. The huge head reappeared in fairly shallow water; he lifted it, looked at the place where I had been before, looked around. This time he did not see me. He took two steps toward the river bank and stopped; he yawned, a slow-moving, happy yawn.

That was my chance. I aimed for that big black and red cavern framed with shining white teeth.

The sound of the shot echoed and reverberated. There was a churning of mud and water; a ribbon of reddish brown rose to the surface and floated down stream. The threshing continued for several minutes, till I wondered whether my shot had wounded and not killed the beast. Then the hippo flopped on his side, half in and half out of the water, one leg sticking up.

The chief and his men cheered and came running down the hillside, but even at a run the chief retained his dignity. The savages yelled and roared, and Derissa explained that now we were their blood-friends; we had provided them with more than two thousand pounds of fresh meat, and to them a hippo means what a Thanksgiving turkey means to Americans.

We backed away, moved up a little distance on the hillside, and watched thirty or more men push and pull the hippo up onto the bank. The tom-toms sounded a strange roll; in response the natives swarmed to the scene like ants, and one of our party named that peculiar rhythm of the drums the "Shankalla dinner gong." Before the men could get the hippo out of the river, the smell of blood attracted the crocodiles. Men with spears and lances waded into the water to guard those who were moving the hippo. A crocodile can spring half out of water, twist his head, and, with one snap of his jaws, drag a man down.

Once our kill was on firm land, the naked blacks formed a procession and came marching toward us; they waved their hands and their spears in a gesture of friendship. They stopped a little distance away from us – but not so far away that we could not smell their strong body odor – and bowed to the ground. This was their way of saying thank you.

They turned and went back to the hippo which lay in an open space just below where we were standing. It was then that we witnessed a veritable orgy of the Stone Age. Time dropped back thousands of years. These savages had steel points for their spears and for their lances and knives; otherwise, they might have been primitive man hunting with flint weapons.

The tom-toms and the hippo horn sounded over and over, racking, monotonous notes, while men, women, and children danced and sang their tribal feast song. Suddenly the singing and dancing stopped. They all ran over to the hippo. Hacking and cutting, they clawed at the carcass. They slapped and struck and bit each other to get to the animal. One of them dug out the greatest delicacy and came and offered it to me – the eyes. The huge beast had been slit and propped open with sticks. Men crawled inside, and cut loose bloody chunks of meat which they threw out to others who fought and snarled like wild animals. One woman, with a child in her arms, dragged out the intestines and tried to get her baby to eat some of the loathsome mess.

This might have been a scene in history before man learned the use of fire. The savages smacked their lips loudly over the raw meat; then they took long drinks of the merissa which the women had brought with them, a potent alcoholic liquor made from fermented honey.

The smells drove us back step by step, but the scene was still so strange that we could not leave. Here were hundreds of savages reveling in raw meat, unconscious of their own strong body odor, the smell of blood, and sickly sweet aroma of the merissa. It was revolting, hypnotic.

The moment the abrupt blackout of an African jungle night fell, the savages lighted huge bonfires.

Satiated with food and intoxicated with what they had drunk, they began a demoniacal dance. The rhythm of the tom-toms took on a faster beat. The natives bleated like animals. Without clothes and without any conception of morals as we know them – although they do have their own standards – they followed any and every animal impulse. Nor did they withdraw into the shadows; in the light from the bonfires these ebony men and women joined as if they were alone in complete darkness. With nerves strained to the breaking point, they made weird noises and turned from one person to another promiscuously.

This was our first contact with jungle Ethiopians in the raw – untamed, bestial savagery. Against the background of flaming bonfires and the cleaned skeleton of the hippo, two figures stood out: a huge Negro with a girl in his arms. He moved toward us, and as he did, the savages opened a path for him. He approached and offered the girl, covered with hippo's blood, as if he were offering a cigarette.

I shuddered. The chief said something, whereupon the black who was holding the girl out to me grinned, turned, and started toward the river. The girl screamed and scratched and bit and clawed, but the Negro was so powerful that her struggles meant nothing. The crowd screamed and roared with laughter. Later I learned the girl thought I had ordered her to be drowned – offered as a living sacrifice to the crocodiles. The Negro plunged her in and out of the water as if he had been rinsing a piece of cloth; then he brought her back and placed her at my feet.

A sharp noise startled me. Men were cracking the hippo's skull with stones. They removed the brains and the marrow from the jaw bone. These were brought and offered to me; when I refused, they were given to the chief. It was then that we turned and left that nauseating, orgiastic scene, and though dinner was waiting when we returned to camp, I found I could not eat.

The chief repaid our courtesies late the following day, but he would not permit us to go on with the excavating. Bearers arrived, loaded with baskets of oranges, bananas, mangoes, containers of merissa – and four black girls. The fruits and liquor were presents, but the four women he wanted to exchange for one more flash-light. He also invited me to attend a public trial.

Just as I was leaving to visit court, an old man arrived with a seven-year-old child in his arms. With dignity he pleaded with me to exchange one steel fish hook for his small daughter. I sent him off with the coveted fish hook, and his little girl.

On our way to the chief's thatched, cone-shaped toucul, Derissa explained that this was a society matter, a trial that involved one of the chief's own, many daughters. He had married her to the son of the head man in a neighboring village, but the husband had discovered that she was not a maiden. Faced with the savage "trial by ordeal," the girl had confessed, and was about to be tried by her own father. In such a trial the accused has to walk over piles of red hot stones; even a slight burn or blister betrays guilt. And the promise of such a trial attracted the people of both villages. Naked, in a circle of excited blacks, the girl had confessed, and stood with her eyes closed and her head lowered.

The father of the cheated husband asked his daughter-in-law to name her lovers. Sobbing, she whispered the name of one. The man stepped forward proudly. He admitted the charge, and offered to pay for his gallantry with cattle. A fine of four cows was imposed. The girl named four other men, one after the other. Each one of them seemed proud of his act, and appeared to be perfectly willing to pay his fine. The outraged husband had been the laughing stock of these savages, but as his wealth increased, he evidently began to win their respect. After each fine was imposed, he would go over and inspect the cows carefully. Then he would nod to indicate that the fine was sufficient to satisfy his injured pride.

After his last inspection of cows he came back and stood inside the circle of savages. His wife came to him and knelt. She kissed his black feet and swore that she would never again be unfaithful, and that if she was unfaithful, her family would forfeit all their property to him. He lifted her up and put his arms around her. He looked around the circle of savage faces proudly. The trial had come to an end.

The chief of these strange people is elected as were men in feudal days. Raiding and stealing cattle and slaves from neighboring tribes and villages proves a man's capacity for leadership: "The greater the thief the greater the chief." It is an honor to be the head man of a savage, jungle village, but it has distinct drawbacks. At the first signs of old age – declining virility, gray hair, or losing one's teeth – the chief is quietly put to death. The man whose daughter had been tried was feeling his years, and was worried. When we were alone, he asked me for drugs, restoratives, and charms to rejuvenate himself.

A great many Africans in all parts of that continent believe in tonics: lion's meat gives one courage, the testes of any animal will quicken the sex urge and fertility, eating the ears brings intelligence, and eating the skin from the forehead of any animal increases brain powers. When an infant is ill, the mother will cut off the tip of its left ear and swallow it; she believes that this will save its life. This custom is so prevalent that it is unusual to see a person with the tip of the left ear intact.

To imitate the head man in everything that he does either in public or in private is a general practice. If the chief sneezes or scratches his head, his warriors do likewise. When the chief decides to spend the night with one of his several or many wives, he hangs out a lion or leopard skin in front of his toucul. His warriors do the same thing. When the chief is quietly put out of the way in favor of a younger and more active man, the chief's wives and daughters become public property. They are put out on the streets. Any children they may have in the next few years are treated with kindness – these children are supposed to be of a superior breeding and blood line, and to possess special virtues.

When our mules were returned to us, we packed and were ready to start on toward the Red Sea, through the province of the Mad Sultan Ghogoli, when the chief arrived to pay us a final, farewell visit. He showed me a festering sore on his right arm – he had been slashed in a slave-raiding expedition a week before. I cleaned the wound, disinfected it, and bound it with sterile gauze. Then each one of his warriors came forward to be similarly treated: each of his men had slashed himself on the arm in the same place where his chief had been wounded.

CHAPTER 8

THE BILI CULT

Three days after leaving Dul, we camped in dense jungle. When just settling down for the night, we were roused by strange, new, and alarming sounds. The sound seemed to be suspended in the air as is sometimes the case with a low-lying bank of fog, and we could feel it as one can feel the distant vibration of a powerful pipe organ. It seemed to surround us with the same pressure that one feels in a deep mine. The noise waked the monkeys, but even their chattering seemed subdued, as if they were anticipating some catastrophe. The hyenas in the bush laughed fiendishly.

The camp hung anxiously listening in that surprised suspense of fear of the unknown. Finally, out of that chaos of collective sounds, which continued to float heavily on the air, we could distinguish the beat of the tom-toms. The monkeys kept up their nervous chatter; the hyenas sounded like the uncontrolled laughter of hysterical women. Through this there penetrated three, mournful, nerve-racking notes. I recognized the "Hippo Horn," a nine-foot bamboo rod which ends in a large gourd of squash. Once one has seen and heard a hippo horn, he can never forget it, but even knowing what it is, it still invariably sends a shiver down the spine.

"Fires out," Stromboli ordered; and while they were being extinguished, he explained, "I know from the cadence of the drums and the blowing of that horn that the natives are going to perform some of their weird, nocturnal ceremonies. We'd better turn in, and get away from here at dawn."

I knew when Stromboli ordered the fires to be put out that we were in some danger, yet those strange sounds had for me the call of a Pied Piper. Summoning Derissa to my tent, I told him that I wanted to witness these ceremonies. He looked surprised, then unbelieving, then clearly terrified.

"Oh, no, Master, you no go tonight," he pleaded. "It is dangerous. Priests of the Bili cult are visiting tonight. Better you not see their rites. If priests saw Master, he would lose his life."

I offered him a drink, and poured a triple tot to buck him up. The whiskey seemed to give him courage. While the others slept, we crept out of the tent into the dense thickness of a jungle night, and stealthily made our way toward the hideous cacophony. About a mile away we came upon the first of three thorn barricades which formed a great circle around fifty or sixty *touculs*. We slipped through these barbed stockades unobserved, the noise of the echoing hippo horns and tomtoms covering every sound. Derissa led me through the village, and guided me to the top of a great rock which looked down upon the *touculs*. From this vantage point, by the light of the rising moon, I was able to see all that went on.

A crowd of black figures was dancing in front of the largest *toucul* in the village. "This," Derissa whispered, was "the residence of the High Priest of the Bili cult." Crouching like animals, the dancers advanced and receded to the savage rhythm. They were not only imitating, they were impersonating lions, tigers, leopards, hippos, elephants, and smaller animals; even to their cries and roars and calls. As they trumpeted and grunted in their dance, the tempo of the rhythm increased gradually until they worked themselves into a state of fanatical frenzy.

I had seen some of these weird, wild, dance ceremonies before, but never anything so nervously disturbing. in the shadows beyond the platoon of dancers I could see a number of naked bodies lying motionless in front of the priest's door. Whenever one of those slim forms started to rise, it was forced down again by the front line of dancers.

"What are they?" I asked Derissa.

"Sacrifices. They are virgins."

"To be killed?"

"No, but there will be a bloody scene. You shall see all, Master."

I recalled something of the cult of Baal and Tanit, and this was undoubtedly a survival. The terrible ceremonies of the sacred groves of that time have been described by Frazer and other authorities on the origins of religion. The early cults ordered the deflowering of virgins in honor of their gods; and in certain parts of Africa the sacrificial maidens were dragged to hideous wooden images and forced into the obscene embraces of these gods.

"It is the High Priest of the Bili cult who performs the sacred act," Derissa explained, breathlessly excited. "Look with all your eyes, for the priest will soon appear."

As if in response to a signal, the hanging leopard skin at the door of the priest's *toucul* was drawn aside, and a horrible-looking apparition stepped out. As he emerged, braziers of some light wood steeped in incense were lighted. In the glare and smoke this monstrous figure raised his arms. Striped with white paint from his neck to his feet, his face was entirely covered with a hideous mask. Except for that he was naked.

When the priest raised his arms, four huge natives sprang out from the circle of dancers and seized one of the girls they had compelled to remain lying prostrate in front of the priest's door. She screamed wildly, fiercely, as she was dragged before the High Priest, and held powerless while he possessed her. The animal imitations softened; the hippo horn and tomtoms seemed to increase in volume; then the grunting increased again like a reviving fire siren. All this brought on an attack of erotomania among the eager-eyed spectators.

The priest withdrew into his *toucul* for a draught of the aphrodisiac with which he is supplied on these nights of sacrificial rites. The inert girl was carried to a *toucul* where aged women would look after her, so Derissa explained. The dance went on, building up again to the climax which would herald the continuation of the rite.

"High Priest recovering," Derissa explained. "Only the strongest, most virile men become High Priests; and even they need merissa and drugs to enable them to continue to carry out their duties."

"What happens when they become old?"

"Priest deprived of office, then castrated," Derissa declared calmly.

"What happens to those poor girls?"

"They retire for a month to pray that they may conceive, looked after by old Bili women. Great honor if they are pregnant. The woman is married at once, and the High Priest's offspring is brought up as a priest.

Both her and her husband's family are very proud; and she and her first child are venerated. Great honor to have a daughter selected for this sacrificial rite – still greater if she bears a child."

With the continuous dancing there was shouting and yelling and frequent stops to drink the potent merissa. It seems unbelievable that so many things used to be and still are done in the name of religion: the association of mystic ideas relating to those gifts of the gods – human fertility and the fruitfulness of the earth. There is a parallel between this ceremony of the Bili cult, with its veneration of the offspring of those women who are taken by the High Priest, and some of the incidents cited by Frazer. At Heliopolis and Baalbec virgins gave themselves up to strangers in the Temple of Astarte at least once – a rite associated with the fertility of the earth, mankind, and livestock. To help build up the treasury of the Temple of Mylitta, free women, known as Azriat in the mountainous regions south of Batna, regard prostitution as a holy act which they perform to assure plentiful crops. Similar rites are practiced among the Kabyles of the Beni Gifser tribe southwest of Bougie, and by other African races. These women are perpetuating religious rites, some of which date back thousands of years in history.

With measured timing the priest performed his rite over and over again; he would retire, refresh himself with some aphrodisiac, then appear with ceremonial dignity and repeat the ceremony before the frenzied, dancing witnesses.

When the last victim had been carried away, Derissa said, "Now they will play and dance until they drop with exhaustion."

Exhilarated by liquor and stimulated by the sacrificial rites, men, women, and adolescents of both sexes joined in an abandon which cannot be accounted for by religious enthusiasm alone.

"Old women busy now collecting blood for charms," Derissa explained.

I glanced at him. From the wild look in his eyes, his controlled excitement, and the things he had told me, I gathered that his was more than a theoretical knowledge of the Bili cult.

"Charms?" I asked.

"The blood makes precious love charms. The old women smear statues with the blood, little ones to wear around your neck, big ones for the house. There's profit in exchanging them for cattle, food, and drink. They bring fecundity to those who buy them. If Master wants one, I can buy."

"We'll talk about that tomorrow," I answered.

I turned to take a last look at that maelstrom of black humanity, whirling and twisting and writhing below me. When I turned around again to ask Derissa a question, he had disappeared; and when he failed to return after a few minutes, I guessed that he had gone to join the worshippers of the Bili cult.

This was an act of insubordination and dangerous disloyalty that would have to be dealt with on the following day. Meantime I had no choice – I had to make my way back to camp alone through the agaves and the thorn bushes.

Late the next morning Derissa appeared before me, dejected and very red of eye, but with one of the charms in his hand. He glanced at me and then kept his eyes lowered; his hands hung loose at his sides, and there were beads of perspiration on his brow.

"Deserting me as you did was an act of disloyalty of which no white man would have been guilty, Derissa. This is a stain on your character." I waited for him to speak – he considered himself and all Abyssinians to be white men. When he failed to answer, I asked, "What have you to say for yourself?"

"Sight too much for me, Master." He wiped the perspiration from his brow, and covered his eyes with his hand. "Had to go – Bili too strong for me."

I looked at him for several seconds before speaking. "I suspected you were one of them, Derissa. To atone, you can tell me what you know about Bili. If you tell me the truth, I will forget and forgive the desertion that might have cost me my life."

Derissa bowed in humble eagerness to redeem himself. He was trembling, and so shaky that I poured him a jigger of whiskey to steady his nerves, and indicated a chair on the other side of the table where I had been making notes.

He told me that I was the first white man ever to witness this ceremony of a very ancient African cult. Bili is the name of one of the many black, secret societies which flourish in various parts of Africa. Its headquarters are supposed to be in the Yambio district; there, particularly among the Zande tribes, are many thousands of members. Witch doctors at the head of the organization, under the guise of religion, aim to consolidate authority over a vast number of primitive and highly superstitious people. They promote immorality and obscene rites at secret meetings throughout Africa, and particularly in the jungle sections of the Belgian Congo and Ethiopia.

Membership is forced in some sections through covert threats and open acts if necessary; superstitious women are particularly easy for these priests to terrify into persuading their husbands and brothers to join the cult. Sworn to secrecy, the men are initiated and branded with red hot spears on their backs; the girls are marked with a line on their breasts. Thus, members may identify themselves and recognize other adherents of this cult in distant parts of the Dark Continent.

Wherever a Bili society is formed, theoretically for mystic and religious purposes, immorality and drunkenness is encouraged by the priests – in some districts they have even introduced the use of hashish to perpetuate and increase their own power and wealth. In Ethiopia, a potent alcoholic drink, the merissa referred to, is provided for this festival of lechery. Actually the Bili societies are so powerful in some places that they form a state within a state which is inimical to the interests of the government and the local men involved in its administration. Claiming to possess supernatural powers, these witch doctors extort payments on the flimsiest pretexts from the poor, ignorant blacks. They also do a very profitable business in charms and fetishes – obscene figures of gods, amulets and pendants made of a special wood, and rattles and reed whistles to which are ascribed magical powers.

When Derissa had told me as much as he could remember by way of expiation for deserting me, he even offered further atonement.

"Would you like to take pictures of the witch doctor, the High Priest? And there are other things not so dangerous, but strange. In the village they will sleep for a long time; now is the time to take photographs. There is another ceremony with the women – this time Derissa will not desert his Master."

When we reached the village with our cameras, we found all the natives asleep, but we waked the priest, revived him with cognac, and posed him in front of the *toucul*. After we had photographed him, we put him back in his *toucul* on his mat. If he remembered it at all, he probably thought it was a dream due to merissa and his other excesses.

Later I learned that two European doctors, who were trying to take pictures of the rites I had seen, were murdered for their attempt. In some regions there is a *toucul* known as the Bili House. This has six doors – one for patients of the witch doctor, one for women, a third for men, a fourth for the priest himself, a fifth for those who come to pay tribute and make the so-called contributions, and a sixth so that one may go without being seen by an incoming caller. It is in that way that the priests maintain an air of mystery and secrecy. In the Kordofan and Arabian provinces of the Anglo-Egyptian Sudan, this cult has been sternly repressed, but that is a small area compared to the great territories in which it still flourishes.

When I asked Derissa what other strange ceremony there was – he had referred to one with women – he informed me that we should see it in a few days, on our way to the Blue Nile, that we were going to see the circumcision of women. Stromboli confirmed this, and added that, although this strange custom was not unusual among the wild tribes in the almost totally unexplored sections of Ethiopia, he knew little more about it.

One night we made camp some little distance from a village in which Derissa said the rite would be performed, so we prepared to remain for twenty-four or forty-eight hours. The next morning we paid our respects, not to witch doctors, but to witches. Stromboli, who was as much at home in these surroundings as any Ethiopian, went with us. He offered to "put the natives, especially the village belles, through their paces" in front of our cameras, and he did a great deal to facilitate our getting some striking pictures of these people. He was so persuasive that some of them removed their very few clothes. These girls, unlike some natives, seemed to have no hesitation or objections to posing before a moving picture camera. It was nothing compared to the ordeal they were about to endure in the *toucul* where the witch women operated. There were six girls waiting to be circumcised by one witch woman, an old woman noted for her skill with the lancet.

"Can you arrange for us to witness one of these operations?" I asked Derissa.

"Old woman jealous of her skill, but I ask," Derissa replied.

"Tell them we insist on it," the resourceful Stromboli ordered. "Tell them that we are medical men – Ferengi surgeons – and will give them the latest thing in lancets," and he pulled from his pocket a half dozen, new, American safety razor blades.

The razor blades won for us permission to see and photograph this strange operation from beginning to end. Female circumcision is believed to have originated in Hedjaz with the sole purpose of pandering to the egotism of the male population. The results of this operation are threefold: the technical virginity of an unmarried girl is preserved and conception becomes unlikely, her sexual desire is reduced so that her chastity is safeguarded, and the later satisfaction of the male is insured.

The operation is performed on girls ranging from four to twelve, usually by means of unsterilized, or even rusty razor blades. Septic poisoning is common because the victims are kept with their legs bound for from fifteen to twenty days. There are serious later effects too. As the records of the European hospitals indicate, a large number of circumcised native women are admitted for gynecological treatment. The worst cases are reported from the Beja, Kordofan, and Drafur districts in the Egyptian hospitals.

There are two forms of female circumcision. In one, known in Egypt as the "Sunna" operation, the clitoris and the Labia Minora are removed, and the opening is not permitted to close; the other, the Pharaonic method, consists of removing the clitoris, the labia minora, and the labia majora – then the opening is allowed to close. The Sunna operation is the one most used among the Arabic-speaking Egyptians north of Shelcal.

Performed without any anesthetic, that operation is enough to rouse pity and indignation in the hardest heart, but it produced not even a ripple of commiseration in those black-skinned, wild-eyed people. When the operation was completed, the wounds were sterilized with a red-hot iron.

Another ceremony that we witnessed was the tattooing and branding of both boys and girls with the tribal insignia. Seized and held to the ground, the girls shrieked and screamed while their cheeks, foreheads, breasts, and backs were branded. Not so the boys, for they had been schooled not to utter a word of protest – their honor and dignity for the future depended upon the fortitude with which they bore their torture. They clenched their teeth and not a sound came from them, not even when their wounds were filled with clay and they were placed in the burning sunshine for the clay to bake and harden. That Spartan courage and patient endurance in the face of intense suffering was one of the most remarkable sights that I have ever witnessed.

CHAPTER 9

ALONG THE RIVER OF GOLD

Leaving Dul, we began to climb through a wild valley of mountain jungle. The temperature was more than a hundred degrees, and humidity was high. We were moving into the territory of the Mad Sultan Ghogoli. The District Commissioner at the last British outpost before we entered Ethiopia had warned me about this man, and had tried to dissuade me from even trying to cross his sultanate. Tales of his savage cruelties were legend; the mere mention of his name was enough to terrorize the natives. Here I was going to meet my first real test in my attempt to cross Ethiopia without passports.

The eastern Beni Shangal country is too wild and too far from Addis Ababa to be controlled. It is a semi-independent kingdom, with the Sultan paying verbal allegiance only to the Emperor. Ghogoli was said to be one hundred years old, and still to be looking for pretty young girls. Parties which had tried to cross his territory had disappeared and never been heard from again.

Without permits to cross the British Sudan, or from the Emperor to cross Abyssinia, they lacked official standing. For that reason their disappearance failed to cause much stir.

The trail was rough, and the heat and humidity such that progress was slow. Danger made it necessary to post guards around our camp each night. Under these conditions the men and even the mules showed bad dispositions; and there were fights every morning before we started moving, soon after dawn.

Day after day we moved up along a ravine cut through walls of heat-radiating rock. One day the ravine broadened suddenly, and we followed the bank of a river that was almost dried up. Working in the bed of the river were nude men, women, and children, bent over in the broiling sun. They glanced up at us, but never for a moment did they stop their labors.

"Slaves," Stromboli explained, and went forward.

Some of them were digging holes in the shallow river bed, some were shoveling, and others were using circular pans to wash out gold. Stromboli, who was in charge of the men, mules, and supplies of our expedition, talked to the head man for a few minutes, and brought him back to meet us. He gave us permission to photograph the slaves working in the Werka Warka – the River of Gold. When he thought he was not observed, he brought out a small bag of gold nuggets from underneath his *shamma*.

Stromboli talked to him for a minute, and then turned to me.

"He wants sixty Egyptian pounds for the nuggets. Offer him forty."

The nuggets appeared to be worth a great deal more than that.

"Let's stay here and get rich," one of the men suggested, getting excited.

"I'd have done that long ago if it weren't for the Mad Sultan," Stromboli laughed.

"Does all the gold that's found belong to him?"

"Yes, but there are a few leaks – like this." Stromboli touched the fat nuggets. "A little gets through to the Greek and Levantine traders, but most of it goes to the Sultan. If he learned that this man had offered to sell us any gold, he would have him hanged by his thumbs till he died, and, that in a place where everyone could see him so as to discourage others from ever cheating or stealing."

Stromboli stopped, and then continued, "Ghogoli makes so much trouble along the frontier with his slave raids that Haile Selassie has threatened to remove him. The Emperor does not want to give outsiders an excuse to come here and take over this gold mine. And as far as buying gold here – well, you know about that pretty Abyssinian custom. That's one reason against buying any gold. Castration would be a mild form of punishment. The Mad Sultan's walls are said to be festooned with the dried relics of his enemies and victims."

"Let's see if we can find some fresh game for supper," someone suggested. We got ready, and started out to hunt.

The gazelles we shot attracted lions, and these roared so loud all through the night that sleep was impossible. With dawn we were on our way again, but the heat was such that men and mules were exhausted by nine o'clock. Again we had to make camp. Occasionally we caught a glimpse of higher altitudes which looked cooler, but the misty, palpitating haze of heat prevented our seeing more than that; and to get there we still had days of hard travel. It was there, somewhere in the distance, that we hoped to find the legendary mines of the Egyptians.

The trail was so well worn that caravans must have followed it for thousands of years. We had picked this little-known route, because it would lead us into the middle of the Sultanate before we encountered the scouts of the Mad Sultan Ghogoli. Alongside this ancient trail were occasional mounds of stones supposed to contain the skeletons of slaves who had died in times long past. Hoping to find a skull or two for our anthropological collection, we camped a little distance from one and began to dig.

The natives with our caravan were superstitious, and believed that strange sounds issued from these tombs at night – the cries of imprisoned, tortured souls. After two hours work with pick and shovel we found an opening. When it was big enough I crawled in. Flashlights disclosed a rude chamber made from shafts of stone and roofed with larger slabs; in one corner lay a pile of bones, but they were so old that they crumbled into dust when I touched them. Under a ledge I found one skeleton intact, and the skull looked like a rare find. It was in such a perfect state of preservation that it must have been embalmed by men who learned their art from the Egyptians. We waxed the skull, and packed it in a benzene can in fine hay. Later we found other skeletons, and strings of carnelians and ancient beads. But we had to stop our digging before dawn – the natives would refuse to go on with us if they learned we had visited a tomb.

As we followed the river bed, we found other groups of slaves washing gold. They were all alike; they had the attitude of whipped, stray curs. Livingstone had written about them seventy-five years before, and there had been no change.

"Where do you suppose those carnelians came from?" one of the men asked.

"Probably from here," I answered, and pointed to the cliffs. The granite was diversified with gneiss, porphyry, serpentine, and other quartz matrix. "The carnelians found in the tombs along the Nile probably came from here, too."

Farther on we came to an unfinished obelisk; it was similar to those we had seen in Egypt and made of porphyry. High up on the purple shaft was a ridge of marble – the *verde antico* of the ancients.

"Greek and Roman writers believed that the emerald mines of the Pharaohs were somewhere in this territory, as well as the gold mines of Solomon," Stromboli contributed.

My mind went back to school days – those Greek and Latin passages that dealt with treasure. Then I remembered Rider Haggard's *King Solomon's Mines, Allan Quatermain,* and *She.* And here we were exploring the lands and routes of caravans which had existed long before the birth of Christ.

As we neared the place where Stromboli expected the Mad Sultan to have scouts posted, we consolidated our caravan. Before that, we had allowed men and animals to scatter out in a long string – now we moved in platoons. Stromboli talked with the head men of the many gold-digging groups of slaves as we trekked ahead. One night we camped near one of these placer mines. The natives told us that there was a small Ethiopian outpost not far ahead, and offered to sell us some fine amethysts.

Stromboli advised rushing the outpost when we got there, before the Ethiopians could start any trouble. We moved ahead, to the tiny town, through it; the town looked as if it were deserted. Then suddenly two excited Ethiopian warriors appeared. They ordered us to halt, but the caravan kept moving.

"Where are your passports?" one of the warriors shouted.

"On the way," I replied, and sighed with relief as the last of the men and mules moved past.

The warriors talked to Derissa, our interpreter, who turned to me and said, "They say you must stop. They have no orders to let you pass without an Imperial Passport."

Stromboli, who had urged the men and mules forward, returned at this moment, and, with the greatest assurance, took an imposing-looking document from his portfolio. It was covered with red seals – actually it was a concession from the Ethiopian Government to cut wood along the Didessa River. While the two astonished men were trying to decipher the Amharic, we photographed them. In the meantime, the mules and men were through the town, and moving swiftly down the hillside.

"Now let's go." Stromboli snatched the document from the men's hands, and we hurried away. The two men shouted for other guards, but they must have been sleeping soundly. Soon we caught up with the caravan and made all the speed we could. When night fell, we had seen no signs of pursuit.

That night we made camp in the lee of the great Gebel Beni Shangal at a point where there were traces of ancient excavations. With our flashlights we found passages that led far into the rock, with beds of marble and mica on either side. This was probably an old emerald mine. On the sides of the rough-hewn passages there were archaic hieroglyphics which we outlined with chalk, and photographed by the light from our flashlights.

When we emerged from these hand-hewn caves, a group of natives appeared as if miraculously. One moment there was nothing to see but a chaos of rocks and boulders, the next, there were six men standing there as if they had been stationed there for a long time. Outstretched hands, palms uppermost, showed that they were friendly. They told us through our interpreter that the two customs men were hurrying to Magali to report our forcing our way across the frontier to the Sultan Ghogoli.

One of the men drew me aside, took a small bag from under his *shamma,* and poured its contents onto a table rock. Here were emeralds, amethysts, and crystals. Neither of us spoke one word of the other's language, but I knew he did not want anyone else involved. Several of the emeralds were really fine stones.

By means of pantomime and pictures which he drew on the ground, he showed me what he wanted in exchange – a drink, a knife, and a gun. I patted a stone to indicate that he was to wait, and went down to camp to get some articles with which to barter. As I went I remembered the words of the Greek historian, Cosmos – writing about the ancestors of this troglodytic trader.

A land of frankincense and gold lies at the farthest end of Ethi- opia. Costly things are brought from there to the Nile, or eastward to be taken across the sea to Arabia Felix by the inhabitants of the neighboring Barbaria or Senna. Each year the King of Axum sends some of his people to join the merchants; together they form a caravan of about five hundred who transport oxen, salt, and iron to the land of gold.

When they reach the mountains they build a barricade of sharp thorns and make their quarters in it. They butcher the oxen and carve them, lay out the pieces of flesh along with iron and salt. Then come the natives who place nuggets of gold beside the meat or iron or salt they have selected. If the trader thinks it is enough he picks up the gold; if not the native adds more gold or takes away the nugget he has laid down. The trade is carried on in this manner, because the languages are different and they have no interpreter. It takes about five days for the merchants and the traders to dispose of the goods which they bring with them.

I uncorked a bottle of Greek cognac. That was something those early Greek traders knew nothing about. I could not give the man a gun, but I carried with me the bottle, a can of bully beef, a package of salt, and a hunting knife. Half an hour later our trading was completed. I was the possessor of several nuggets of gold, rough emeralds, rock crystals, obsidian, and amethysts. Later the emeralds, which were light in color, proved to be duplicates of those found in the tomb of Tut-Ankh-Ahmen. They must have come from those rough-hewn stone passages we had explored.

The next morning we began an almost perpendicular climb to the top of the great Ethiopian plateau. This is the great divide between the British Sudan and the watershed of the Blue Nile. The temperature had dropped from well over a hundred degrees to ninety-nine; and now and then one could feel a very gentle breeze. This was the first promise of cool air without humidity we had known for weeks.

Breathless, we topped the ridge a mile above sea-level. There was a tonic breeze blowing from the highlands of the Blue Nile to the west. Torrid desert and plains, and fetid jungle heat were left behind; ahead was a panorama of mountains covered with lush green. Barren, sun-blasted canyons, with thick heat-haze, gave way to valleys spread with trees and flowers, and live, clear air. For the first time in days everyone looked cheerful.

The Nagradas and Derissa reported that there were two ancient ruins, at a tangent to the main trail, which I would want to see. The caravan went on to make camp, while I followed a guide through a paradise of birds and trees and flowers. We went through three recently-deserted villages – household utensils were lying inside the *touculs* as if they had just been dropped. We were probably following a late slave-raiding trail of the Mad Sultan Ghogoli.

To save their women and children, the people had fled toward the Blue Nile and British freedom, so Derissa explained. This confirmed the stories which had been told me in Khartoum and Kurmuk. To escape the clutches of the Mad Sultan, these people tried to reach a land where order and liberty prevailed.

"Any young girls would have been put in the Sultan's harem; and the men and women would have become slaves at the River of Gold," Derissa said.

When we reached the region of the first ancient ruins, it looked like a high pile of stones. We had to cut our way with machetes through thorns and bamboo to reach the crumbling fortifications. There were foundations for two circular edifices of some size, probably temples. We found a number of flint implements including adzes, and some Neolithic arrowheads made of shale. Some of the larger blocks of stone were covered with symbols and drawings of great antiquity. Small hatchets were made of hematite or bloodstone.

The things we found indicated not one, but several epochs. The Neolithic implements represented one historic age; shards of pottery suggested the proto-Pharaonic period. Systematic digging there might prove a partly Sabean and partly Ethiopian civilization dating from 1500 to 1000 BC

On our way to the second ruined city we went through a forest of giant lobelias. In that city we found an inscription, in a language totally unknown to me, which may prove of real importance in deciphering the history of early civilization on the upper Blue Nile. Photographs of that inscription went to linguistic experts at the *Institut de France*. I also found two fylfot signs – Sanskrit and Indian swastikas. It was clear that the people in this region were connected with the Egyptian, Sabean, and Axum civilizations.

The nearer we approached the Blue Nile, the more difficult it was to cut our way through. Aloes, thorny acacias, cane, and bamboo made passage awkward. Giant sycamores measured twenty to thirty feet in circumference. Cacti and palms were scattered everywhere.

We reached camp to find it pitched on one of the most beautiful spots in all the world. We were camped under huge trees on the edge of an emerald pool. The men were swimming in crystal clear water, the white men above and the natives further down the stream.

The cook was calling for wood while he skinned an antelope for dinner. The horses and mules were cropping lush grass along the river bank. Ethiopians with long spears were standing half-concealed by bamboo; they looked astonished, but appeared to be friendly. The phonograph with Negro jazz records failed to move them, but it did have one surprising result. Several nude women came swimming downstream from around a bend in the river.

Their naked bodies glistening with water, they giggled, climbed out of the river, and came up to camp. Some of them wore ancient necklaces which they were eager to exchange for mirrors and strings of red beads. It was too dark to photograph them that night, so they returned the next morning, and in exchange for more beads they allowed us to take pictures.

The advance scouts returned to inform us that the Mad Sultan Ghogoli himself was waiting for us at the village of Abu Moti. We had almost crossed his Sultanate. Beyond lay the well controlled province of Walaga, just across the Babous River.

We considered making a wide circle around Abu Moti and trying to get into Walaga, but both Stromboli and the Nagradas advised against it. The next afternoon at three o'clock we climbed to the top of a small hill; from there we could see a group of *touculs*, with dirty, white-clad figures carrying spears moving back and forth in front of one of them. This was Abu Moti, and the Mad Sultan Ghogoli was lying in wait for us there.

CHAPTER 10

THE MAD SULTAN

At the foot of the hill leading to Abu Moti, we organized our party to make as impressive a showing as possible. I rode the white horse, with Derissa on one side of me and a Nagrada on the other; then came the gun-bearers. Behind them came Andalamu, carrying the flag of the Explorers' Club; following him were the men, horses, and mules in groups of twelve.

The white-robed soldiers whom we had seen had disappeared. It was past the middle of the day, but still terrifically hot, and most of the villagers were asleep. It looked for a moment as if, by marching through boldly, we could repeat our success of Wadi Dul.

Slowly we moved through the silent town, and no city has ever seemed so long. At the farther side I pulled up, and waited for the rest of the caravan to pass me, counting the animals and men. One of our men was missing, one of the Nagradas. That might mean trouble, or he might have stopped to ask for a pass for his mules and his men, to be used on his return to the Sudan. We moved with all the speed we could, but tried not to look as if we were running away.

Before we had covered any distance beyond the town, we heard shouts and saw a cloud of dust behind us. A man on horseback, with several followers, galloped up. Through Derissa he demanded that I return and show my passport and permit at the Sultan Ghogoli's headquarters. I ordered the men to unload the mules and make camp on top of a low, rounded hill, and to get out the cognac and other presents.

The head man, who looked like a pirate and appeared to be half Arab and half Negro, protested. He tried to order the whole caravan to return to Abu Moti, but the men were fast making camp. To gain time, I pretended not to understand what he wanted.

"The Crown Prince says his father will force us to return," Derissa translated. Questioned, he explained that the head man was the favorite of Sultan Ghogoli's four-hundred-and-some-odd legitimate sons. It seemed better to make a show of force; all the guns were brought out, and placed in a defensive position around the camp. Foot soldiers with spears had followed the Crown Prince and his mounted guard, and they surrounded us, talking loudly and making war-like gestures.

"Tell him we shall camp here until relief comes, that Haile Selassie, the Emperor, is sending a large military escort to meet us."

The British at Kurmuk had told me not to give way by even an inch while we were in Abyssinia, or we would never get through.

"Tell him that I am now ready to go with him to call upon his father, the Sultan Ghogoli," I said to Derissa. With our guns arranged in a fairly wide circle around the mules, horses, men, and supplies, the warriors could see that we meant business – that we were not afraid. I started off in the middle of a howling, hostile escort, with Derissa following.

"These people are all Shiftas," Derissa whispered. "Brigands."

They looked it. They brandished antique guns, daggers, lances, and revolvers. It is difficult to imagine a more war-like set of desperadoes. The mixture of Arab, Negro, and Abyssinian blood produces the perfect African gangster. Surrounded by this mob, we rode back to Abu Moti, across the town again, and into the Sultan Ghogoli's compound. Guarded by a high wall of long and sharp cactus thorns, it was a large yard filled with bodyguards and dignitaries. We entered a large, but typical *toucul.* It was like a great silo, with a thatched, cone-shaped roof.

I was ushered over to a little man who was seated on a mat, surrounded by a number of fat little boys. When my eyes got used to the dim light, I saw that he was wrinkled and wizened, but that his eyes were piercing, vicious, malevolent, and calculating. There was something evil about his wiry vitality that had endured through his reputed hundred years. When he spoke, his voice was a cross between a bark and a snarl.

He said something to Derissa, and stuck out his hard, claw-like hand. Derissa took the low stool a Servant handed him, and indicated that I was to sit down. Then he said, "The Sultan asks what the hell you are doing in his country."

"Tell the old devil we are just passing through on our way to visit the King of Kings."

The Sultan Ghogoli listened, snorted, and said something I gathered to mean, "Not to visit this King," and that he did not welcome visitors.

Derissa translated – the Mad Sultan had said just what I thought he had – and continued, "And he says that Haile Selassie is only the King in Addis Ababa."

"Tell the Sultan that I shall be glad to inform His Majesty, The Emperor, of his words when I reach there."

"The Sultan asks," Derissa said after talking to, and listening to him, "What makes you think you will ever get to Addis Ababa?"

"Oh, tell him I'm the son of the King of France."

"He says," Derissa translated, "that fat French missionaries came here long ago – when the Sultan's people left the restaurant they said there never were such good missionaries."

I wondered if the stories of cannibalism we had heard were true, or whether the old devil was having fun at my expense. Just then one of the boys pinched another, who let out a squeal. Quick as lightning, the old man tapped the offender on his shaven skull with a knotted stick.

"Are these his sons?" I asked Derissa.

"All Abu Moti are his sons," he answered. "Big *fantasia* tomorrow. New boy born in the Sultan's harem."

I looked at the hundred-year-old man again. "Please congratulate him for me."

Derissa did, and then turned back to me. "The Sultan is pleased. He wishes to know how many wives you have."

"Tell him, one."

The old Sultan snorted in contemptuous disbelief. "Ask him how many wives he has," I demanded. "Better not," Derissa advised. "He is touchy about such matters. He has government-controlled harems in every village."

The Sultan snarled again, and Derissa translated, "He wants to know how many bottles of cognac you have with you. And have you come to steal his wives or his gold?"

"Tell him I'm not interested in his wives or his gold, but that I have plenty of cognac for his *fantasia* tomorrow."

"The Sultan is pleased. I told him you were interested only in science and history, old stones and pictures, and antiques."

The Sultan's snake-like eyes glittered, and he made some sharp request of Derissa.

"He wants to see your passport."

"Tell him that The King of Kings is sending permits and passports to me with an escort."

Sultan Ghogoli looked at me suspiciously while Derissa translated. He talked to my interpreter for several minutes. Then he called one of his lance-bearing warriors and barked an order.

When the man had gone, Derissa said, "He is sending runners to the Dabous River to learn if you are telling the truth. You will have to remain here until his runners return." My heart fell. If all the letters and telegrams had brought no answer over a period of months from Addis Ababa, was it likely or even possible that there was an escort on its way to meet us now? We had waited in Alexandria, in Cairo, in Khartoum, and in Kurmuk. One by one, six scientists had deserted our party, unwilling to risk their lives in this savage, jungle country without permits and passports. I wondered if I had been foolish in risking the lives of the other members of the expedition.

The Mad Sultan was looking at me, like a hooded cobra from under his eyelids; a shiver ran down my spine, but I managed to smile. "Thank him for his courtesy," I said to Derissa. The Sultan snapped another order, and stared at me. I did not know whether to stay where I was or attempt to leave.

Slaves – men, women, and children in Northern Africa – are usually marked by a single gold earring. In response to the Sultan's order a huge Negro slave entered with a chest and placed it in front of the aged Ghogoli. The old man opened it, removed several bags of what appeared to be gold nuggets, and lifted out two bronze statuettes and several gold coins. Even at first glance I knew they were extremely old and Egyptian. I tried to remain calm while examining them – they were exciting finds. One of the coins was very ancient Roman.

"Ask the Sultan where he found these things." Their historical value depended on that; their intrinsic value was considerable.

"For a thousand thalers he will show you the place," Derissa explained after talking to the Sultan.

"Offer him five hundred for these pieces *and* to show us the place."

"For six bottles of cognac and five hundred thalers he says he will do it."

When I nodded, the Sultan laughed maliciously, and spoke to Derissa.

"He says all right, the laugh is on you. They were found right here in Abu Moti. He will show you where tomorrow morning. And now we can go."

The Sultan barked an order as I rose, and his voice was sharp and mean. In a moment I was out in the compound, surrounded again by the brigand escort. A slave held my horse and waited for me to mount, but he did not let go of the bridle. I waited. Derissa had disappeared in the crowd; the slaves were staring at me and talking loudly. It was not till several minutes had passed that the Sultan came out and mounted his horse. I wondered if I were being taken prisoner.

We rode out toward camp. Just before we reached it, the Crown Prince drew the side of his hand across his throat. That may be amusing as the "cut off" sign in a radio studio, but with savages it has a less humorous implication. The Crown Prince repeated his gesture, and grinned wickedly.

The Sultan, two aides, and the Crown Prince rode into camp with me; the rest of the escort circled around outside.

"Keep them covered, and give them cognac," I said to Browne as I dismounted and gave my horse to one of the Nagradas. "Where are the money chests?"

"Don't look! Buried under the boulder on the right," Browne answered. "Are we prisoners?"

"Yes. I'm afraid of treachery. Give me your revolver and warn the men. The Sultan has sent runners through to the Dabous River to see if the Emperor's escort is really coming."

The Sultan and the Crown Prince looked over our baggage and stores appraisingly, covetously, while they drank cognac. They did not try to conceal their interest in our guns and ammunition, so I suggested a shooting match. Africans generally are bad marksmen, but they love to shoot. Tactfully, we permitted the Sultan and his son to win the prizes we offered for hitting a bull's eye. But nothing seemed to satisfy them. They made it clear that if the Emperor's escort did not arrive –

While they drank our cognac, they counted our men and guns, and carefully appraised our supplies. Finally they left to return to Abu Moti – probably to sleep off the effects of the liquor. The Crown Prince left in particularly good humor. I let him think I had not seen him hide two bottles of cognac under his burnous. Just before he left, he asked me to visit him in the village that night. There seemed to be little danger, at least until the runners returned from the Dabous River with news, so I accepted. The future and life itself had never seemed so promising – and so discouraging, but I had to pretend, and try to maintain the morale of the rest of the men.

I had scarcely given orders to keep a watch and a guard, day and night, and that no man or men were to visit the village on any account, when the Crown Prince returned. He was so drunk that he was scarcely able to stay in his saddle. Without his saying so, I expected him to show me more antiques. He led me on a wide detour, in an almost complete circle of the town. Finally we dismounted, went through a narrow passage, and entered the second largest *toucul* in the village, but not before the Crown Prince had posted guards outside. And we had not come to see antiques, as I had hoped; he had brought me to visit the harem – not his own, but his father's harem.

It was a large, round, dimly lighted room, full of fat, giggling females. The one old kerosene lamp showed low couches all around the wall, eighteen or twenty of them; and mine was the privilege of seeing the travelling seraglio of His Majesty, The Sultan Methuselah Solomon Ghogoli. What would happen to the

Crown Prince if he were found there, I didn't know, but there was no question of what would happen to me – and it was not death of which I was afraid.

We sat on a rug and opened a bottle of the cognac I had brought with me; I poured a stiff drink for myself, for if ever a man needed liquor, I needed it at that moment. Still drunk, the Crown Prince wanted to show off in front of me and these women. He opened another bottle of cognac for them, and ordered two of them to arise for approval. He put them through their paces as if they were prize horses in the ring, and in a manner that was wholly revolting. The women giggled, and – it must be said – appeared to enjoy it thoroughly. There seemed to be no escape from the hot, dimly lighted room, for I could not afford to offend the Crown Prince.

The tempo of the soft music increased with the drinking. The overtones that characterize African and Chinese music, with their minor harmonies and discords, have an exhilarating effect, once one becomes accustomed to their cadence. I was already thoroughly uncomfortable when we heard a low whistle from the guard outside.

The Crown Prince jumped with surprising speed and seized the bottles. The nearly nude black women rushed and pushed us out through the back entrance. The move was so sudden and abrupt a release from an embarrassing situation that I wanted to roar with laughter. The women and the Crown Prince were plainly terrified, and I would have been too, if it all had not seemed so funny.

The Sultan Ghogoli was on his way to visit his harem. I hoped that he was still so inebriated that he would not notice cognac on the breath of his favorite. We stumbled around in the darkness, which was full of cactus thorns, made a circuit, and finally reached the horses. I wanted to return to camp, but the Crown Prince insisted that I visit his *toucul* first. He showed every sign of wanting to make a night of it.

His own harem had fewer and less attractive women than his father's. Obviously, the Old Sultan selected and kept all of the more attractive ones for himself. The Crown Prince sat on a rug with a fat concubine on either side of him, the bottle of cognac

between his feet. Both of these women wore massive gold ornaments in the form of entwined serpents. My interest in the ornaments brought a hiccoughed explanation from the man. The
necklaces and bracelets came from Abu Moti, and were very old.
He handed me one of each so that I could make sketches of them
and of the unfamiliar symbols on the charms.

I stood up and handed them back, explaining that I would send
presents for his favorites in the morning. He was too inebriated or
too occupied to protest, but he did draw the side of his hand across
his throat, and make a gurgling sound. That was his pleasant way
of saving good night.

I rode back to camp, unaccompanied and unmolested, to the
sound of the tom-toms and the strum of the quarter-tone music –
these punctuated by singing and occasional shrieks and yells. The
noise kept the whole camp awake most of the night, in spite of the
sentinels we had posted. Even the Nagradas were restless, as if
they expected some devilish treachery; they showed more uneasiness than at any time on our long trek across the desert and into
the jungle.

While we were prisoners of the Mad Sultan, there seemed to
be nothing we could do but wait. But in spite of that, breakfast
was ready at dawn; and we had just finished coffee and lighted
our pipes when the Crown Prince came to get me. A hangover and
too little sleep had left him in a bad temper; but a couple of drinks
and presents for his favorites improved his mood. We started off
to find the ancient ruins his father had promised to show me.

Two miles north of Abu Moti there were several large mounds
which were undoubtedly the remains of some ancient city. These
ruins belonged to the same period as those we had visited earlier.
There was the same kind of masonry, the same design and
construction, but everything of value seemed to have been
removed by the avaricious Sultan.

When we climbed down to the tombs, I saw that they were
similar to the sepulchres of Gebel Moya and Axum. Just as we
began to photograph them, the Sultan arrived with his warriors
and shouted for us. "The tombs are sacred," Derissa explained.
They did not even want us to photograph the mounds. The Sultan's brigands followed us around, and every time I picked up a

stone or a broken piece of pottery, they jumped at me. After an hour we gave up in disgust, and rode back to camp.

While we stayed in camp, Derissa told us stories of the Sultan's cruelties: refinements of torture that have been going on for nearly four thousand years – two thousand years before the coming of Christ and more than nineteen hundred years since. The mildest is the *Lex Talionis,* the law of an eye for an eye. If a man is adjudged guilty of a major crime such as murder, the nearest male kin of the victim is required to kill the offender while the family and friends look on. Until Haile Selassie changed the law, the ordinary thief or robber was hung to a post in the middle of a village till he was dead, left there for three days as a warning to others, and then dragged through the streets to a dump where his body was left to the hyenas and the vultures. With his ears and nose cut off and bleeding, a man could be buried alive up to his neck in an ant heap, and, as the Greek trader had told us, his screams could be heard for miles.

Death by cotton is reserved for assassins or would-be-assassins of an Emperor or Sultan. This ceremony is performed in an open square or amphitheater, and hosts of people are invited to come to witness it. This, too, serves as a lesson to discourage regicides.

The prisoner is stripped, his hands tied behind him, and he is staked out in the center of the enclosure. Soldiers with knives and lances form a large circle around the outside the circle the people gather to watch the show, and there are roofs and elevated stands for selected guests, and a dais, resembling a box at the opera, for the nobility. It could be a horse race or a football game from the way this hideous ceremony attracts and holds the crowds.

The criminal is compelled to watch while a slow-burning fire is lighted underneath a cauldron in front of him. The fire is kept small in order to prolong the ceremony. Tallow is put in the kettle and melted; then men dip narrow cotton bandages in the liquid, and wrap them around the victim carefully. This, too, is a slow and formal proceeding. With his hands tied behind him, the prisoner is released from the stake. He is swathed in several thickness of these tallow bandages from his chin to his hips, and on halfway down to his knees. The bandages are not unlike mummy cloths. He is hobbled, but is left free enough to use his legs and run. Finally, one piece of tallow-soaked cloth is twisted, and caught under the other layers of bandage on his back, in such a way that it hangs like a tail. This serves as a lamp wick. At a signal from the Sultan this wick is lighted. The moment the cloth is ignited, the crowds cheer and yell as if they were seeing a home–run. It is believed that being boiled alive in oil is quicker and less agonizing than the death by cotton. The slow-burning bandages burn, smoke, break into flames, smolder, and then blaze again. The prisoner runs when he begins to burn; he strikes against the solid wall of spears and lances that the warriors hold. He rolls on the ground. He screams.

When the prisoner runs against the wall of blades, the warriors are very careful not to let him slash himself in any way that would shorten his agony. The victim keeps throwing himself against the blades, bounding back, hurling his body against the knives, trying to kill himself. The crowds keep on cheering and jeering.

Gradually, the smell of burning flesh increases, but there is a limit to human endurance. The victim goes mad. In the intensity of his suffering, he does not know what he is doing. The pungent odor of roasting meat spreads; the aroma is unmistakable. At last his suffering is ended, from insanity he goes into unconsciousness, then into his death throes. Haile Selassie was opposed to this death by cotton, and wanted to do away with it entirely, but the powerful Coptic priests prevailed upon him to keep it alive as a law.

These tales of suffering and torture added to our discomfort. If the King of Kings did not send an escort with passports and permits, what was our fate going to be? I noticed that all the other men in our party seemed to care as little for the meals when they were served as I did. Even the century-old Sultan's *fantasia* – for which we supplied the liquor – failed to relieve our worries.

We listened to the music and the tom-toms, the screams and laughter and the singing for hours after we had returned to camp and retired. Several times that night I got up and smoked my pipe; once I even made a tour around the camp to make sure that the men were keeping watch. The night seemed endless, and the morning dragged as if all time had stopped.

About eleven o'clock that morning, in the shimmering heat, a man galloped past us. At noon the Crown Prince rode out with several men. Again he was in a bad mood, and looked as vicious as usual till he had consumed several drinks. Then he talked to Derissa for several moments, and kept motioning toward me. Several times the interpreter tried to get away, but the older man kept on talking and gesturing.

Finally, Derissa came over to me. The runners had met Haile Selassie's escort on its way to meet us. The Crown Prince and his father, the Sultan Ghogoli, had never for a moment doubted the truth of my statement, and we were invited to remain for as long as we would as guests of the country. I sent Derissa out to tell the rest of the men that we were saved. They had been as worried and anxious as myself.

The Emperor's escort was made up of one hundred and twenty people with horses, mules, huge parchments covered with red wax seals and ribbons, and carrying flags and elaborate umbrellas. At its head was an important Prince, who presented us with gifts, passports, and permits. We decided to break camp, and leave the following morning.

Late that afternoon I rode in and paid my farewell visit – with presents – to the Sultan and his son. In the evening the Crown Prince returned my call, and announced that his father was coming to pay his official farewell, and was bringing gifts.

With pomp and ceremony the Mad Sultan appeared at the head of a slow-moving procession. He and his son had accepted presents – and had exacted them in a way. Now he made return as became the Sultan of a great province doing honor to his Emperor's honored guest. The things I should have really liked were few and not valuable – ancient beads, coins, pottery, and finely wrought miniature figures of pre-Christian gods and goddesses. His gifts of fruit and supplies were more than ample, but his personal gift to me was, from his viewpoint, truly regal.

At the approach of his father, the Crown Prince disappeared – , with a bottle of cognac. Derissa translated a long, ceremonial address which the Mad Sultan made. Later I learned that that was to impress the Prince who had come as the head of the escort, and to ward off a contemplated military occupation of the Beni Shangal which would have done away with this savage old Sultan's power. Then came the speech of presentation. He built it up to a climax, offered me his claw-like hand, and left as soon as I could express my appreciation.

He had assured me that his gift to me was completely fresh, unsullied, and untouched, but he had not told me what it was, though he explained carefully that it was for me alone. He had departed with a wicked snort and chuckle. I was not prepared for the surprise and the shock it gave me. Soon after the Mad Sultan had gone, the camp literally rocked with laughter. Browne and Stromboli ceremoniously ushered me over to see my personal present. The Mad Sultan Ghogoli had presented me with twelve of his virgin wives.

It took several minutes to adjust myself to my predicament; meantime all twelve black beauties simpered and giggled. To return the Sultan's gift was clearly not possible; that would be the most insulting thing I could do. It might even offend the Prince whom Haile Selassie had sent to meet me.

Derissa suggested a gracious way out. He explained that each girl probably had a sweetheart among the soldiers; a tactful suggestion would bring the right soldiers to "steal" their girls that night. The men would conceal their wives till we were some distance on our way; but it devolved upon me to furnish them with trousseaux – beads and mirrors. He added that each would name her first-born son for me.

On our way to the Dabous River the next morning – without my gift – we passed the gruesome evidence of a battle. The troops of Sultan Ghogoli had met the neighboring Gallas there. Thirty Gallas had been killed, and their grim, mutilated remains were hung so that you could not fail to see them. While Browne was taking photographs of these grisly souvenirs of cruelty, I asked Derissa if the victims had been dead when they were operated upon.

"Probably," Derissa answered laconically, and shrugged.

At the Italian disaster at Adua, Abyssinia, in 1898, several thousand Italian soldiers had been operated on in the same way – the Ethiopians had sterilized them, and had sent them home eunuchs. That is what Haile Selassie meant when he asked his troops to be merciful to the Italians they captured in 1941. Italy has never forgiven nor forgotten the insult of 1898.

With a shudder, I turned from the Galla's grisly remains toward the majestic, winding river. I regretted being unable to explore and search for historical treasures buried in the Beni Shangal country, but it was a relief to get away from the power of the cruel Mad Sultan Ghogoli.

CHAPTER 11

WILD BEES AND BUSH FIRES

One of the most terrifying and painful experiences of my life occurred on the Didessa River. Alone I went on ahead of Stromboli and the rest of the party, hunting for game. As I was aiming at a gigantic crocodile steaming leisurely upstream, a couple of bees got under my helmet. I brushed them away, and was raising my gun again when something stung my arm. Looking down, I saw that my arms and legs and hands were covered with bees. An attack by a swarm of wild bees may sound funny, but it is genuinely dangerous, since the consequences may prove fatal.

I dropped my gun, rushed into the thick cane-grass, and rolled; but it was too late. The bees were already crawling all over me, stinging my eyelids, my lips, even my nose. They were down my neck, in my nostrils, into my ears. In a frenzy of terror and pain, and partially blinded, I rolled over and over in the cane and elephant-grass, and still those diabolical insects went on stinging. Though I knew that the river was full of crocodiles, I would gladly have thrown myself into its water to escape this burning fire if I could have found it – but by now my eyes were too swollen from the stings to see anything.

In excruciating pain, I stumbled into a mud hole and plunged my whole head into water that stank, got out, and then in my blindness could not find it again. I screamed in agony; opening my mouth allowed the infuriated bees to get in and sting my gums and tongue. I pitched into a hippo hole, got out, fell again; that was the last I remembered.

Late that afternoon, when camp was pitched, and I had not appeared, Stromboli organized a party to search for me. Luckily they found my gun, and later my swollen, unconscious self. There could be no question as to what had happened, for as soon as the searching party arrived these infuriated bees turned, and attacked them. Stromboli had had experience with them before, and succeeded in fighting them off; he wrapped me in *shammas* which he took from the porters, and they carried me back to camp. When he told me about it later, he said that those angry bees had followed them for several miles.

Once they got me into a tent, Stromboli and two men set to work with tweezers to extract thousands of stings before I regained consciousness. When I came to, they were bathing me with ammonia; but my fever was so high that I alternated between delirium and consciousness. The venom of the bee is formic acid, and formic acid poisoning causes cramps and colic. In a conscious moment I heard roars of laughter, and Stromboli saying, "He looks like a swollen, putrid hippopotamus."

Soon I saw lights, and heard the characteristic clicks of the camera; they were making pictures of me – I even tried to laugh before I slid into unconsciousness again. That wild bee attack held us up for more than a week, and it was more painful than any accident I have ever had.

Once, going through the swamps of the Sacred Lakes of the Libyan Desert, I had been bitten by a snake and had had to spend ten days in the hospital in Siwa. In Mexico, my arm had swollen to the size of a balloon-tire as the result of a tarantula bite. Another time, I had made the mistake of putting my hand into a knapsack without looking; as a result, a scorpion bite made me dangerously ill, and put me in the Fort Sudan Hospital for a month. But none or all of those was as agonizingly painful as the wild bee stings.

With our escort from the Emperor, the dangers from unfriendly natives had been reduced to a minimum, and on February 14th, we reached the great Abyssinian Plateau, eight thousand feet above sea level. Here we met another of our many complete changes of climate; the nights were freezing, and the days were scorching.

Necessarily, we were travelling in the dry season; at that elevation and at that particular time of the year, the whole landscape was dry and dusty.

Our caravan traveled in three sections of about twenty mules and men; three Nagradas controlled or owned between them the mules and sixty men. But it was our escort which was interesting; it was made up of more than one hundred Abyssinians. They are a proud race, but cruel to their slaves and animals. The leaders are moderately intelligent and very brave, but so jealous that they are ever ready to draw a knife and start a bloody struggle with any rival. Fights occurred daily; to avoid these, and the constant racket and wrangling which went on day and night, I pitched my tent a hundred yards away from theirs.

What a contrast were these people to the Indians of Mexico and Guatemala; there they are uncomplaining, sad, and stoic. Abyssinians sing and fight and chatter all day, and generally throughout the night; around the camp fire they talk and talk, going over and reiterating every trivial episode of the day's march. As a result, one is exasperated to the point of frenzy during the night – an exasperation which reaches a climax each morning when attempting to overcome the lethargy of the men and the after-effects of their drinking the night before. A white man frequently does more work on an expedition than does a native porter.

Abyssinians are expert stalkers of game, but bad marksmen. Of course, the latter may be due to the fact that most of their guns are relics of the Franco-Prussian War. They are inordinately proud of their country, and profess disdain for a number of European races. Toward the Italians they feel a vast superiority because of the ignominious defeat they were able to inflict on them at Adowa. The upper classes practice an old-world courtesy characterized by sweeping bows, wide flourishes with their hats like cavaliers, and exaggerated manners.

The poorer people are apt to kneel every time you meet them in the villages or on the trail, and some of them even touch their foreheads to the ground. The only exceptions to these courtesies are the wild, pure-blooded Beni Shangal and Shankalla – pagan Negroes of the Blue Nile – both of whom are cruel, cunning, superstitious, sensual, and even sometimes vicious.

While we were crossing the territory of these bellicose people of the upper Blue Nile, we discovered some prehistoric rock drawings. Deeply cut into the rock and boulders were scenes of warfare and hunting. These clearly depicted the prehistoric peoples who had inhabited Africa from the Atlantic to the Red Sea thousands of years before. Superimposed on these deep etchings were Egyptian hieroglyphics of a much later period. These dated from the epoch when gold was being exported from this part of Ethiopia to the Pharaohs. And they were overlaid with yet a third series of pictures of the period of Sabean culture.

A few miles beyond, on the top of a hill, we came upon hundreds of human skeletons which, our Nagradas told us, were the result of a comparatively recent battle between the Shangallas and the people from "across the river." While we were looking at this eloquent symbol of war, we ourselves narrowly escaped death, on this sun-blasted North Abyssinian Plateau.

Most of the animals and men had gone on; and some one probably dropped a lighted cigarette into the dry elephant-grass. Andalamu, our guide, believed it was done intentionally to satisfy some grudge, but whether or no, we were cut off from the rest of the caravan by a wall of flame that swept up that Hill of Skeletons with incredible speed. The burning bamboo and grass were just as dry as kindling; the flame and smoke sprang toward us and towered over us like a tidal wave. As it came, it sounded like some tremendous waterfall.

Our only chance was to get to the river before that wall of flame strangled us. We started to run. Soon we were being passed by terrified gazelles and antelopes. Overhead, kites and vultures – ever on the lookout for carrion – flapped their wings.

When we thought we had gained a little on the fire, we stopped for a few seconds to catch our breath and to take some photographs, but as the fire surged and jumped nearer in a great seething roller, our cameraman said dryly, "You never engaged me to photograph hell." Then he ran.

The heat swung at us like a veritable inferno; blazing sparks and brands, carried by eddies of heat, started fires ahead of us. Two men tried to save the moving picture camera, the mules that carried it, and the films. The heavy smoke dimmed the sun, and it grew dark. In panic-stricken confusion, we became separated. When I looked around, I seemed to be enclosed in a circle of fire.

It is strange how one's mind reverts at a time like that – (*or does* one only *think* he remembered it all later?). However that may be, I remembered flying over the Tabascan jungles trying to locate Mayan temples when we had discovered that there was almost no gas left in our tanks; in a diving suit, four fathoms below the surface of the Mediterranean in the submerged ruins of Tipasa, the life line had become entangled; when my canoe over-turned in Lake Pitha, I had been surrounded by crocodiles; once I had been entombed by a cave-in among the mummies in the Hill of the Dead at Siwa; several times I had been attacked by fanatics; and the time I was most afraid in all of these experiences – the time when I was lost for three days in the Western Sahara.

Hillier had been forced to slash his own wrist and drink his own blood once – which gave him eighteen hours' more of con-sciousness and saved his life. Another time, when we were both lost in the Sahara, we had killed a camel and drunk its store of water. That water proved to be green; it made us both sick, but it probably saved our lives in spite of the fact that later we, too, turned a sickly green and remained that way for days. But all expeditions mean facing danger and death from the known and the unknown.

To beat that roaring wave of flame ceased to be a matter of stopping and looking back; it became a race for life, with every man and beast running, on his own, without thought of supplies or future needs. When finally I plunged into the river, my coat over my face to keep from breathing flames, I was black and singed. We hailed others of our party as they joined us from up and down the river, thankful that so many had escaped.

When every thing had been burned or killed by that fire – grass, bushes, trees, and animals – we had to wait for hours for the earth to cool. For the next few days we searched for missing men and mules. Some of them had covered great distances; some of them had been burned to death; some of them had escaped only to be killed by the savage beasts of the jungle near the river. Looking for them was a sad, slow business.

A large part of the caravan had gone ahead, and because of this fact enough of our supplies and equipment were saved to enable us to carry on. And – wonderful luck! – the films were spared, which made a real and precious addition to our pictorial account of the Gold Trail in Ethiopia.

Some cults, such as Bili, seem to spring up and thrive all over Africa like weeds; others, highly individualized, seem never to spread beyond a certain tribe or area, though one hears of them in far distant parts of the world. Buda is one of the latter cults, a pagan survival of which I had read and heard fantastic accounts. Stopping on the summit of a mountain, we looked down into one of the many picturesque canyons which lead to the Blue Nile.

"Can we visit the villages of the pagan Negroes who live in this district?" I asked Derissa.

"Buda! Buda!" Derissa was so frightened that he spoke in Amharic, before he remembered and continued in English. "The evil eye is here; these people are bad. Not Christians, Master, they worship the sun and animals. They are cannibals who fight with poisoned arrows. No go to those villages, Master."

Looking at that vista of beauty, it seemed impossible to believe it concealed gross cruelty, and ugliness, and ignorance. Before us lay a tangle of tropical vegetation, studded with rare orchids and brilliantly colored flowers and birds.

"You know about this animal cult?" I asked.

"The Dog People live down there." Derissa sounded sullen and resentful at my question.

I suspected that he was talking about lycanthropy; curious instances of this superstition had been brought to me in Haiti. After a few seconds of hesitation, Derissa began to talk, and as he progressed he grew more and more excited and so eloquent that I wondered if there were any basis in fact for this and other weird legends of the district.

As he talked, the Dog People became a race of monsters, a cross between human beings and beasts who lived hidden away in the Mountains of Shan. "Children of the Devil," he called them. After a long palaver, without which these natives are never willing to cooperate, Derissa admitted that there was one chief who was a great friend of his. The man had become his friend when he bought from him, for an Abyssinian who lived in Mendi, two Shankalla virgins and a first-class eunuch.

With the moving picture photographer and five porters we left our escort, while the main body of the caravan prepared for a fairly long stay. This is one of the worst sections in all Ethiopia for malaria, so we took plenty of quinine and mosquito nets as well as provisions and gifts.

When we reached the village of which Derissa's friend was the chief, the man professed to have nothing whatever to do with Buda. Upon receiving gifts of electric flashlights and Greek cognac, he admitted that this cult was practiced in a village two days' march beyond, and offered to provide us with a guide. Banboo, the chief and Derissa's friend, warned us that he would not be responsible for the consequences if we showed ourselves during the ceremonies. If we followed his guide's advice, we would be able to see the rites from a distance, but at any false step or sound on our part, the natives would murder us without compunction. He said that convincingly.

When we left, he was getting a little drunk on the liquor, and playing like a child with the electric flashlight, which he turned toward his own face and flicked on and off, over and over again. We headed back into the jungle through thorns that formed a particularly dense barrier. Led by a guide who knew the secret trail, we followed the bank of a river which was half dried-up. From the deep pools the snouts of crocodiles protruded menacingly; one would occasionally slide off the sun-baked mud and slither into the water holes. We had to keep a sharp lookout for enormous snakes which coiled at the sound of our approach, and waited to strike. At the end of the second day's circuitous march over ground which fairly vibrated with danger, we came within sound of the village tom-toms. We made camp among some great boulders and waited for the rising of the moon. Until then, our local guide and Derissa assured us there would be nothing to see. Toward midnight, when the moon was at its height, we could go, and not before. Not until the natives had had enough to drink and were achieving their fanatical frenzy, would it be safe for us to approach, not until their guards and watchmen had been enticed away from their posts by the orgiastic ceremony.

The moon was high over those somber, volcanic mountains when we started stealthily toward the village. The guide led us by a roundabout route toward the sounds, and finally found us a position on high ground which looked down on the clearing. Full and almost overhead, the Abyssinian moon gave us as much light as does the sun through haze. Neither the jungle trees, towering into the sky around the clearing, nor the *touculs* cast any shadows; in the background lay a chaos of volcanic rocks, and around them flowed the river like a gigantic silver snake.

Before us in the clearing, as if it were on a stage, the dark native figures moved or stood. The night was still, and the air was so heavy that we could smell the pungent odor of merissa, mingled with the stench of raw flesh and perspiration from long-unwashed bodies. In front of us was the carcass of a huge hippo, and as we anticipated, the Buda rites began with a feast; not until great quantities of raw meat and merissa had been consumed, would the formal ceremonies commence. The tom-toms increased in volume and in tempo after this, till the noise was deafening. Strange chants, which filled our hearts with fear and sent cold shivers down our spines, pierced the beat of the tom-toms.

In spite of having seen a hippo feast two months before, this one was so fascinating that time seemed not to exist in my consciousness. It was as if I were hypnotized – living in a state of suspended animation – and with it I felt the kind of suspense which keeps one leaning tensely forward.

Abruptly, the tom-toms and the poignant chanting ceased. The natives, who had been moving about stopped, as if they were automatons. It was a pregnant silence, of evil augury, the suspense of awful dread. The queer light from the moon seemed to take on a faint green tinge.

Slowly, officiously, ceremoniously, the leopard skin over the door of one of the *touculs* lifted. With measured tread a gigantic, well-proportioned man moved out into the moonlight. The essence of evil could not have been portrayed on any stage in so loathsome a form, and so horrifying a countenance. Satan himself seemed to stand there, satirically looking over his dupes before he spitted them. This was the Dabtara, the medicine man of the Buda cult, a worker of evil spells. His tall, broad-shouldered, naked body was painted with an intricate pattern of white circles and mystic symbols.

"Worse than the evil eye," Derissa whispered. "Listen! He is going to make his call."

The Dabtara turned toward the clean silhouette of a ridge of rocks and brushwood above the village. After several seconds of tense suspense he began to howl – the call of a jackal in the rutting season. It ran and echoed with a foul, sensual quality that made me shudder. As the echo faded, there came an answering rutting call – unmistakably filthy and obscene in its significance. That was the signal for an amazing scene.

Wholly unobstructed by scud, the moon poured down a clean, white brilliance, a celestial spotlight. With the answering howl, those people who had stood for minutes without moving, threw themselves down on their hands and knees. They groveled and impersonated scavenger hyenas and jackals. They acted like dogs at mating time. They may well have been hypnotized – without inhibitions – and truly believing that they were jackals and hyenas, so completely were they dominated by the most animal of instincts.

Here was a bestial variation of Walpurgis Night: the howling of the Dabtara, the groveling animals around his feet, sent chills down my spine. Superstitious feeling welled up from my innermost depths; was there still a tie-link between man and the animal kingdom? Was there something more than hypnotic trickery in this survival of a rite which indicated that once man and animal were one and indivisible?

"Probably all arranged by the Dabtara with an accomplice in the woods to answer his jackal mating call," one of our men suggested skeptically. "It's his way of keeping his hold over these poor, superstitious people." But the events of the next few minutes swept away his supposition.

The next act was like one incident of the Bili cult, but this time the woman cooperated willingly. Voluntarily she "sacrificed" herself to the person of Satan, the Dabtara – not in a normal manner, but like animals at mating season.

And worse was still to come. I literally kicked myself to be sure I was not under some hypnotic power or illusion. Mass hypnotism is not unusual in the wilds of Asia and Africa; I was not sure we were free of it.

"Are we hypnotized – under his spell?" I asked Derissa.

"No, Master. You can believe what you see," he answered. From out of the forest there came running – jackals, real jackals – foul, scavenging beasts. I could see their eyes blazing with excitement, tongues hanging from foam flecked mouths, gleaming teeth, amorously wagging tails. They mingled with the blacks, lapped wine, and joined with them in a manner which, even while witnessing it, I seemed not able to believe.

Before, I had thought I was going to be sick; now, there was no time for thought. I turned away and vomited, nor could I turn to face that scene again. As we moved away along the river bank, two jackals stopped near us, then at our smell or from the unexpected sight of whites, they ran off howling. We were evidently not of their clan.

Again I retched, and it was with a whirling brain and tottering legs that I returned to camp. I have seen many strange things on the Dark Continent; the Aissiawas pierce their bodies with swords and swallow hands-full of nails, or scorpions, or deadly snakes, with impunity; the veiled Tuaregs go through the unbelievable performance of the Ahal; the firewalkers of Tibous are interesting. But this bestiality on the snake-infested banks of the Dabous River still haunts me.

Stromboli and Derissa taught me a great deal about those African superstitions in addition to the many things I saw. Pearce and Coffin have written about them at some length; and so has C. H. Walker who was British Consul to Western Ethiopia for many years.

The men who work in pottery and metals in Ethiopia are looked upon with superstitious awe. Most of them are Falasha Jews who came to Abyssinia untold centuries ago bringing their knowledge of crafts with them. Whether they came as slaves or free people is not known; through the ages they have kept apart, practicing their religion and their arts. They were so isolated in Ethiopia that not until a comparatively few years ago did they learn that there were other people in the world who believed as they did, and who followed their faith in the same way.

One reason for the native's strange aversion to these artisans is that they believe they have the power to change themselves into hyenas and other ravenous beasts. Convulsions of hysterical disorders are attributed to the evil eye of these unfortunate workmen. Many of them are known by the name of Buda; and even men of superior intelligence attribute marvelous exploits to them. The Budas are distinguished by a peculiarly formed ring worn by the whole cult; and Coffin declares that he has frequently seen such a ring in the ears of hyenas he has shot and trapped.

How these rings found their way into the ears of the hyenas he has been unable to discover. Besides the power these people are supposed to have of transforming themselves into wild animals, they are imagined to possess the still more dangerous attribute of inflicting disease and sickness merely by directing a malignant look towards their victims.

The Ethiopians also believe that the metal workers while they are in the form of hyenas are in the habit of rifling graves; and Coffin tells this remarkable story of a man transforming himself. Among his servants he had a man who belonged to the Buda cult. One evening, while it was still daylight, the servant asked for leave of absence till the following morning. Giving the asked-for leave, Coffin dismissed the matter until one of the other servants called to him, "Look! He is turning himself into a hyena." Coffin turned instantly, a matter of only a few seconds after he had given the Buda leave. He missed the transformation, but the young man had vanished, and a large hyena was loping off at a distance of one hundred paces. This occurred in an open field where there was not a bush or a tree to intercept his view.

The Buda returned to camp in the morning; accused by his companions of this strange metamorphosis, he did not deny it. Russell states that a similar superstition existed among the Greeks and the Romans. Pliny discredits it. Sir Richard Burton likewise comments on the magical practices of the metal workers and potters among the Abyssinians and the Somalis.

C.H. Walker quotes a statement made to him in Amharic:

When a man is eating of a meat sauce at the midday meal, a Buda passing his door may gaze upon him. He will fall ill and will send speedily to the scribe who sells medicines and charms. These, his friends will sew for him inside some for-

eign leather; hung on a cord around his neck this packet will heal him. Some scribes are cunning workers of spells, having parchment of the skin of a goat on which they can inscribe holy texts and charms against the Evil Eye, shooting pains, rheumatism, and blindness. Also a scribe may sell medicine from the root of a tree, and, if a man lie sick from the Evil Eye, his bread companions will cast the drug upon the embers and, when the fumes arise, will cover the sick man with a shamma and hold him over the fire till the smoke enters his mouth and he begins to rave, saying: "So and so looked on me as I ate." Thus will be revealed to them the name of the Buda. Then, hiding their knowledge, they will give a feast to which in ignorance the Buda will come, and when all are assembled, one of the kin will cry, "Come, all of you! Spit upon the sick man before our eyes." When the spittle of the Buda touches him, he will be healed. But, had he worn a writing down his neck upon a cord, he would not have been struck down.

(C. H. Walker is the author of the invaluable English-Amharic Dictionary.)

CHAPTER 12

PLAGUES AND PESTS

Ethiopians are secretive about their historical antiquities, but after two or three hours palaver one evening, and with the adroit presentation of gifts at an opportune moment, I learned that we were camped near their Sacred Mountains, fairly close to some noted caves and ruins. But there was one outstanding handicap to our exploring; the Governor was a "bad man" who hated the *Ferengi* – foreigners. Further, it was said, he did not discourage cannibalism.

Undaunted by the danger of being served as the *pièce de résistance*, I argued that, if there were antique stones with etched inscriptions, I should be able to tell him the history of his ancestors. Unwillingly persuaded, some of the natives led me to the Governor. When I offered him this gift in exchange for an opportunity to see and photograph, he frowned and his eyes blazed. Through my interpreter he made it very clear that he was in no way interested in his forebears, and that he already knew too much about them. After a long session, however, he grudgingly granted us permission to explore.

The first night after we left the Governor's headquarters, we camped in a region so wild and so beautiful that it was breath-taking. We pitched our tents on the edge of a vast, rugged canyon looking down over a fairyland oasis – an oasis of graceful palms and wild mimosa, of strange trees on which hung brilliantly colored orchids, of other flowers of many vivid shades. It was a multi-colored tangle of vegetation, alive with creatures of the tropics. Blue and white birds flecked with silver and gold flashed up and down the valley; monkeys and baboons swung happily from tree to tree. Looking down, with the sun slowly sinking, it seemed to be a magic valley, not unlike the traditional Garden of Eden, an ideal spot for prehistoric man to have left traces of his activities.

The next morning, long before sunrise, and before the night voices of the forest had been stilled, I was out with a small pickaxe and a specimen-bag, exploring the strange boulders and needles of volcanic rock. I heard the roar of a lion on some plateau above me, and the unmistakable sound of leopards prowling in the thickets. The lower precipices were on a level with the tops of the tallest palms, and dark fissures under overhanging rocks indicated caves.

Pushing my gun ahead of me, and worming my way into one of the caves, I recognized the stench of animals. My flashlight showed smoke-blackened walls where, obviously, man had lived centuries before; the floor was covered with soft earth. Starting a preliminary trench, I soon unearthed crude implements of obsidian, that dark, volcanic rock which resembles bottle-glass; we had made collections of this months before in Mexico and Guatemala. The workmanship was identical, thus supporting my theory of the Atlantean civilization having spread from east to west.

I carried the obsidian lance-heads and other objects into the daylight. The similarity of workmanship linked them not only to those of Mexico, but also to those of the Atlas Mountains, Carthage, the Hoggar Mountains, the Valley of the Nile, and the British Sudan.

From those finds I knew that this part of Ethiopia was some day going to be a fertile field for archeological research; an untapped source of history, it may even be one of the centers of the origin of man. That Abyssinia is the birthplace of African man is becoming more and more apparent with increased research. From there he moved and spread to the Valley of the Nile and on across the whole of Africa, until he reached even the Grimaldi Caves of Mentone.

We explored these local caves for several days. When we started westward on our journey, I saw for the first time one of "The Seven Plagues of Egypt." Fairly frequent in tropical countries, it is a phenomenon which is said never to lose its strange interest. It was a plague of locusts.

"The curse!" shouted the natives, "the curse!"

For fifteen minutes all progress was halted. Those insects came at us in serried battalions, hundreds of thousands of locusts following other hundreds of thousands. They flew in great clouds pursued by other clouds. When we could see and begin to move again, they lay six inches deep under our feet; they made the going so slippery and difficult that even our sure-footed mules skidded and slid.

While they were still advancing, the camera-man set up his machine and began to film the sight; but soon that living cloud was so thick that it obscured the light of the sun and made it seem like early evening. In the semi-darkness we were almost smothered and blinded by the locusts flying in our faces and around our heads.

The hum of those countless wings sounded like the drone of a multi-motored plane approaching; and through that noise you could hear the natives calling to the Virgin Mary for protection.

Our local guide got the other men to help him shout and wave arms in an effort to keep the insects from landing there in his province; he wanted to frighten them so they would pass over his homeland – and land on the property of others. This stampeded the mules, just at the moment it had grown light and clear enough to start moving, and had no effect whatever on the swarms of insects. The baggage, food, and medical supplies were tossed right and left. The mules took off in a dozen different directions; the men shouted and prayed and waved their arms.

Before we could again collect the mules and reorganize our party, the locusts had devoured every visible speck of the lush, jungle green. The mimosa and other bushes were stripped of their leaves; not a flower or a blade of grass remained. All that had been colorful and beautiful was reduced to a drab, dry desert. From the six-inch carpet of bugs, the Ethiopians selected the fattest, cut off wings and legs, put the body inside a date, poured honey over it, and washed it down with *tedj*. This is a great delicacy for them.

(One author says that the Abyssinian locust is called *Terad* in Yemen and *Anne* in the Danakil country. During his stay on the Bay of Amphila, so he writes, a plague of locusts landed on one of the islands and in a few days destroyed nearly half the vegetation, not even sparing the bitter leaves of the Rack Tree. These insects "are frequently used as food by the wandering tribes who broil them and eat them in the same way Europeans eat shrimps and prawns.")

Storks, eagles, hawks, buzzards, vultures, and all kinds of brightly plumaged birds wheeled down like swallows to feast on the insects. Exploring in Ethiopia presents more problems than one encounters in almost any other country; every day brings some new tangle which has to be straightened out before one can move on. When our mules and supplies – most of them – had been collected, we followed a winding canyon into the Sacred Mountains.

The local Governor was less hostile than we had anticipated, but he was sharp-tongued and to the point. He wanted to know exactly what we were doing there, and why. Derissa explained that we were making a courtesy visit to the Emperor – and pointed to our Royal Escort. Despite the usual exchange of gifts, the Governor retired to his *toucul* looking suspicious. He did not offer to help in any way, but neither did he try to hinder us.

To get to the inscribed stones, we had to cut our way through the jungles with the machetes I had brought with me from Mexico. After hours of cutting paths, one of the workmen on the summit of a hill unexpectedly pointed to the ground. "Here is one of the sacred tombs," he called.

When the vegetation had been cleared away, there were the slabs, covered with strange hieroglyphics. Here, buried in the jungle, were traces of man in his unrecorded and long-forgotten past. Every archeologist feels a thrill when he discovers some long-buried historical remnant, which may throw light on ancient times or confirm some existing theory. In addition to the writing, there were some well-designed pictures of skulls; and on the top of some of the nearby boulders were cup-like troughs which may have been used in connection with sacrifices. These troughs were similar to others I had found at Siwa and at a number of other spots in Africa.

It took hard scraping and rubbing to uncover the entire surface of those stones. What at first we thought was an unknown language, proved to be etchings made in three different periods, one superimposed over the other. With paper especially prepared for this purpose, we made squeegees, not unlike newspaper mats. We found rough, underlying drawings of prehistoric man in the time of the Stone Age, Sabean writing, and the Old Amharic characters of present-day Ethiopia, usually to be found only in the ancient ecclesiastical documents of the country. Casts made from these squeegees can be seen in the Museum of the University of Pennsylvania at Philadelphia, and in the *Institut de France* in Paris.

This was an exciting find, for it showed a definite link between the Egyptian and prehistoric periods. So we set to work with a will.

"You must not touch any of the tombs in these mountains," our local guide announced. "Evil spirits dwell in them."

To take the photographs we wanted, we had to cut down trees and brush to make a clearing – a kind of forest studio where the operator could work. To facilitate the taking of pictures, we outlined the inscriptions and drawings with chalk. Several of them were clear-cut, lunar drawings showing different phases of the moon. They might have been a calendar used in sacred ceremonies of the past.

Another complete drawing showed a battle scene. Figures with lances and circular shields were like those seen in the land of the Tuaregs and the Libyans. One sketch was distinctly Egyptian in character, while near it was a worn cartouche – the inevitable Solar disk and Ram's horn which was almost the hallmark of the ancients all over Africa.

Absorbed in our work of copying, deciphering, and photographing, we suddenly became aware of the rhythmic note of approaching tom-toms. Our guide looked worried; he feared the priests from a nearby monastery were coming to this sacred spot with an escort to inspect our work. He urged us to hurry.

Speed in the face of tom-toms coming nearer and nearer is nerve-racking. We worked as long and as hard as we could, until the tom-toms were almost upon us. Then we waited to receive the unknown enemy, with our backs against one of the biggest boulders, our escort around us, our guns ready in case we needed them.

The men who appeared through the bush took us by complete surprise. A fanatical-looking man with a long face, wearing a towering turban on his head, marched toward us, followed by a number of white-robed monks. The High Priest – he carried the gold-headed cane which is the insignia of his office – moved majestically to within speaking distance and pointed at the motion picture camera. For a moment I thought the priests and the excited group of natives with them would rush at our camera and smash it. Our escort and the pointing guns carried them past that moment of mob hysteria. A minute later they all began shouting angrily at once.

"Why are they so angry?" I had to yell to be heard, though I had waited several minutes for the din to quiet.

"They say this is the Sacred Mountain of the Moon," Derissa shouted into my ear. "These are the tombs of the ancestors of ancient Ethiopians. The priests are very angry. By cutting down the trees, you have committed sacrilege, for in them live the spirits of the dead. They do not understand how you came to know of this place – the Devil must have told you, and now he is cursing you and will send you to Cahannab – the Ethiopian Hell."

"Tell the *Ecagei* (the head man) that we have removed nothing, and that our interests in these stones is only that of a *Liq* (a professor). Say that I will give funds to the monastery."

These were the strangest Christians I ever met. They talked about evil spirits and haunted tombs, and of spirits who lived in trees – a confusion of pagan practices and Christian ideology. The promise of a contribution to their funds, and profuse apologies, calmed their rage; but they took us with them, theoretically as guests, virtually as prisoners. Fortunately, Derissa and Andalamu concealed films and other records we had made underneath their *shammas,* so unless they were searched, we had at least something to show for our long day's work.

This was my first contact with the redoubtable Abyssinian clergy, whose power is so great that their hints and suggestions are virtually laws; they even dictate to the Emperor. They own almost one-third of the country; 10 per cent of the population is directly or indirectly employed in or by the Coptic Christian Church. Here is an Empire in the heart of Africa that was Christian long before Europe. While the Britons and Gauls were wearing hides, eating raw meat, and making sacrifices to the gods of nature with the Druids, these Abyssinians were wearing clothes, building magnificent obelisks and temples, and constructing monasteries to house and preserve their ancient manuscripts.

The power of the clergy in Ethiopia offers one of the more serious political and economic problems which retards this country's growth and development. Forming a state within a state, a government behind the government, the majority of the population bows down to a group both ignorant and bigoted, and permits it to drain their little monies. Ethiopia is more priest-ridden than even Spain was in the days of the Inquisition.

Surrounded by these white-robed priests, we marched down to the monastery through the gaping crowds of an awe-struck village. When we reached it, we were shown into spacious guest-quarters, and told that, until we explained fully, we were prisoners. The quarters were dirty and near the privies – six holes in the ground.

When we were summoned to pay our respects to the Bishop, we found him on his patriarchal throne in oriental splendor. The Coptics belong to the Monophysite branch of the Christian Church whose teachings reached Ethiopia in the third century after Christ. In the seventeen hundred years which have passed, the teachings have become distorted and infused with paganism. The gorgeously-attired Bishop began by scolding. He could not understand why the Emperor was so foolish as to allow foreigners – *Ferengi* – to enter his domains. This was only a part of his arraignment of all foreigners.

"Historical research!" His indignation made it clear that he did not believe us.

"What you are really interested in is the gold and platinum and wealth of the country. I declare," here he shook his fist in Derissa's face, "the Emperor Haile Selassie is wrong. He will deeply regret his imprudence."

That the priests wished to acquire and keep the treasures of Ethiopia for themselves, against the interests of a backward people, was manifest. The old Bishop ranted on until he had talked out a good part of his indignation. Then I asked him for his opinion of the Emperor's plans for educating the people along European standards with free schools.

"Nonsense!" he retorted. "Only the priesthood should be allowed to learn to read the manuscripts. Educate the common people and they will follow in the ways of the Devil."

His mention of manuscripts gave me an opportunity. I assured him that we were fellow students, that I belonged to a class of men who venerated ancient documents relating to the history of the Church; through Derissa, I explained something of the organization of the Protestant and Catholic Churches in America. He was amazed when he heard that there were two hundred and forty-odd branches of the Protestant Church. Gradually his attitude changed from one of indignation to at least an approach toward friendliness; and eventually we were informed that we were no longer prisoners.

Descending from his throne he led us into the great library of the monastery where thousands of precious manuscripts were rolled and filed in pigeonholes. He ordered that some of the most ancient be shown to us. Here was a treasure house of historical and bibliographical information and data. These parchments were covered with clear, fine writing in ancient Geez – an antique, ecclesiastical language reserved for the use of the Church and certain educated classes. Some of these biblical parchments dated from the seventh and eighth centuries, and one that was decorated with primitive drawings in gold, red, and purple, belonged to the fifth century.

When I told the Bishop something of the immense value of these manuscripts – that there were bibliophiles and libraries in the United States and England which would pay hundreds of thousands of dollars for such specimens – an unmistakable gleam of avarice showed in his eyes.

"Purchase, yes, but not robbery," the Bishop complained. "Do you know that a French expedition last year came upon a half-abandoned monastery and carried off the manuscripts?"

I shook my head, no; but I did, for they had been on display in Paris when last I had been there.

"Ethiopia for the Ethiopians, I say," he declared, but what he meant was Ethiopia for *his* Church.

Those precious manuscripts were put back in their respective pigeonholes, when they should have been preserved from dust and damp in a museum's air-conditioned glass case. After we had contributed many thalers to the poor box, we were offered food and *tedj*. When we returned to the guest-quarters after dark, the floor had been strewn with fresh leaves, and we were most ready for sleep after the work and excitement of a day that had begun before dawn.

The moment I lay down, I heard a curious sound. It was as if hundreds of grasshoppers were skipping in the leaves. As I listened, trying to discover what was making that strange noise, something bit me. I felt another bite, another, a dozen simultaneously. The other men were twitching and turning in the darkness, too. As I groped for my flashlight, several others clicked on. We were being attacked by thousand of fleas.

Never have I seen so many together. They hopped collectively and individually, and in those few minutes since we had first lain down, they had penetrated our clothes. They seemed to bite every part of my body at once. Cursing and scratching, I started for the door, followed by the other men. In the darkness I stumbled, fell over the prostrate body of one fat monk, only to land with a crash on the fat belly of another. In falling my flashlight flew out of my hand. Later we learned that several of these monks had been assigned to guard us, and they had stretched out and gone to sleep in front of our door. The men who were following me did not have time to stop either; they fell and stumbled over the sleeping clergy who set up an unholy yelling and shouting for help. In a few seconds half a dozen slaves appeared in the darkness armed with clubs. Before we knew it, we were in the thick of a melee that would have done honor to Hollywood.

"Derissa!" I shouted, as soon as I could get my breath, "Explain that we are only trying to escape from the fleas."

When we finally found our flashlights, Derissa succeeded in explaining, but this only led to more trouble. The monks were insulted. Never before had anyone complained of fleas in their guest-quarters.

"No white man ever tried to sleep in that room," the cameraman commented. "But I'd give a lot for lights to film this show."

Unfortunately, Derissa overheard him and growled resentfully, "We Abyssinians are all white men."

That night was ruined for us, and so were the next few days. Those fleas infested our clothes, and they are devilish to catch. Our bodies were a mass of bites. Worse still was the fact that that part of our supplies which contained the insect powder had been lost in the plague of locusts when the mules stampeded. After a long talk with the Bishop the following morning, we were permitted to leave on the agreement that we would not touch or photograph any of the graves while we were in his bishopric. It was a genuine pleasure for "The Scratching Expedition" to take its leave from there.

CHAPTER 13

DAJJAZMAC MARIAM
GIVES US A DINNER

From the flea-ridden monastery we moved on toward Lekempti, the first town of any importance since we had entered Ethiopia. The Emperor's personal escort had joined us long before; now, while we were still on the trail, we were welcomed by his personal representative, Prince Galata. He arranged to introduce us to Hoppit Makial, Commander-in-Chief of the military forces of the province of Walaga.

From the Prince I gathered that the Commander-in-Chief was a man of considerable importance, and we made preparations accordingly. But we were not prepared for the spectacle we saw. Outside the town we were met by a procession made up of the General and his escort, a thousand warriors and one hundred slaves on foot. Hoppit Makial was a tall, haughty, fierce-looking man with a fine beard. Dressed in the barbaric costume of an Abyssinian general, high on his head he wore a crown made from a lion's mane, and his medieval clothing was encrusted with precious stones. His escort, who rode mules, were dressed with equal splendor, and were shaded by immense green umbrellas which their slaves held over them.

We dismounted, according to Abyssinian etiquette, and waited to be introduced. First the General ordered his chair, which had been brought for the purpose, to be placed, and leopard skins to be arranged in front of it. When he had taken his seat, we were ceremoniously introduced, and photographs were taken. Then the procession reformed, and we started toward the town, in all the splendor of an oriental pageant, to make a noisy and triumphal entry into Lekempti.

There was a great display of banners; the warriors carried antique shields and lances; the immaculate white *shammas* of the dignitaries were in sharp contrast to their green umbrellas. Numbered among us were the ecclesiastical dignitaries, the General and his gorgeously caparisoned escort, Prince Galata, and our very shabby, travel-stained selves.

We were invited to stay at the Governor's palace, but remembering the monastery with its fleas, I begged off. Instead, I asked permission to camp on a hill nearby in a particularly lovely eucalyptus grove, where there flowed a stream of clear water. That request was granted, and we were officially informed that Dajjazmac Mariam, Governor of that very rich province, expected the members of the expedition to attend a dinner in our honor that evening. *Dajjazmac* in Amharic means "one who camps near the door of the Emperor's tent in time of war." Evidently, this was a Governor of more than usual rank. Proffered as an invitation, it was more nearly a royal command.

It took hours of mending and cleaning and brushing to get our clothes into presentable condition, and even then we must have looked like beggars on horseback. Shortly before eight o'clock the horses arrived to take us to the dinner party, they were Arabian thoroughbreds, caparisoned for princes and kings. Over their saddles were thrown long streaming cloths of purple and gold; and around their necks were bells of solid gold and silver.

The palace was a sizable structure with wooden verandas and a galvanized-iron roof, but its foundation was stone and so were its walls; the sheets of galvanized iron had been carried on the black, curly heads of slaves for hundreds of miles. A flight of steps formed a grand staircase up to the door.

At the entrance to the palace a court chamberlain met us, and led the way into a waiting room in which the furniture and carpets were a confusion of the styles of East and West. While we were still looking at this strange mixture, a white-robed attendant entered carrying a silver tray; on it were crystal glasses containing the last thing in the world we might have expected in this wilderness of Ethiopia – perfect, properly-iced, Manhattan cocktails.

My surprise did not delay my drinking one immediately, and fortunately, for almost instantly the wooden doors to the throne room were thrown open, and we were ushered into the presence of the Governor, Dajjazmac Mariam. As we advanced, he descended from his throne to greet us, dressed, not in the gorgeous Ethiopian attire, but in evening clothes with a white tie. He shook hands and invited us in perfect French to sit around him. He was a young man, handsome, with very black eyes, and with one foot bandaged. When I asked him if he had had an accident, he replied, *"Non, mon cher Monsieur,"* and, smiling to reveal a number of gold teeth, "I suffer from the hereditary complaint of my family – gout."

"Then we are fellow sufferers, Your Highness, and I have a remedy that has worked well for me. It is at our camp and at Your Highness' disposal if you care to try it."

Dr. Laville, a specialist on gout in Normandy, had given me the prescription. French people came to him from great distances for his cure. Dajjazmac Mariam was so taken with the idea that he sent a slave immediately with a note to Derissa to get him some of the medicine. Just then the Governor's wife entered. Slender and beautiful, she wore an exquisite Abyssinian costume.

Her red lips had something of the contour of the Orient, her slanting eyes were soft and shining, her complexion olive. Shyly she spoke a few words of French to welcome us; after that she remained a silent, beautiful picture beside her husband. This Princess of Ethiopia wore a soft, clinging gown in a shade of green that emphasized her pale, olive skin; around her neck and in her ears were rough-cut emeralds such as we had seen in the tombs near the River of Gold in Werka Warka. Tinted nails on her slender feet showed through her open sandals. Her hair was done in the Abyssinian fashion, brushed away from the forehead and formed into a high, wavy crown. She was the first exquisitely gowned and beautiful woman we had seen since we left Khartoum.

After a second round of cocktails, the doors into the banqueting hall were thrown open. The table was perfectly appointed with silverware, crystal glasses in front of each place for different wines, and with low vases of orchids and rare flowers from the jungle as decoration. Behind each chair stood a footman in his picturesque white *shamma*.

Dinner was as much of a surprise as were the appointments. The Governor had imported a Russian chef who had formerly worked for a Grand Duke. He, in turn, had trained the native servants in such fashion that even the caviar was served in the approved Russian manner. The list of wines to be served – beginning with chablis and ending with vintage champagne – was appropriately read aloud by the major-domo. Once dinner had begun, conversation swung onto the subject of the Italian menace. The Governor asked my opinion.

"The Italians claim that you are not united and that you are badly governed by the Negus," I answered.

The Governor laughed. "That is funny, for the Italians are trying to bring about our disintegration."

"Would your Highness enlarge on that statement?" I asked.

"Yes – " he thought for a moment before he answered. "We are honeycombed with paid agents, spies and propagandists, here in Ethiopia. Count Vinci, at Addis Ababa, and the other Italian consuls pay two-faced respect to the Emperor."

"Is the Emperor, Haile Selassie, aware of this?"

"Ah! His Majesty does not wish to offend. He chooses to be diplomatic, and relies on God and the League of Nations to maintain peace. The Great Meneuk would have arrested these agents, had them shot as spies, and asked God's forgiveness afterward."

"You *know* that the Italians are trying to undermine your national solidarity?" I asked.

"It is pretty plain, though we have no counter espionage here. We are without experience in spying and the propaganda methods in which your civilized nations are so proficient." He laughed. "We know that the consulates are hotbeds of intrigue, supplied with funds and plans sent here under cover of their diplomatic privilege. If I could, I should violate those damned privileges and meet trick with trick. But the Emperor will not listen to me. He says that would cause an international incident which could be used as a pretext to start war. Our King of Kings is honest, he keeps his word, he is without guile. Some day we will find an Italian force in Ethiopia; and our tribesmen will retaliate. The Fascists will use the usual civilization pretext for another war of conquest."

This was a prophecy which soon came true, for the Italians used the Wal Wal incident as a pretext for beginning the war not long after.

"What do you think of the League of Nations?" I asked.

The Governor scowled for the first time that evening. "We gained admittance to the League, thanks to a diplomatic trick and a lie. Due to the eloquence of Senator de Jouvenel, France got us in, but not for the benefit of Ethiopia. At the time, relations between France and Italy were strained, and Jouvenel, knowing that Italy might try to conquer us, got us into the League in an attempt to keep the Fascists out of Ethiopia."

"You think this war with Italy is near?"

"They have increased their propaganda and their spies recently. Here is one incident. Near here at Gondar there lives a charming, white-bearded, Italian merchant, married to an Abyssinian. He has become a real Ethiopian and is highly esteemed, for he gives our people medicines and does a great deal of good. But underneath, he is backing a certain Ras, saying that he is the real ruler, and that he will keep foreigners out of our country."

Stromboli got angry at this, but before he could speak I changed the subject.

"Your Emperor is very religious," I said quickly.

"He still has faith. You see, we are a primitive people, spiritually inclined. Unlike materialistic and spiritually-dead Europe, most of us believe in God. But then," he smiled, "we are considered to be a backward people."

After a moment's silence he continued, "Have you heard that Monsieur Laval made an agreement with the Duce on the 5th of January? It is my impression that the new Franco-Italian rapprochement is at the expense of Ethiopia. Laval may be going to finance Italy's project here in return for her support against Germany." He sighed.

"What about the League of Nations and the Pact?"

"I have no faith in the Pact. Italy had her eyes on Tunisia; in order to protect her French Colony, Laval is prepared to sacrifice some other land, some country France does not own. We have been sold out."

"What about England?"

The Governor thought for a moment, "I trust England, and I believe she will stand by us. Anyway it is to her interest not to have Italy in control of the head-waters of the Nile or predominant in the Red Sea."

"If war should come, is Ethiopia prepared to fight?"

"We will fight, but we are totally unarmed. In 1928 we signed an agreement with England, France, and Italy in which we agreed not to import more than five hundred rifles a year. We must rely on God and England; though Napoleon said, 'God is on the side of the strongest battalions.'

"How could a war be possible without arms?"

"If the arms embargo were raised – we could hold out while Italy mobilized."

A moment later he answered a question which was in my mind, but which I had hesitated to ask.

"Our methods of warfare are different, but they are no worse than the use of poison gas. League Members have agreed not to use this, but planes, tanks, and flame throwers, too, are unknown here."

All through dinner the Governor's Lady had maintained silence. Coffee, Havana cigars, and liqueurs were served in the throne room, and still she did not interrupt. It was not till it came time for us to go that she spoke, and all she said was a very shy good night.

CHAPTER 14

A NICE ASSORTMENT OF HORRORS

A young servant of the Governor, Dajjazmac Mariam, was eager to speak his "Mission French," and in talking, he told me about some secret caves near Lekempti. He spoke of an underground fortress which he had seen once when he was hunting, and of some legends about it. As a child, he had been threatened with being left there if he did not behave. It was supposed to be full of evil, mystery, wonder, and horror. "Death Birds" were said to nest in its entrance.

"No man has ever dared to enter," he told me, "because of those birds, and the thousands of hyenas that have their lairs there."

With gifts he was persuaded to take me to the place, but I had to promise not to hold him responsible for anything that might happen and never to tell anyone who had led me on that path of evil.

We mounted and rode for an hour into a wild region with deep canyons, vast boulders, and strange-looking pinnacles of rock.

"We leave our horses now and climb," my young guide explained. "Evil spirit cave up there." He pointed to some towering rocks where I could see the suggestion of a cave's mouth in the gold and crimson walls of granite.

We climbed and scrambled through jungle undergrowth and over a chaos of rocks, up and still on up. Here was an ideal spot for prehistoric man to have lived and struggled and died. High in the rocks, we overlooked the river and the jungle below; all one needed to do to stop anyone from climbing up, was to roll a few rocks down. The site seemed impregnable.

The entrance to the cave had been blocked by boulders, obviously the work of men. I mentioned this, but my guide only shook his head and said, "No. Devil's work!" But he reconsidered, for in a moment he said dubiously, "Maybe *shiftas"* – brigands.
"Devil or brigands, I want to see what is behind those stones." When I took my gun from his hands, he was trembling with fright.

He remained outside while I stooped and entered the low cave mouth, gun in one hand, my flashlight in the other. After a few yards the cave opened up into a vast grotto lighted by rays of the sun which came through crevices in the rocks high over my head. These also supplied ventilation.

From outside, the boy begged me to come back.

"Master, Dajjazmac Mariam will be angry. Please come back, Master."

But I was looking for prehistoric rock drawings on the walls and feeling for flints with my stick. Thirty or forty yards inside the cave, I came to a fork where two passages joined. They, too, looked as if they had been carved by man.

While I stood there, wondering which passage to follow first, I heard loud, strange sounds. At first I could not tell what caused them, then I recognized the noise for what it was – the savage yelping of wild animals, and the sound of their feet echoing in the cave. Holding my gun ready, I turned my light down one of the corridors toward the sounds. I waited; then, with a speed that took my breath and gave me just a second to flatten myself against the stone wall, a pack of hyenas came fleeing through the passage as if panic-stricken. I got one shot at the evil-smelling beasts, but if I had not hugged the wall, they would have run me down.

That was exactly what did happen to my youthful guide. Stampeding from the cave, the animals knocked him down and ran over him. From his howls you would have thought he was seriously injured. However, he was only frightened. He had been rolled a little distance down the slope, and was just lying there jabbering with fear. When I picked him up and stood him on his feet, he was angry and let off steam by throwing stones at the hyena which my shot had struck. It was a huge, foul-looking beast, that stood, some thirty yards from us, snarling and occasionally licking its wounds. I put the animal out of its misery, cleaned and bandaged my guide's great toe, which he had scratched, and turned back toward the cave.

The long-lived echoes and repercussions of my shot rang up and down the canyon. Before I could re-enter the cave, two strange-looking men stood before me. Thin to the point of emaciation, they were pitiful in their tattered rags. They looked at me as if I were some animal which they had never seen before.

"Who are these men?" I demanded.

"Goatherds. Dajjazmac Mariam's men who come to protect him against evil spirits."

"Tell them to go back to their goats," I ordered and started to re-enter the cave.

The men protested, gestured, jabbered; frantically, they tried to keep me from going in.

"Don't go! Please don't go, Master," my guide pleaded.

"The hyenas have come out and run away," I answered.

"Yes, Master. Devil-men turned into hyenas have gone, but these Death Birds still remain – these men say horrible, evil birds with claws are still in there. Don't go in, Master."

"By Death Birds do you mean eagles?"

"No, Master. Death Birds are big and black and sit upside down."

"Oh, bats. They aren't dangerous." I entered the cave, leaving the three Abyssinians jabbering excitedly.

At a turn in the passage, I heard a queer, whirring roar which startled me. It sounded like a great waterfall beyond, there in the darkness where my flashlight did not carry. For a moment I was afraid, and then the logical explanation came to me: hundreds of huge vampire bats were whirling over me. As they made for the exit en masse, they brushed the top of my head. Startled, I fired haphazard into the dense cloud. I heard shouts of fear and alarm from outside, then all was silent, and I knew the men had fled.

The shot and its repercussions caused something to start dripping from the roof; it kept dripping on me, and at the same time a stench began to fill the air. It proved to be a rain of bats' excrement, accumulated for centuries and loosened, either by the shot or by its vibrations. I tied my handkerchief over my nose and pushed on down the length of the corridor. It was a cul-de-sac, but at its end were a few drawings and a crude altar. In spite of the stench, I managed to make some sketches in my note book before I was compelled to go outside for air.

When I did crawl out, my guide and his two skeletonic companions came creeping back up the slope. I inquired why they were so afraid of harmless bats, and they replied that these bats were blood-suckers who sometimes killed cattle or people in their sleep. I scoffed at such an idea.

"Come, Master. The men will show you," my guide suggested. "They will give you proof."

I brushed off all the filth from my clothes that I could, photographed the entrance to the cave, and prepared to follow the three men. Up the steep side of the canyon we crawled till we reached a path that had been chipped out of the rock. These goatherds were so thin and frail that I wondered how they could keep on climbing such a steep path. After half an hour's climb, we reached a wretched *toucul* on a rock-strewn plateau. When we entered that squalid camp, I saw bloodstained rags and clothing strewn on either side of two small cots.

"Murder?" I asked my guide.

"No, Master. Work of the Death Birds," he replied solemnly.

I had first heard of these vampire bats killing people in South America, and I had considered it a "tall tale." But what I saw in that hut made it begin to seem credible. These bats are said to fly into a hut silently, remain hidden until people fall asleep, and then settle on the sleepers very quietly without waking them, sucking the blood from their veins. They are enormous creatures with a wing spread of from twelve to sixteen inches.

"Where do these Death Birds bite you?" I asked.

One of the living skeletons showed me his bony arm on which there were a number of small wounds.

"Don't you feel them when they bite?"

"No. There's no pain, but every day you grow weaker."

"Can't you keep them out of your *toucul?*"

One of the men showed me how every hole in the roof and walls had been carefully filled.

"They come at dusk when the door is open, then they hide until you fall asleep."

"Must you live so near the caves?"

"The Governor's orders," the men answered apathetically. "We must be here to watch the goats."

"How long does this leech business last?"

"Until one gets so weak and sick one dies. Then a new man comes. This man is very sick;" he pointed to a bundle of rags lying in the corner.

There a thin hand was stretched out, an arm whose blood had been sucked from it night after night by the vampire bats, till the man was no longer able to stand. I presumed that the Governor knew nothing about this and resolved to tell him, believing that he could correct the situation. Sickened by this sight, I went outside to find that my shots had attracted other Abyssinians besides the goatherds. One of the men among the newcomers had a mule which I borrowed to ride back to where we had left our horses.

As we made our way along, my guide said, "Don't speak about the sick man. The Governor will be angry with me if you do." Then he began to translate for the others, and I learned why the mule had been lent to me so readily.

"Headman says you are a great man, and brave. The Governor will make you a chief. No man ever entered the Devil's Cave before." My guide waved something bloody that smelled badly; he had cut off the tail of the hyena I had shot and was waving it wildly.

"Throw that stinking thing away," I ordered, but he pretended not to understand and continued flicking flies with his evil-smelling memento.

Scarcely had I returned to camp there in the shade of the eucalyptus trees, when the Governor's secretary arrived with a very serious look on his face. He explained directly and without preamble that I had offended His Highness. I had visited the Devil's Cave. That was no place for me, and anyway I should have asked for a permit. He told me that the boy who guided me would be severely punished.

"What of the sick man in that lonely hut? Will you do something about him?"

"There are lots of sick men," the secretary replied callously. "You only cause trouble if you interfere."

But before he left, he at least promised to take some medicine and money and to see that it reached the poor goatherd.

The next day once more we were invited to the Governor's palace – this time for a luncheon in our honor. Again we were treated like royalty, but all through the meal Dajjazmac Mariam seemed to avoid the subject of vampire bats. Over coffee and liqueurs in the throne room I asked him if he had taken the medicine and if he felt any relief from his gout. He answered that he had, and that he thought he was better.

That gave me an opportunity to refer to the poor goatherd. I explained that I knew a little about medicine and wanted to help anyone who was sick. I told him of finding on a mountain plateau a poor goatherd, who really needed medicine. The Governor smiled enigmatically, and I knew that he had understood my oblique rebuke, even though he did not reply to it directly. But nearly all Abyssinians seem callous to the sufferings of man and beast alike.

Dajjazmac Mariam apparently bore me no grudge for visiting the Devil's Cave without permission, nor for my implied criticism of his inhuman treatment of the goatherds, for he supplied us with an escort to the farthest border of his vast estate, and extended every possible courtesy. Starting at dawn, we had to halt every morning at eleven; the heat was unbearable, and by that time both mules and men were near exhaustion.

At every village we were greeted by the headman and almost burdened with presents. So many gifts were offered that I could easily have started a cattle and poultry farm. Each chief would make his presentation as if it were a token of respect and admiration from his little community; but I knew that these offerings from the people were not altogether voluntary. We did our best to return as much as we could, and for the rest, we tried to compensate the people with gifts or money. But eggs, bread, *tedj*, and some of the fowls, we were very glad to get.

On the banks of the Gosta we bade farewell to both our escorts; one turned back toward Lekempti, and the other toward Addis Ababa. From this point on we could travel toward the capital with little risk. So Prince Galata, his lieutenants, his court, and our military escort left us. They had come to us almost magically when we needed them most, but now that they were no longer of any use, I did not regret their departure.

We had been told that we would not find water in Abyssinia, but hardly a day passed without our crossing some river or stream. Our difficulties came, not because of thirst, but because of the leaders of our caravan. Under Stromboli there were three men, each of whom was responsible for twenty mules and ten men. Rivalry and jealousy led to constant wrangling and fighting which seemed to go on day and night.

At Mendi we had an experience that proved to be funny, but it might have been very painful for the men involved. An antelope had been stolen, and three of our men were arrested. They were hauled off to be tried at an impromptu court under the largest tree in the village, and I was invited to share the bench with the local judge. Each one of the three accused men had a lawyer of sorts to plead for him, and the trial began. There was a great deal of noise and confusion, for the entire village attended and loudly expressed opposing opinions.

At first it was amusing. But when the three men were found guilty, they were sentenced to a fine of one thaler each, and to be hung by their thumbs from a tree for two hours. By paying for the antelope and making a present to the judge, I succeeded in defeating Ethiopian justice. Hanging by the thumbs in a public place is an everyday punishment in Abyssinia, but one which I did not care to have inflicted on my men.

Ethiopians are as stoical as were the American Indians. At the end of each day we had to have an inspection and spend considerable time in dressing injuries and wounds of which there had been neither mention nor complaint. The danger of infection is greater in hot climates, yet these men treated injuries, even serious ones, in the most casual manner. Sometimes they would apply live coals to a serious wound. Without a groan or a moan they would stand immobile until the cut or scratch was thoroughly cauterized. Scarcely a day passed that one of them did not have a crushed toe, and we were constantly cutting out huge thorns and sterilizing their gashes.

Our greatest pest, one which demanded attention every day, was the *ermoli*. This is a small tick that worms its way in under the skin and lays its eggs. If not extracted at once, it may cause a serious infection. *Ermoli* come from the mules; and it is particularly unsafe to camp on any site which has been used before or where mules have been herded. In the Mexican jungles one has to combat *garapatos;* but in Ethiopia our worst enemy was the *ermoli,* and every night you could see the men digging with needles at each other's feet.

Jungle animals, snakes, scorpions, poisonous plants, and ticks are only part of the questionable joy of exploration. In nearly every village, and sometimes along the trail between the towns, the sick were brought to us to see if we could cure them. Never have I seen so many hideous diseases. Nearly every person seemed to have something the matter with him. Almost 90 per cent of the population suffers from skin trouble; venereal diseases are widespread; very frequently we had to drive away lepers.

A Swedish mission doctor at Nejo told me that at least 5 per cent of the population of Ethiopia is tainted with leprosy. To see fingerless, toeless, or even uglier disfigurements was an everyday occurrence, not an exception. We tried to help those natives whom we felt competent to treat – the two hundred or so to whom we gave aid were only a small percentage of those who came to us asking for treatment or medicines.

Tapeworm is one of their commonest ills; it is so prevalent that most of the population must be treated for it every two or three months. Some doctors claim that this is due to the general practice of eating raw meat; others believe it is caused by the climate and the water. A native plant called *cusho* offers a certain but harsh cure for the disorder; without this active remedy, the health of the whole population would be even more undermined.

Raw meat served bleeding in a hot climate may be revolting, but cut from a living animal it is sickening. I did not see this myself, but Bruce states that in the vicinity of Axum he overtook three men who were driving a cow. He saw them throw the animal to the ground and watched one man with a knife make a deep gash. Thinking they were going to butcher the beast, Bruce tried to buy some of the meat for his party; but he learned that the cow did not belong to these men – they were not killing her, only cutting off a steak while she was still alive.

Stromboli told me that Bruce did not exaggerate, that he himself had attended a banquet at which the famous raw meat had been carved from living animals and served warm.

"When we had taken our seats at the banquet, a bull was brought in and tied firmly by the feet; the butchers selected the most delicate morsels from that living larder. Before they killed the animal, they cut all the flesh off the buttocks in square solid pieces. These were served to us instantly on slabs of Abyssinian bread, with plenty of *tedj*. The butchers were still carving when the animal let out a final roar of agony and died."

The night that Stromboli told me that story, I saw evidence of the secret slave traffic for the first time. Stromboli's story and the mosquitoes inside my net had succeeded in keeping me awake. We were camped at the foot of a hill near a stream, under some giant, monkey-bread trees – *Adansonia digitata*. Down the hill toward us came the muffled sound of an approaching caravan. That did not seem alarming, for we were in comparatively safe country near the crossroads of the trails to the Sudan and Eritrea, and from the Red Sea to the West. But the stealthiness of that mysterious caravan, as it drew nearer, made me suspicious.

Abyssinians on the trail are usually noisy and quarrelsome; there was something very queer about this caravan travelling in comparative silence in the night. As they came nearer, I could hear the jangle of chains. I was almost certain that slaves were being run through secretly.

Silently I crept through the trees and waited to see the curse of Africa; slavery has been practiced there for at least thirty centuries. Though officially abolished, Ethiopia still has three million slaves. And slave traders steal or buy these black humans and move them over secret trails, from hideout to hideout, to the Red Sea, where they are shipped like cattle to Arabia. There they are sold to the buyers of that country and of the East.

From my hiding place, I saw an armed escort with guns and lances, then a long procession of drooping, footsore prisoners, dragging their hopeless bodies along to the sound of shuffling feet and clanking chains. Without our armed escort, which had left us to return to Addis Ababa, there was nothing we could do. There was no authority, police or military, for us to summon. All we could do was wait until we reached the capital and inform the authorities there. It was just possible that this illegal caravan of slaves could be overtaken and brought back before it reached the Red Sea.

The mournful procession of men and women, moving slowly toward some secret hiding place, was swallowed up by the darkness. At dawn they would be herded like sheep until the following night. When night came again, they would be driven along once more on their hopeless way.

CHAPTER 15

AN AUDIENCE WITH HAILE SELASSIE

For the first few days, after months of camping along the slave and gold trails, it was a relief to live in a comfortable hotel in Addis Ababa. Soon I wanted to continue on to the Red Sea. But courtesy demanded that I wait until I was summoned to the Imperial Palace for at least one audience. After I had said goodbye to Derissa, the interpreter, Andalamu, the guide, the Nagradas, and Stromboli, there was nothing for me to do but wait for a summons from Haile Selassie. Addis Ababa may be the world's strangest capital, but after a few days it ceases to be entertaining.

One morning in the Imperial Palace Hotel I was awakened by the sound of marching feet in the corridor just outside my door. I heard the order, "Halt!" followed by a loud knock. In my pajamas, I opened the door to find the Foreign Minister of Ethiopia. The late Ras Mougalata stood there smiling, with his guard standing at attention against the farther wall, their "Made-in-Japan" rifles on their shoulders. He was to take me to call on the Emperor Haile Selassie. This was the summons I had been waiting for.

Breakfastless, I hurried into clothes. The Foreign Minister waited, ushered me down the stairs and into an ancient limousine. He was evidently proud of his guard, which kept us surrounded as we bumped over the rough streets. The huge old car rolled and lurched into holes in the street and over mounds of rubbish.

Ras Mougalata wore a white robe lined with red silk and trimmed with gold – in vivid contrast to the ragged, poorly-clothed people on the streets. His plump, well-fed figure emphasized the poverty and squalor of the mud huts and tin-roofed, wooden buildings we passed. Donkeys and mules led by shouting attendants – without halters or bridles – were carrying produce from the outlying districts to the clamorous din of the market place. Crowds thronged the hard-baked, earthen sidewalks, and the broiling sun cast black shadows on the sweltering streets.

At the top of the hill which commands the city, stands Haile Selassie's Imperial Palace with literally hundreds of rooms. The Negus is known as the Lord King of Kings of Ethiopia, the Conquering Lion of the Tribe of Judah, the Elect of God, and the Light of the World. Around the Palace and its park and grounds is a wall with guarded gates.

When the car stopped for the gates to be opened, white-robed guards salaamed to the ground. Ahead of us the gardens were magnificent. The sunlight created rainbows in the fountains; the tropical plants and flowers of many colors contrasted brilliantly with the green lawn. The Palace and its grounds constitute a city within a city; slaves and servants alone number six thousand.

In addition to the Palace itself, the grounds are so large that the feudal nobles maintain "town houses" there. Lacking telephone and telegraph communication with their distant kingdoms and principalities, the nobles keep a staff of runners to supply information when they are at the capital. It is from the Palace that the rich clergy of the Coptic Church hold their control over so large a part of the population.

As we drove through the grounds up to the Palace, I could see nobles, court attendants, and priests walking through the gardens. Tall, stately, and dignified, they wore white robes such as the senators wore in ancient Rome. When we got out of the car, I could hear the soft, well-modulated voices speaking Amharic, which I could not understand.

At the Palace doors a group of dignitaries greeted the Foreign Minister and me, and led us into a white and gold reception room. It was not till I was summoned for my audience with His Imperial Highness that Ras Mougalata left me. I followed a court chamberlain through a maze of corridors into a vast hall; at the farther end, under a purple and gold canopy, on a gold throne sat a small, solitary figure – The King of Kings.

Antique, oriental carpets of great value covered the floors; massive chandeliers hung from the ceiling. Along the wall, singly and in groups, were enormous chairs; the top of the back of each was crowned with the carved figure of the snarling Lion of Judah. As I walked down the long room toward the Emperor, I noted that he was wearing a long, black cape over white breeches that fitted close to his legs below the knees. The cape was caught at the throat with a massive, gold clasp, and it was lined with purple and gold.

The Negus dismissed most of his attendants and indicated that the chair at his right was intended for me, but he did not speak. He never talks to a foreigner directly; he speaks to his interpreter, who, in turn, addresses the visitor. I was sorry for the Emperor; he looked tired and sad, but I was amused when he listened to the translation of my conversation, for he understands French, and speaks it perfectly.

White, even teeth flashed through his beard as he inquired about the success of my expedition. My passports and permits were the first he had ever granted to any foreigner to cross his "Forbidden Lands." He asked many questions about the parts of his country we had visited, the welfare of his people, their customs, and their way of living. When he spoke about the future of his country and the things he hoped to do for his people, his eyes had a faraway look as if he were seeing it done.

"Give us time," he said, "and we shall have more roads, abolish certain customs that have prevailed since pagan days, and introduce a modern system of education. In time I hope you will collaborate and help us to found an archeological and historical museum and library in our ancient land."

When I expressed my appreciation for the help he had extended, he dismissed it with a gesture, but he asked about how many miles we could travel in a day. I told him, and expressed thanks for the escort he had sent us.

"We are passing through anxious times just now," said the Emperor. "Our land, the land of chivalry, is wealthy, and there are those who covet our wealth. God and the Brotherhood of Nations will, I trust, help us to retain our independence. God and the League will aid us in our efforts to improve the lot of my people. Time is all we need – even Rome was not built in a day." It was a sad-eyed, wistful, weary man who had spoken, an Emperor who still retained hope, profound trust in God, and faith in the promises that had been made to him. And these he has never lost.

My audience was a long one. We spoke of the next part of my travels through the north-eastern part of his Empire, of the people and their customs, of the possibilities of there being oil. Never directly did he mention the Italian menace, but from his indirect allusions I could see that he was worried. Finally, he said:

"I hope that our joint collaboration and scientific work may continue in the future. We welcome all interests, provided they work for the mutual benefit of science and my ancient Ethiopia."

With that he extended his finely-shaped hand, and I knew that my audience was over. He smiled and his kindly, noble, ascetic face lighted pleasantly. Haile Selassie is an optimistic, far-seeing, patriotic leader. Educated by the Jesuits, he is the cultured ruler of an ancient race. His people are backward and in need of reforms and improvement, but the Negus recognizes this and wants to help them.

I wanted to say, "God help you in your great task," but somehow words would not come. I bowed and backed away.

I was not to see the King of Kings again for several years, and then under tragic circumstances for him. The arrangements I made later were with various of his subordinates who got the Emperor's consent. When next I saw Haile Selassie, he was in his railroad compartment en route from London to Geneva – and in exile. This was in 1936. He was a defeated Emperor, but he was not broken, nor had he lost his faith and courage. He was on his way to plead for a cause already lost. Perhaps it is his unfailing faith and courage that has led him back to rule his people once again.

At Geneva he appealed in vain before the League of Nations. With all the force of a mystic prophet, he spoke of the doom which was hanging over the smaller nations: "You abandoned me in my hour of need, and now you will soon see the end of all the small countries of the world." His voice was tired, but proud and clear; his faith in his people, in future events, and in himself was unbounded. "In five years I shall regain my throne," he said.

On the three hundred and sixty-fifth day of the fourth year, he re-entered Addis Ababa on a white charger. Haile Selassie is a mystic, a psychic, and a prophet. His gift of prophecy is uncanny. As a child, he surprised and astonished the Jesuit priests at Harrar, under whom he studied, with this strange gift.

He is a direct descendant of the ancient, Semitic Sabeans who settled Ethiopia four thousand years ago. They came from the great unknown empires of southern Arabia, which I had explored – they are proud, fighting, noble Amharis who kept their independence and religion through the ages. King Ibn Saud of Arabia, a relative of Haile Selassie, is six feet, four inches tall.

The Ethiopian Emperor seems too frail and too delicate a man to rule so fierce and individualistic a people. Before his exile, he spent six hours each day in solitary prayer.

How he survived the fogs and cold of Britain, I shall never understand, unless it was that his faith in his destiny kept him alive. When I saw him at Bath, he had a racking cough and was living in penury. It made me very angry when people said that he had left his native land carrying chests of gold. He took with him only the sacred verses of his church. The few thousand thalers he did take were gone in six months – given to his faithful followers. His servants received the last of his family jewels.

Haile Selassie possesses great pride, courage, and a strong feeling of race. He was both insulted and shocked when he was offered a fabulous sum for his memoirs while he was in England, and though he was nearly destitute, he refused. He was so poor that he could not afford coal to heat his house in England, and the tradesmen dunned him for the modest sums he owed.

Some writers have stated that Haile Selassie was cruel, but that is not true. Some of his leaders were Fascist-minded – especially after civilization had brought poison gas and tanks to Ethiopia, along with the ruthless bombing and machine-gunning by young Mussolini and Count Ciano – but never Haile Selassie himself.

Coming from a long line of rulers, some peaceful, some great fighters, some mystics fanatically religious, Haile Selassie has the bravery of an intellectual, he hates war and cruelty, but for sheer physical courage there has been no one like him since Richard the Lion Hearted.

He has regained his throne with the help of the British, and now Ethiopia should progress. He should have put himself under the protection of these colonizers long ago as a military precaution. Under the British Colonels, Sandford and Wingate, Haile Selassie is training and arming an army of a million warriors. If it should become necessary, this army will fight with tanks, machine-guns, and airplanes.

No man ever felt more deeply for his people than he did during the Fascist conquest with its unspeakable horrors, but he never lost his sense of kindness nor of humor. He is reported to have been agreeably surprised at the improvements the Italians had made, and to have said, "It was worth my forced exile these five years to return to such an improved palace and splendid roads, buildings, model farms, hospitals, and hundreds of fine edifices."

He has been lenient with the traitors who betrayed him, particularly with his brother-in-law, who acted as a puppet ruler for the Italians and is known as the Judas of Ethiopia.

CHAPTER 16

SLAVES EN ROUTE TO THE RED SEA

For seven months we had been exploring one of the least-known sections of the world. Very little had been known or written about Abyssinia, still less about the western half of that Empire. It is made up of almost independent, feudal states with great natural, mineral, and agricultural wealth. The population is made up of savage, superstitious blacks who claim they are white.

Ethiopia was an old, important, and rich country in Biblical times when the glamorous Queen of Sheba reigned, but our historical knowledge of it is incomplete and vague. Almeida and Lobo, Rudolf and Bruce, Salt and Nathaniel Pearce, and the mysterious Prester John have written about it, and still it is a nation little known. It became world news when the bellicose Emperor Menelik conquered the Italians at Adowa just before the turn of the twentieth century. When Ras Tafari visited France and England in the days of Miller and and George V, Ethiopia again made front-page news. When he was made Emperor, the oriental splendor of his semi-barbaric coronation was again world news; and still no one anticipated that Ethiopia would one day play an important, a leading part in the politics of the world as a whole. Not until intelligent, educated, and altruistic Haile Selassie came to the throne with his great faith and eagerness to better conditions for his uneducated people, did Abyssinia become a progressive, forward-looking nation. But as stories of the country's fabulous wealth in jewels and gold and deposits of oil percolated into European countries, it became a rich prize which nations coveted.

England, France, and Italy scrambled for it, at first under cover and secretly, then diplomatically, and finally openly. France and

Italy failed to conceal their avarice, though they maneuvered under the guise of diplomacy; England's appeared to be a more kindly interest. Ethiopia finally became a pawn in the game of international politics under the pretense that her people were savage, downtrodden, and uncivilized. The lost land of Ophir, King Solomon's gold and emerald mines, rich deposits of oil, and great agricultural wealth – real and potential – were too much of a temptation. The country was poorly prepared to defend itself, and Italy still writhed under the ignominy of her defeat at the hands of the savage Ethiopians at Adowa.

Along the ancient gold trails I had seen things which, perhaps, no other explorer had ever viewed. So far, my journey had supplied even more than my long years of anticipatory waiting had promised. In all my work of exploring and digging for historical data, from the Atlas Mountains to the Red Sea and from buried Carthage to Timbuctoo, no land had shown so much remarkable promise in its dead cities and lost civilizations. I could only hope that someday I might return to excavate and examine them more thoroughly.

"The Land of Burnt Faces," the ancient Greeks called it, and it offers rich treasure to the historian and archeologist. I have located those places on the maps I have made, and have seen many of them that one can visit only on foot. Long before the birth of Christ, Ethiopians were building tall obelisks and inscribing on these and other monuments the story of their conquests of a hundred nations and their progress "toward the light."

Perhaps she has retrogressed; the tanks and poison gas and brutality may be symbols of a civilization which has changed, but are they less or more cruel and savage than the ancient tortures? When the Italians came to Abyssinia, they asserted that it was for the purpose of abolishing slavery. But the slavery they imposed was worse than any the poor, unarmed, uneducated people had ever known. That the real purpose of the invaders was to acquire jewels and oil and gold was clear to even the least-educated slave.

I was lucky enough to see one of the first discoveries of oil in Ethiopia, unfortunate enough to be present when the last caravan of slaves was sold to be delivered to Yemen – a sight that will haunt me as long as I live. Leaving Addis Ababa, we intended to follow the old caravan route along which the Queen of Sheba is supposed to have led her Arabian followers. Between eastern Ethiopia and the Red Sea lies the Danakil Desert. It seemed probable that Phoenicians, Sabers, and Romans, too, had crossed this treacherous waste. One of our objectives was to look for signs of their crossing.

Along those trails I hoped to find archeological treasures. I wanted, too, to film the stealthy, criminal, slave caravans which stole across the land by night and hid by day – going from the western jungles to the wild and desolate coasts of the Somaliland, where traders anchored in secluded harbors, waiting to take these forbidden cargoes to Arabia. And I wanted to see if we could locate oil deposits. Haile Selassie had promised me a five years' concession to explore archeologically in exchange for a geological survey of that part of his empire with particular regard to oil.

The secret survival of slavery I have previously referred to as the curse of Africa – perhaps it is its most dominating, characteristic feature. In carrying out the promises he made when he joined the League of Nations, Haile Selassie did everything he could, and with great thoroughness, to stamp out slavery. He tried to wipe out a feudal custom which had persisted for more than thirty centuries; the country is vast and honeycombed with secret paths through the jungles and deserts. And the Danakils, with their desert and mountains, are so fierce that even the Fascists later found it judicious to leave them strictly alone.

Other explorers who had proved inquisitive as to the strange practices carried on in the land of the Queen of Sheba had been deported, or had started and never returned. The Ethiopians are violently opposed to foreigners who want to investigate the barbarous customs of their little-known land. In setting out to obtain accurate and detailed information bearing on the infamous slave traffic, I knew that extreme caution must be exercised. But the wily, unscrupulous Levantines are eager to act as secret intermediaries – for a price; having acquired the habit of cheating and robbing the happy-go-lucky, indolent, and dreamy Abyssinians, they are willing to do anything which has no risk and yet will pay a profit.

Planning and consulting with them, after having acquired all the information I could elsewhere, led me to decide to leave Addis Ababa, in the early autumn of 1935, by train, and go to Diredawa. Between these two cities there was nothing of interest which had not already been explored. From Diredawa we could make for the Aussa Sultanate, cross the Danakil Desert, and proceed on through the wilderness of Somaliland to the Red Sea.

Two of the explorers I had known, Baron Franchetti of Italy, and N. E. Nesbitt of England, had traveled across this infernal region of the Danakil Desert, and both had met violent deaths. One had followed the northern route across the desert and the other had taken the middle path. I wanted to go along the unknown, south-east trail. While we were making the geological survey for the Negus, we could search for the chained victims of the slave traders, photograph the game and other characteristic and individual things we might meet.

Thanks to Papadipoulos, in Diredawa I met Mohammed ibn Achmed. We met secretly like conspirators, as one so often does in Africa, in the back room of a Greek hotel. Arabian Achmed was the most notorious slave dealer in all East Africa. He had inherited his trade from his father, who in turn had learned it from his father. Achmed had himself been in the business for thirty years.

Under the back room of the Greek hotel, I learned later, was a huge cellar; this served as a storeroom and warehouse for a few legitimate and many illicit commodities. It was from here that hashish and other drugs were distributed. Firearms and ammunition were smuggled in and out by a secret entrance. Young girls and women, kidnapped or enticed away from their native villages, were imprisoned in that cellar until a propitious hour arrived for their transfer to the coast, a boat, and then Arabia.

Papadipoulos was a dark-skinned rascal, fat and oily, with a tendency toward excessive perspiration – the more he struggled to make me pay a few more pounds sterling than seemed fair, the more he sweated. The slave dealer, Mohammed ibn Achmed, was not much better, though he was neither fat nor greasy, and bore himself with imposing dignity. As an Arab, he appeared to have a certain refinement, but this was only a role, a part that he played;

biologists call it "protective coloration." His gray-black beard emphasized eloquent, searching eyes – eyes constantly on the lookout for any conscienceless opportunity. Achmed looked into my eyes, at me, through me. He studied me till I felt that he was trying to read my inmost thoughts; and in part he seemed to succeed.

Without being told, he knew what I wanted, how much I was prepared to pay, and how great were the risks I was willing to take.

In spite of that, my meeting with him was one of the longest sessions of my experience, and most Arabs enjoy long periods of discussion. When I left him, after midnight, we had discussed the most minute details of the plan we had worked out together. I handed him a considerable sum, and walked out of that notorious hotel with the feeling that Mohammed ibn Achmed would do all of the things he had promised, and do them exactly. He had not minimized the risks he thought we were taking.

CHAPTER 17

THE MAN IN THE IRON CAGE

While I waited the five days Mohammed ibn Achmed had told me it would take to make arrangements for my caravan and supplies, Papadipoulos entertained me with stories of the most extraordinary character in modern Ethiopian history – the infamous ex-Emperor, Lidj Yassou, who was known as "the prisoner in golden chains," and "the Man in the Iron Cage."

Sadistic, ruthless, cruel, despotic, the former Emperor spent three weeks in the Arrousi in September 1916, hunting down criminals. One of his prisoners had been a man who had tried to assassinate him – the father of a young girl whom Lidj Yassou had ravished. The ex-Emperor had waited in Arrousi to witness the execution of this would-be assassin by the torture-death usually reserved for regicides – "the death by cotton."

Lidj Yassou reveled in inflicting and witnessing tortures; the anticipation of seeing a man turn into a living torch and slowly burn to death, delighted his twisted, perverted sense of pleasure. He had just arranged to force the daughter to witness this hideous execution, when a messenger rode up on a lathered horse.

"Your Majesty," the messenger began when he had been ushered into the Royal Presence, "Addis Ababa and Ethiopia are in revolt. The Abouna (Church council) has excommunicated you. The Princess Zaoditou is on the throne. Your cousin Tafari has been proclaimed Ras, Regent, and heir to the throne of your fathers."

Lidj Yassou whipped out his revolver, aimed at the messenger and fired. That irascible tyrant would kill any man who brought him a message which irked him – even slightly. But the messenger had anticipated this – one of His Majesty's pleasanter little idiosyncrasies – and dodged as soon as he had delivered his message. He waited to see if the Emperor were going to shoot again, but the King of Kings had satisfied his mad impulse. The messenger watched him slide his revolver back into its holster. "I don't suppose it is your fault," His Majesty commented casually. "Off with you. I shall proceed to Harrar and my faithful Mohammedan followers; then we'll go and cut off my cousin Tafari's tiny organs and string them over the Altar of St. George." The Emperor's eyes began to blaze in anticipation of the tortures he would inflict; flecks of foam formed and spread on his thick, sensual lips.

But he had failed to consider several things: the attitude and the power of the Coptic Church, the reasons for the revolt, and the fanatical following of his idealistic, but clear-visioned cousin. Controlling a large part of Ethiopia's land and riches, the Church was eager to be rid of a man who had been converted to Mohammedanism. His tyrannical, arbitrary rule and his completely uninhibited joy in torture had alienated a large number of his people. His quiet cousin, Tafari, had been made to feel that he should take the risk and make the sacrifice for the good of Ethiopia and its people.

On October 8th of that year, 1916, Ras Tafari – now Haile Selassie – had led his army to meet that of the excommunicated Emperor. Small of stature, wily and cautious, the Ras waited for Lidj Yassou to attack. A fanatical Mohammedan army, led by the despot, advanced to attack the Ras' forces on the outskirts of Harrar.

Impatient, foolhardy, fearless, Lidj Yassou charged with the red and yellow banners of Mohammed flying – straight into the devastating line of fire from twenty newly-arrived machine-guns. These were weapons which the Mohammedans had never seen, had never even heard of. Instead of retreating, they yelled and charged again; they kept on charging. Men fell in waves, like grain behind a reaper with the bundles neatly stacked.

When he saw that he was hopelessly defeated, Lidj Yassou called out his defiance, turned on his white Arabian stallion, and made his escape with twelve or fifteen of his bodyguard. Ras Tafari then unfurled the flag of the Lion of Judah surmounted by a cross, and was photographed standing on a high mound made of the bodies of Lidj Yassou's defeated Mohammedans.

Supported by the Coptic Christians, Ras Tafari had then quickly won the cooperation of most of Ethiopia. His decision to join the Allies in the first World War automatically defeated German and Turkish plans for the invasion of Egypt and the probable capture of the Suez Canal. But so long as Lidj Yassou remained free, he had represented a potential danger, both to Ethiopia and to the Allies. Whether it was due to tyranny, sadism, or one of his many other vices, he had been, at last, betrayed. Captured, he had been fettered with golden chains and imprisoned in a palace in Titchi. There he was supplied with all the women he fancied, and all the drugs and liquor he cared to consume. It was assumed that he would die like a Roman Emperor from a surfeit of carnal pleasures.

Everything that could be thought of had been done to avoid his becoming a martyr in the eyes of his people. He had been imprisoned and kept under strict guard, manacled with golden chains, but his harshest punishment was that he was never permitted to see his official queen-wife, nor his son and heir.

Faithful to her degenerate husband, the former Danaku princess had begun to intrigue for his escape; and finally, she succeeded by a ruse. Learning that Lidj Yassou was entertained each evening by a troupe of dancing girls, she arranged to have his guards drugged and to have her husband escape in the disguise of a veiled bayadère. One can only think that Lidj Yassou must have made an extraordinary dancing girl. His wife arranged for horses to be waiting in relays, and the ex-Emperor made good his escape. Managing to get to the Blue Nile in western Ethiopia, he there joined forces with the traitor, Ras Hailu.

But his freedom did not last long. "The Mad Dog of Abyssinia" was traced, discovered, pursued, and tracked down like a vicious animal. He fled from place to place. Finally, he was cornered in a cave. In chains and manacles, iron ones this time, he was taken to Garamoulta. There in a mountain fastness, near Harrar, he was imprisoned on the second floor of a huge cage of wood and iron. The former Emperor was on display in such manner that he could be seen from every side, both day and night. A military guard of nine thousand men was stationed there and held responsible for his permanent imprisonment.

He was still in this cage when I reached Ethiopia. In spite of the fact that it was strictly forbidden, I decided to try to see this man in his strange prison. It was not very far from Diredawa. When I first suggested this, Papadipoulos shrugged, but later he introduced me to a Greek named Zaphir. He, in turn, managed to put me in touch with one of the officers of the guards responsible for Lidj Yassou's custody. The officer promised to get me past enough sentries to enable me to see and, perhaps, photograph "the Man in the Iron Cage" at Garamouka.

How Zaphir arranged for me to meet this officer I did not inquire. I doubt that the man could have been bribed, though the Greek exacted a considerable sum from me – the penalty for anyone discovered breaking the strict, prison regulations was the choice of having his tongue torn out so that he could never again tell tales, or having his eyes gouged out so that he could not see anything to tell. Both penalties might be inflicted – and, in point of fact, often were.

The Greeks and Armenians were the "trusted" agents and spies for the government in Addis Ababa, but they could be bribed if the amount was sufficient to interest them. Thus I learned that a special supply truck went up to the mysterious, mountain fortress at Garamoulta once each week to carry special foods and liquors to His Majesty. The provisions were supplied by a Greek; the driver of the truck was a young Armenian, who was said to do a thriving business on the side with illicit drugs and arms. He was persuaded to take me with him – as his new assistant mechanic.

The road up the mountains from Diredawa to Harrar was so narrow, steep, and rocky that a sure-footed mule would have been a happier means of travel. At one moment we were on the edge of a chasm a thousand feet deep, tilting toward it with the car wheels on the very brink of the precipice. A second later, the chauffeur had to skid his rear wheels around a curve to make the next grade. The views were awe-inspiring, with vast perspectives and harsh ruggedness. The tropical climate was tempered by the high altitude, but we rolled through coffee and banana trees surrounded by purple, crimson, emerald, and silver-winged parrots and aigrettes.

In the background was an immense cyclorama of red and brown mountains.

Every few miles we could look down and see some enchanting oasis where the primitive people worked just enough to provide themselves with clothing, food, and shelter. The driver explained that their many idle hours were spent in singing, dancing, and in making love. These were the Harraris, a simple, peace-loving people who had never been disturbed by the advances of civilization.

We passed the plantation of a French nobleman whose career was both thrilling and romantic. Bored with his secluded, half-ruined, ancestral castle, and with almost no funds, he had come to Ethiopia twenty years before in search of adventure and a fortune. In an earlier age Henri de Monfried might have turned pirate, but like Lord Byron's friend, Trelawney, his gift seemed to turn in his middle years toward writing. He began to put down episodes of his strange life, episodes which included gun-running from the Red Sea, slave raids, dope-running, and political intrigue. His stories were both fascinating and convincing adventure-romances. With the publication of his first book, he had become well-known; with the next, he became a vogue; and successful novels followed one after the other. Unexpectedly, he was ordered to leave his beloved, adopted Ethiopia – because of his secret negotiations with a foreign power, so it was rumored.

Some distance beyond De Monfried's plantation we passed the ancient Coptic monastery which is the home of the celebrated Bishop of Harrar, Abu Hanan. He was one of the most important men in all Abyssinia. With the brilliant mind of a politician and with the wealth and the power of the Church behind him, he was one of Haile Selassie's staunchest supporters.

A few miles beyond the monastery we came to the first of the sentries, the one farthest from Lidj Yassou's prison cage. At the sight of the two bottles of cognac I held out, the sentry smiled, came forward and took them, and disappeared without asking a single question.

At the second outpost, the soldiers needed several drinks of cognac before they were willing to accept the bottles and close their eyes to my presence.

"Our difficulties are increasing," the young Armenian driver explained, "because they have orders to search all cars for messages that get through from outside; that even includes myself, though I come up here every week." He said it so guilelessly that, in view of the fact that he had been bribed to bring me with him, I smiled.

"Mohammedan and Italian agents are working to free Lidj Yassou and to start a civil war. They want to make him a puppet king," he added. "Tinker with the motor, clean the spark plugs, and keep busy when we reach the Military Governor's Palace. You'll find an oil can and wrenches under the seat. It'll take me some time to unload."

Soon after he had given me those orders, we drove into the courtyard of a good-sized house built of stone and mud. When we stopped I got out, lifted the hood, and did as I was told, still managing to look around and see what was going on. Under the sharp eyes of a boss, a dozen Galla slaves began removing the cases of cognac and champagne. Through the trees, on the summit of a hill I could just see the Iron Cage. There was an air of excitement around, which seemed greater than could be explained by the mere arrival of the regular, weekly truck.

The driver came over and pointed to the carburetor as if he were explaining something.

"You're having luck. Lidj Yassou is celebrating another of his birthdays. He's giving a grand gibr, a banquet in honor of his women and his guards. He conveniently forgets the day on which he was born, so he can celebrate a number of times each year. It helps him to kill time, too."

I began wiping down the motor with cotton waste, excited at the prospect of seeing Lidj Yassou when he was celebrating. The strange parties I had witnessed in this land had been genuine, but they had lacked the social prestige of royalty! "The Mad Dog of Abyssinia" was an Ethiopian Nero and Rasputin combined in one person.

The feast was to take place inside the enclosure which surrounded the prisoner's cage. Under the strict and constant watch of spies, soldiers, and priests – several millions of the Mohammedan population still venerated him – Lidj Yassou was compelled to enjoy the spectacle from his second-story prison.

As the men unloaded and checked the supplies, I counted twenty-two cases marked "Pommery and Greno" and "Hennessy." Tables and benches were being carried from the barracks to the enclosure, and huge slabs of raw meat were placed in piles on the tables. Containers of odorous intschera – Ethiopian red pepper – and big barrels of tedj were brought out. The strong body odors of the workers combined with everything else to create a stench worse than that of a slaughterhouse.

The cases of luxury drinks were taken up the hill to the Iron Cage. When the imprisoned ex-Emperor began to sip his first drink, the tedj was served to the natives below in the compound, and the feast began. Only Dante's description of Inferno offers any parallel to the spectacle. Heavy-lipped, gory mouths slavered from the reeking chunks of purple flesh and the copious draughts of tedj. One old man tried to emulate the death of the Duke of Clarence (who had drowned in a vat of Maimsey); he fell into a hogshead of tedj, and had to be pulled out by the feet by his shouting, laughing grandchildren.

In all the excitement, I slipped away from the truck, moved up nearer to the Iron Cage, and found a place from which I could see its occupants well. Lidj Yassou was lolling against a pile of silk cushions, surrounded by ten or twelve naked women who were offering him champagne and drugs. This fantastic prisoner, was a mountainous, Bacchus-like figure with a bloated face – the result of twenty years of inaction, imprisonment, licentiousness, and drugs. In the hope of even a momentary restoration of his declining powers, he indulged in hashish and other drugs, and in obscene spectacles. From the Iron Cage there came a scream, followed by lewd laughter, which was far from pleasant to hear. Panic-stricken by my disappearance, the Armenian driver had searched until he had found me.

"Quick. We must get away from here before it gets any worse." He took my arm.

"What's going on up there? Why did someone scream?"

"I'll tell you on the way." He looked around anxiously.

We moved down the hill and got into the truck. Still the driver kept looking around. But whatever it was that he feared, nothing happened. We drove off just as the sunset turned the mountains purple, and no sentry delayed or searched us. As the driver maneuvered the truck down the steep grades and hairpin turns, he talked as calmly as if he were sitting comfortably on some verandah.

"That scream you heard – Lidj Yassou is no longer capable of his favorite pastime, so he takes his pleasure by proxy. He has a male court favorite whose duty it is to take his pleasures while the former Emperor and his court look on. His present favorite is a huge Shankalla slave, and the scream you heard probably came from a young girl. Allah is supposed to bestow on the Emperor's diseased nerves and imagination the delights of the houris of the Mohammedan paradise while he watches."

In the silence that followed this explanation, while we were getting farther and farther away from the horror house of Garamoulta, some lines of Keats stood out in my memory:

The Shark at savage prey – the Hawk at pounce,
The gentle Robin, like a Pard or Ounce
Ravening a worm –

Those simple, Harrar and Galla people, who lived in the valley oases, were soon to be victims of the caterpillar treads of tanks, and vomit up their lungs from the poisonous chemical gas the Italians used. Intrigues between the Fascists and Lidj Yassou had been started; worn-out with disease, drugs, and excesses, he would have made a weak, easily-managed puppet. But the Coptic priests were too intelligent to let this go on for long, and the Iron Cage was abolished. A sixteen-room palace was built for the ex-Emperor within the enclosure of a Coptic monastery. So far as she could, the ex-Emperor's sister, the Empress who is Haile Selassie's wife, protected her brother, but she could not prevent his being moved to the monastery grounds.

One attempt to kidnap Lidj Yassou was made after he had been moved, but only one. Italian agents arrived at Harrar prepared to bribe the Governor and the Danaku warriors. The conspirators and kidnappers met at a spot in the mountains which looked down upon the monastery, where the ex-ruler was waiting to be freed.

But the wily Bishop too had spies, and was not afraid of drastic action. The conspirators were surrounded, and every one of them was killed or captured.

The fate of those who died was the kinder one, for those who lived were "persuaded" to talk; and time-tested methods of torture were employed. The Italians had done the bribing. Dajjazmac Mariam, the Governor of the province of Walaga, whom we had visited, and who had talked so frankly about the Italian menace, was involved. The astute bishop, Abu Hanan, wired this information to the Empress, Lidj Yassou's sister, which led to the strong man of Ethiopia, Ras Nasibu, being sent to Harrar. From that time until his death, "the Man in the Iron Cage" was bereft of even a slight hope of escape.

Back in Diredawa my friend Zaphir added to my knowledge of the ex-Emperor. He referred to him as the "Anti-Christ," and told me how his downfall had been accomplished – he believed, by the rich and powerful Coptic Church. Lidj Yassou had surrounded himself with native and foreign counselors as depraved as himself. One of his pleasures had been to gallop through Addis Ababa on his white stallion, shooting his revolvers right and left for the sheer joy of hurting people. Another of his delights had been to insult white women. At three o'clock in the morning he would sally forth and raid the Grand Market Place, where the Greeks, Turks, Armenians, and Levantines had their shops, helping himself to their women and to their goods.

"What finally brought about his downfall, Zaphir?"

He thought for a moment before he answered, "His Mohammedan marriage and tendencies, and German and Turkish intrigues during the last World War. Caucasian and Turkish beauties had been introduced into his palace as agents of Turkey and Germany. These two countries, working together, wanted to make the whole country Mohammedan, have it join them in their war against the Allies, march into Egypt and Arabia, and close the Red Sea and the Suez Canal. There was a time when the history of the world and the outcome of the war hinged on this "Mad Dog" and his plans for marching on Djibuti and the Red Sea.

"Lidj Yassou was an easy victim for the Turks and their Islamic ambitions. His father had been a Mohammedan who turned Christian, conveniently, to better his political fortunes. Under the influence of the Germans and Turks one drunken champagne party followed another; receptions for dignitaries featured naked, Turkish dancing girls. As a Prince, Lidj Yassou had won public favor in his successful struggle against the insurgent Danakils and Somalis. That was in 1913, when his father was still alive. He always had ridden a white Arabian stallion covered with blood – Abyssinians cut out the heart and liver of their defeated opponents and feed them to their mounts – the Prince had been a human whirlwind with his lance. He became the idol of the battle-loving Abyssinians; when he returned to Addis Ababa wounded after another victorious battle, his popularity reached its height. The people welcomed him as Menelik the Second.

"On December 13th, 1913, the death of Menelik the Great was officially proclaimed. He had been dead for three years, but fear of revolts in the provinces had kept his death a secret. During those years an old man who resembled the deceased Emperor was carried to the palace windows to be exhibited and to reassure the adoring, but vaguely suspicious people. It was then that Lidj Yassou was proclaimed Emperor, but he became a mad tyrant the moment he donned the royal purple. At one of the reviews he joined the soldiers in their feats of prowess. To the horror of the foreign legations he threw his lance at captured Danakil prisoners, and showed obvious pleasure in doing it.

"Italy, France, and England would have taken joint action in Ethiopia if the World War had not begun in 1914. This Abyssinian Nero and his atrocities offered the ideal excuse for intervention. The partition of the Empire had already been decided upon by the three powers, and during the first years of the World War, Addis Ababa became a hotbed of intrigue. It would have been simple for half a million Ethiopians to march down the Nile to join the Army of the Central Powers at Suez – the British Empire would have been crushed.

"In 1916, Germany and Turkey thought they had persuaded the Emperor. They promised him Djibuti for a seaport when the Allies were defeated, together with Italian and British Somaliland,

Eritrea, and the British Sudan. Picturing himself as a second Menelik the Great, Lidj Yassou had dreamed of an all-African Empire under the banner of the Prophet.

"At that time a strange, little man arrived in Addis Ababa, an archeologist and a linguist. His understanding of the oriental mind made him an ideal member of the British Intelligence Service."

My friend Zaphir's description of the man's abilities fitted remarkably with that of the author of The Seven Pillars of Wisdom, and Revolt in the Desert – Lawrence of Arabia.

"This mysterious Englishman was closeted with the British Minister for several days – only a short time later things started to happen – and things changed abruptly for the Emperor. First he became less popular, then unpopular, and then the whole country became anti-Lidj Yassou. This had been accomplished in a very adroit manner. Thousands of the most obscene photographs were circulated all over the country simultaneously."

"Pictures of Lidj Yassou?" I asked.

"Yes – that's what they were supposed to be. One showed him dressed as a Mohammedan and surrounded by Moslem priests at prayer; the others showed him in a harem with dozens of beautiful white women in vile poses. Lidj Yassou was the key figure in every group, and beneath each picture, written in Amharic, were the words: 'The Anti-Christ.'

"The Coptic Church is the single, strongest power in Ethiopia. It probably was delighted to use the idea suggested by an Englishman. The photographer who faked the pictures was an Armenian named Leon. He may have felt that his was an act of patriotism, since his race has always been persecuted by the Turks. The Germans and Turks had persuaded Lidj Yassou to join with them, but before he could move the name, 'The Anti-Christ' echoed and re-echoed throughout the Empire. People began to speak of him as Shaitan – the Devil. Then one day the streets of Addis Ababa swarmed with thousands of armed men. The Revolutionary Party had marched up to the Imperial Palace, led by the head of the Coptic Church, Abouna Matheos. When they reached it, they learned that Lidj Yassou was away – collecting virgins in the Aroussi Province, it was said.

"The Abouna Matheos pointed to the flag of Ethiopia and stated, 'Our glorious flag is sullied by the Mohamadans. In the name of the true Cross, the Maskal, and the Ethiopian Church, I excommunicate Lidj Yassou; and I absolve you all from your oath of fealty and fidelity to the Anti-Christ.'

"The revolution was accomplished, and the Anti-Christ was doomed. In due time the new Emperor, Haile Selassie, was enthroned; and Lidj Yassou was captured, escaped, was recaptured, and imprisoned in the Iron Cage. That is why Ethiopia did not join with Germany and Turkey in the first World War."

CHAPTER 18

RENDEZVOUS IN THE DESERT

Mohammed ibn Achmed arranged for us to meet his illicit caravan out in the Danakil Desert. He gave me to understand that he would be convoying a particularly fine selection of slave girls from the jungle of Jimma. We planned to meet at the Danakil village of Killalu, about a hundred miles north of the Djibuti-Addis Ababa Railroad. From there we were to cross the dangerous country toward the Red Sea.

Zaphir arranged for six mules and ten pack-horses to be waiting for us at Saram, where we were to leave the train. We were to be supplied with canned foods and cognac, an interpreter, a Nagradas, eight Danakil guards, and the mule boys – all these for the geologist, the camera-man, and myself. This was considered to be the smallest number with which one could cross the country to Killalu and still be safe from attack. All of us were sworn to secrecy.

To make our leaving the train seem plausible, we announced that we were getting off to do some shooting.

A rare species of gazelle had been reported in that neighborhood, and several European museums were eager to obtain specimens.

As we left the train, friends of ours from Addis Ababa sang, "Mad dogs and Englishmen go out in the mid-day sun." With that song ringing in our ears, we watched the train pull away, and heard its departing whistle while we checked the pile of baggage dumped out on the hot sand beside the tracks. Saram is one of the most desolate flag stations in the world. The temperature was 120 degrees in the shade, and the air seemed alive with flies thirsting for blood. Except for a few typical Abyssinian *touculs* and the ever-present, staring, naked children, all that could be seen was a shimmering, blinding, heat haze, with mirage-like mountains at a great distance to the north. It was there somewhere that we were supposed to meet the slave caravan of Mohammed ibn Achmed. Zaphir's Armenian representative, Walodia, had come on in advance with the mules and part of the supplies. While he had one of the *touculs* swept out for us – this was the only shade – we checked guns, cases for archeological specimens, medicines, gifts, clothes, and camp equipment. The heat was so intense that we would not start to travel until after dark. Even the hardy, native mules could not endure the heat of that fierce Abyssinian sun.

Our Danakil guards were more villainous-looking than any set we had encountered in all our trek across Ethiopia.

"They look like devils out of hell," the geologist said when we were sitting in the *toucul*, sweating and scratching.

"You've got hell on the brain," the camera-man answered. He too was sweating and scratching. "Look at those things around their necks."

Tall, long-nosed, almost naked, with their long curly hair worn like a crown, the Danakils strung necklaces or chaplets around their shiny, ebony necks – human relics which suggested unspeakable horrors and the shrieks of victims echoing through the African bush. Naturally curious, those savages crowded into our *toucul* to stare at us with hungry eyes; to them we were very strange – white men.

"They look like starved jackals, dipped in tar and perfumed with brimstone," the geologist said.

"We'd better kill a cow and feed these fellows before we leave," the camera-man suggested. "I don't like the way the one with the filed-off teeth is slobbering at us."

Walodia laughed. "You'll be safe. They're in mortal fear of their master, Mohammed ibn Achmed. Never have they eaten any of his friends."

But we did kill a camel to feed those Danakils before we left that night. When we started, they were gorged with raw meat. Single file, we moved into the cool night air of the desert, accompanied by the unearthly yelping of the jackals and the snarling laughter of the hyenas which echoed in that melancholy, sun-blasted desolation. When the telegraph poles along the railroad faded into the darkness, I knew we had left our last link with civilization.

In the wake of our silent, swift-moving, desert guides, we stumbled through the darkness. Now and then I caught the glint of light on the spearhead of one of the men ahead of me. They kept some distance ahead to make sure that the trail was free of marauders, wild animals, and particularly of any roving bands of savage Shiftas.

Our party was small for so dangerous a section of the country. We had tried to preserve secrecy, but news travels with incredible swiftness in the desert. That several other caravans and expeditions had started out over this trail and never been heard from again was an accepted fact. So great is the speed and accuracy with which news travels in the desert that the mysterious method is referred to as the "Native Wireless."

For seven hours we marched steadily, until we reached the first low foothills of the mountains. There we camped beside a muddy water-hole; in the background were towering precipices and tomb-like perpendicular walls. Silhouetted against the gray, morning light, I could see a long-haired Danakil sentinel; tall and panther-like, he seemed to be some jungle animal stalking its prey.

Walodia built a small fire and cooked a meal which consisted almost entirely of rice, washed down with *tedj.* The Danakils ate and drank enormous amounts, threw themselves down on the stony ground and went to sleep. But there was no sleeping so far as we four white men were concerned; our nerves were too taut in spite of the terrific heat of the day and our long night's travel. We smoked and stared into the embers, or out into the fearful, thick darkness, while we waited for the dawn.

When dawn came, it was unbelievably beautiful. The gray rocks turned to pink, and then kept changing tones as the light increased with the rising of the sun. It was like looking through a kaleidoscope at changing opalescent shades. Before the sun was up, we were on our way again. The lithe Danakils were soft-footed and silent – very different from the men who had brought us from the Sudan to Addis Ababa. The mules' hooves clicked and threw stones and pebbles; sounds carried back and forth across the canyon walls with tireless monotony. For three hours we kept moving up along a flinty river bed.

For a time the high walls of the canyon protected us, but when the sun rose higher, the heat became unbearable. Suddenly in the intense heat and that chaos of small echoing sounds, a rifle shot rang out. Its echo repeated over and over again, as though it would never stop.

Our caravan came to an abrupt halt. "Got him," I heard the geologist say jubilantly, and saw the body of a gazelle – a dig-dig – come rattling down into the canyon.

The Danakils shouted and gesticulated wildly.

"What's wrong?" I asked the interpreter.

"Should not shoot or make noise here. This is an evil place. Lots of bad men hide here."

How any roving bands or tribes could live or hunt in such a wilderness, it was hard to imagine; but events followed so rapidly that I saw there was plenty of cause for caution. Guns and spears were unslung instantly. Two guards climbed up to the highest peak to act as lookouts.

It was only nine o'clock in the morning, but it was already so hot that it was necessary to stop for the day. While Walodia skinned the dig-dig, we found whatever shade we could; there seemed to be nothing to do but eat and sleep till sundown.

But sleep had to be postponed. Within the hour our guards, who had gone out scouting, returned with twelve, long-haired, emaciated, savage Danakils; these vulture-like humans had been attracted by that one heedless shot. Three of them had old guns and a very few cartridges, not all of which fitted their guns.

The head man came into camp, while the other eleven stood around menacingly. We pretended to clean our guns in order to have them ready for whatever might happen. The chief and our interpreter talked for a very long time. The warriors were fascinated by our modern rifles, for never before had they seen any like them. And there are only two things of primary interest and importance to a Danakil warrior: killing an enemy and wearing the dried sex organs for trophies as a sign of courage, and stealing a rifle with a good supply of cartridges, which indicates wealth.

Everything else in life is secondary. Our guns and ammunition offered them a temptation that was understandable, but dangerous to us. After a long time, peace was concluded with the Danakil chief, partly because of some shells we gave him, which did not fit his guns, but more because we were on our way to meet the armed and ruthless Mohammed ibn Achmed.

Never have I seen covetousness shown as openly as those savages displayed it. Their own weapons were Mausers of about 1880; and two of them bore the name of Greek traders on their stocks. When I asked Walodia about that, he explained that thirty years before, a party of twenty Greeks and Armenians had attempted to open up the trail from Harrar to the rich Aussa Sultanate; as pioneers, they had opened up trails to many of the distant parts of the Empire. They had started, loaded with many rich presents with which they hoped to please the Sultan enough to persuade him to permit trading.

"But their gifts were too rich and too many," Walodia told me. The advance escort became intoxicated with the vision of so much wealth within its grasp. The men decided to betray both the expedition and their tyrannical Sultan. Only one young Greek managed to escape, and he crept back to Diredawa weeks later, literally on his hands and knees. "I heard the story from the Greek himself," Walodia said. "We shall reach the water-hole where the expedition was massacred in two more days."

Bleached bones, animal and human, lay near every waterhole. Sagelle, Abaiton, Nehelle, and Traiti were the names given to these places; and we moved from one on to the next. Travelling by night, resting two hours, then going on for three or four hours in the morning, made for slow going. Never were we able to endure the heat after nine o'clock in the morning. We passed through canyons of bronze-colored rocks and opaque lava, intersected by the beds of dry rivers. It was like a cauldron of burning brass with fire above and below. The sun beat down on us from above, and the rocks radiated almost as much heat under our feet. At 156 degrees of temperature our brains felt as though they were sizzling.

The heat dried out the cord and thongs which held the baggage on the mules' backs, and they sometimes snapped with the sound of a firecracker. Startled by the sound and maddened with the heat, the mules stampeded, strewing our belongings all over the rocky river bottom. Packs of snarling hyenas made the mules bolt too. Two ran away in the night and were never recaptured.

At one water-hole where we expected to stop, we found the Danakil sign of danger – a long knife stuck in the bole of a skeleton palm tree. This meant that the water had been poisoned; our guides thought that the poisoning had been done only a few hours before we arrived.

"Here we are in the land of Issa, and we must stay closer together. Look for a hidden enemy behind every rock and in every fissure," Walodia ordered.

We had the feeling that we were being stared at by unseen eyes. Now and then we passed curious alignments of stones which served to mark the trail; and we saw the geometric, phallus-like cairns which marked the burial place of Danakil and Issa warriors. At night they looked like giant fingers pointing to the sky – symbols of the dead whose soul still appealed for mercy. Those who die in this wilderness do so horribly – from thirst, poison, madness, or maiming.

One morning we made camp on the site of the Greek massacre of which Walodia had told us. The atmosphere of the place was oppressive. We had nothing to look at save the melancholy, precipitous, heat-exuding walls of stone. To kill time, three of us began to build a cairn in memory of those poor butchered men. Suddenly I had the feeling that I was being watched. I looked up to see three nude savages staring at us, their spears in their hands. They snarled at our frightened interpreter.

"Stop," he told us. "They think you are members of a punitive expedition come to avenge the death of the *Ferengi* of long ago."

"They will be avenged," Walodia muttered under his breath. "The hour is drawing near."

"This place smells of blood," the Nagradas said. "Let's get to Mohammed ibn Achmed as soon as we possibly can."

As we moved away from the place of the massacre, the howling of the hyenas and the jackals sounded like the anguished cries of the ambushed pioneers. So many heroic explorers have died in the desert: Colonel Flatters perished with one hundred men at the

Wells of Garama; Pére Charles de Foucauld, van Bary, Major Laing – they were martyrs to the lure of adventure and the spirit of the wilderness.

We crossed the scorching, lacerating flints of what seemed to be an endless trail, and came upon another poisoned well. Two of our men were incapacitated by the thorns of some poisonous bush. The endless hills of rock opened out on other, farther ranges of rock hills, radiating heat.

Weary, blinded by the glare, mouths black and cracked and bleeding from the lack of water, we plodded on. And then two horsemen appeared. They were almost upon us before we saw them. Mohammed ibn Achmed had sent his son out to find us, and guide us to our secret rendezvous.

CHAPTER 19

THE CARAVAN OF THE LIVING DEAD

As soon as we reached Killalu, a Danakil massaged my swollen, blistered feet with oil until I fell asleep. That was the first unbroken rest I had had in more than a week. The heat was less intense in Mohammed ibn Achmed's hide-out, though it was still well over 100 degrees. In spite of that, we slept for almost twenty-four hours. When I awakened the following afternoon, the aroma of broiling steaks made me forget my fatigue, though I was still suffering from sun blindness.

Killalu is one of the legendary camps which the Queen of Sheba is supposed to have used on her visits to King Solomon. It was an important stopping place for the slave caravans. Killalu was different from other Abyssinian towns; instead of being straw-thatched *toucals,* the houses were built of rough stone and were arranged in a circle on the summit of a hill, thus forming a fortified citadel, an inner line of defense. Further down the hill was a twelve-foot stockade of thick, almost impenetrable, thorn bushes.

"Welcome to Killalu, the village of the Aragoubas," Mohammed ibn Achmed said when we emerged from our quarters. Later, while we were eating our steaks, he told us something of the people.

"The Aragoubas are a branch of the Galla race; next to the ancient Amharas, they are the proudest and the most intelligent of all the many peoples of Ethiopia. They neither buy nor sell slaves, but their villages on the fringe of the desert and the jungle serve as stations for the traffic. They used to be able to live on the toll they levied for concealing the slaves on their way to the coast. Under the rule of the cursed Haile Selassie" – he spat on the ground venomously – "they have grown poorer and poorer. And my own business in slaves has become less and less."

I knew that Haile Selassie had taken drastic measures to carry out his promise to the League of Nations to suppress the slave traffic in his country. By his orders, slave traders who were caught were hung to the nearest tree, just as criminals in the early history of France and England were hung. Pictures of these hanging men have been introduced as evidence of Abyssinian atrocities, but in many instances they show proof of exact and strict justice. An examination of the remains and the tattered clothing shows that most if not all of these criminals were Arabs; they alone seem to control the slave traffic in Ethiopia and all East Africa. The true Abyssinian is too proud to engage in any kind of commerce. The Negus not only did everything in his power to suppress the traffic within his own Empire, but also offered every possible aid to the English, Italian, and French gunboats engaged in trying to stop this illicit trading in the Red Sea.

When we finished eating, it was nearly sundown, so we walked through the village. To our surprise there was not one single person to be seen in the maze of narrow passages between the stone houses. It was a dead and abandoned city. When we climbed to the roof of the sheik's house, we learned why it was deserted; all the Aragoubas were working on the slopes a little distance away – threshing millet by hand.

"Are those people slaves?" the camera-man asked.

"No, those are the villagers working there. If you want to see my slaves, I'll show you where they are. They're resting." Achmed started and we followed. "They have come a great distance and they still have a long way to go."

Before we left the roof, I looked at the desert region to the south through which we had come. In the mystic light of an African sunset it looked enchanting. The rugged, monotonous, naked mountains were transformed into a fairy-tale castle. That which had actually been a scorching hell, now looked like paradise. Their lithe bodies glistening in the sun, the Aragoubas sang in unison as they swung their flails near us; the cadence of their rhythmic African chant drifted softly on the clear, warm air. Yet this far-off, lonely oasis with its songs had been an outpost of human bondage and suffering for centuries.

Achmed led us to a door which opened on a courtyard shaded by palms. Lying on the hard-packed, earthen floor were over twenty women, sleeping soundly. So completely exhausted were they that not one of them opened her eyes when we entered. They had no manacles or chains; those were no longer necessary so far along the road toward Arabia. Surrounded by the terribly desolate and waterless country, escape was almost an impossibility. They were all young, and almost without clothes. Their heavy, thick-lipped faces were drawn with pain and strain; occasionally one moaned in her sleep. From my European standard of beauty, I could not discern one single redeeming feature in the faces of those sleeping slaves.

But their sleek, youthful, ebony bodies were as graceful as those of the most beautiful of white women, though their feet and legs were scratched and swollen from their long tramp over flinty ground and through thorny forests.

"Only four of them are sick in spite of the fact that they have walked six hundred miles. You white men covered less than a hundred," Achmed almost sneered. Through our interpreter I later learned that six women had died along the trail.

"We keep the men and women apart," the Arab slave trader continued, "for most of the journey. The men are in another depot. The last month of our journey we permit them to mingle – at least the more experienced women. These and the ugly ones may become more valuable when we do that. Should Allah will it, they arrive with child. They then fetch almost twice as much when they are sold. The very young and beautiful maidens are kept scrupulously by themselves; they have a high value in Arabia."

This callous agent of the devil was not entirely to be blamed for his attitude; he had been brought up in a country where slavery had always existed, by a family who had been in that trade for centuries, under a religion that does not frown on slaves.

The next morning, as soon as it was light enough to see, we followed him and his caravan of slaves across the plain of Killalu. In single file we stumbled and sweated our way across a wilderness of razor-sharp flints and volcanic rocks. Only the Danakils seemed to negotiate the trail with ease; they glided through the low thickets of wild mimosa and its dagger-like thorns, with the ease of snakes. The barefooted, weary, hopeless slaves tried to keep up the pace the Danakils set, but they could maintain it for only two hours before they had to slow down.

We went through a land of Satan; thorns tore our legs and shorts and shirts; our black sand-glasses were useless because they were always covered with perspiration. After two hours we had to mount our mules, our feet were so swollen. The Arabs endure it better by continually taking a drug which they chew – *khat.*

Soon after we had mounted our donkeys, I noticed several strange-looking piles of stones – a kind of monument.

"What do those mean?" I asked Mohammed ibn Achmed.

"Those are the tombs of ancient Issa chieftains."

I got out my camera to photograph one of them, but Achmed stopped me.

"To photograph them is dangerous; to touch them is death," he said succinctly.

"Dangerous to take pictures of them?" I couldn't believe it.

"Allah protect us! There are evil spirits about."

"Why would touching one mean death?"

"Because we are being followed by a band of Issa – their course parallels ours." He made a gesture toward the north.

I looked across the barren lands and could see no sign of any living thing. When I turned to look at Achmed, I saw that he was seriously troubled; and he was a man not easily alarmed. My camera went back into its case without having been opened; we were under the protection of the Arab and had agreed to obey his orders. When we neared an ancient wall, I inquired if there were ruins near.

"Not here," he replied, "but according to the Nagradas there is a white-walled city to the north – the ancient capital of the Danakil kingdom."

I had heard of that ancient city before, but it is so far from traveled trails, and in so savage a country, that it has gone unexplored.

As we moved along the rocks, the depth of the smooth-worn tread in the flat stones showed that the trail was thousands of years old. I had followed other, aged trails, cut and worn-down through centuries of use, from Carthage to Timbuctoo, and from the Atlas Mountains to the Nile, and now we were going from Alexandria to Khartoum and east across Ethiopia en route to the Red Sea.

Jungle growth and shifting sands, recurring storms and landslides partially obliterate these trails, yet there are always signs for the trained eye. A worn groove in a rock, drawings on the side of a canyon, a piece of pottery, a worn ornament or coin are pieces of a puzzle to be solved. The hunt for lost cities and ancient civilizations can be fascinating work. The early historians – Herodotus, Pliny, and Polybius, among others – point the way, and in spite of the handicaps of their times, are strangely accurate. The natives, especially the Arab and Berber nomads, are another source of information.

"My grandfather told me," a native will inform you, "that when he was lost in the desert he saw a great, deserted city halfway between the Hoggar Mountains and Timbuctoo. For one hundred francs I will guide you there."

Nine times out of ten the city or tomb he promised is not to be found, but one often finds something of rare and real historical importance. Tin Hinan I had discovered through a legend; Garama came as the result of deduction; the tomb of Siwa came through a bead I found on the trail; submerged Tipasa we saw beneath the clear water from an airplane. And now here I was on the ancient trail that led from Arabia across Africa to the valley of the Nile and the very heart of the Dark Continent. That night we camped beside a well, the walls of which showed indications that they had been constructed by masons whose craft exceeded any that we had seen in Ethiopia, dating from a far earlier age.

The slaves in the caravan were really poor specimens of the black race; they were descendants of countless generations of servile, degenerate humans. Debasement was imprinted on their flat-nosed and wholly animal like faces. In their eyes and in their whole aspect was that haunting fear seen in a homeless, beaten dog. Only the very young had decent bodies. All of them moved like cattle, without spirit, hope or intelligence. The men were being sold to do manual work in the fields, the women to be the playthings of men so long as they remained young – later they, too, would be compelled to work in the fields until they died.

Our days of marching involved stops to rest, and time to examine the sands for traces of oil. We moved over briny sand, rotting lava, through thorny bushes in blistering heat. We passed Lake Assal where caravans had come for centuries to get their salt – the lake is not unlike the great Great Salt Lake of Utah. The waters of Assal, supposed to be bottomless, are a miraculous blue; inky, blue-black mountains are reflected on its surface, and around the shore, as if it were a frame, is a silver band of salt. Two of the slaves were so ill here that prophetic vultures flapped their funereal wings not far above our heads. One wretched woman was with child, and near her time. Exhaustion, fever, and her condition were too much for her. We made a brief halt, scooped a shallow grave in the sand, buried her and her unborn child, and raised a pile of stones over them. Without a sign of mourning they were left behind, like hundreds of thousands of other victims of useless cruelty – many of whom never received the decency of burial.

Achmed shook his head and said, "There goes one hundred and thirty English pounds, but it is the will of Allah."

Nearing Gubut, we ran into a company of Danakils – tall, with cruel, aquiline features and fuzzy hair worn long, they were armed only with lances and daggers. They proved to be friendly; in exchange for knives, cartridges, and empty tin cans they gave us goats and milk. Meanwhile, the geologist made maps and notes on the many places where there were indications of oil pools. Each day there was time to take samples and search for oil-bearing rock and sand, but slowly we moved along through the desolate wilderness toward French Somaliland, the Red Sea, and the Gulf of Aden, where an Arab boat was to be waiting in a hidden cove for Achmed's caravan of slaves.

After three weeks of bare, volcanic mountains, blistering desert, and gloomy canyons, our first look at the Red Sea from the heights seemed enchanting. But the slaves were so apathetic that they did not even look up. They had never seen the ocean before, or any really large body of water, yet it awakened no slightest interest in their minds. They sat dully in a circle around the fire when we made camp, waiting to be fed and to fall asleep. The rest of us were soon splashing and wallowing in the salt water, in spite of the danger from sharks. After so many weeks when every drop of water counted, the sea was irresistible in spite of the risks. At least half of the next day we spent in the water, while the slaves prepared a farewell feast. The Gubbet Kharab is one of the wildest spots on the face of the earth. A vast, inland bay, it was once the crater of a volcano, and is surrounded by high mountains. It is said to be haunted and cursed by the ghosts of hundreds of thousands of slaves who have perished through the centuries on its melancholy shores.

The depth of the bay is fantastic; in some places close to shore, there is a sheer drop of a quarter-of-a-mile to the bottom – as in the Norwegian fjords. A mile-long channel connects the bay with the Gulf of Tajurrah; in the middle of the channel is an island known as Hell's Gate, past which the tides rush at the rate of seven or eight knots. Many of the Arazig pirate and slave ships have foundered on its shores; volcanic disturbances occasionally cause the death of thousands of fish which wash up to rot there.

Another name for the place is the "Pit of Perdition." It is said to have been a fiery hell until a follower of the True Prophet came to let in the sea and drown the Devil and the members of his court. None of the superstitious Somali or Danakils will bathe there; they claim that demons of the deep will seize them by their legs and drag them down into the great depths.

Gubbet has been used as a port since the time of Himerite and Sabean migrations into Ethiopia. The caves and canyons show evidence that Paleolithic and Neolithic man lived there. Later it became a pirate haven, a depot for the shipment of slaves to Arabia, and a base for gun-runners and spies. Someday the Danakil oil may flow down through pipe lines to storage tanks and refineries there or in Tajurrah, or perhaps both.

Two wild and warlike races live in the region, the nomadic Danakils and the sedentary Somalis. I was told that the Danakil's cranial formation shows that they arc dolichocephalic – suspicious, sanguinary, and treacherous. The importance and significance of their murder victims can be distinguished by the trophies they wear. A bronze bracelet signifies one murder; earrings show a claim to three; a necklace from which hangs a dried phallus indicates the murder of some nobleman or military officer; a red ostrich plume shows the killing of a white man. Nevertheless, it is interesting to note that the half-breed Danakil-Arab women are both beautiful and graceful.

With sunset we gathered round the fire in that silent period which comes with dusk. Again we were startled by the exciting beat of tom-toms. Soon a boat rounded the point; it was evident from all the excitement on board that something unusual had happened. No sooner had it glided up on the beach than we learned that there had been a massacre on the frontier. A young French officer, named Bernard, and one hundred and fifty Somalis had been killed by a raiding party of Assaimara – Danakils. It seemed impossible that we had been so near at the time it had happened.

I looked around and realized that our farewell banquet had to go on. Whatever our feelings might be at hearing of the death of a white comrade, they could not be allowed to stand in the way of our promise to these poor slaves who were going to be shipped to Yemen and perpetual servitude the following morning. The killing of the oxen and the sheep brought the first look of genuine interest into their eyes that I had seen in the weeks we had been with the caravan. They licked their lips over and over again, like wild beasts slavering. When the signal was given, they made for the raw meat as if they were animals. They tore at it with claw-like fingers; as they gorged themselves, they rolled their eyes in ecstasy, and cracked the smaller bones between their teeth with gusto.

Without the illumination from a bonfire no African feast is complete. The beating of the tom-toms and gasoline cans, raw flesh, fire, and the fierce urge of sex characterize the native celebrations everywhere in the savage world. Leaving them, we went into our tents, but not to sleep. With dawn we packed our kits, breakfasted, and waited for the boat that was coming to take us to Djibuti. When it came, it brought us word once more of Bernard's gallant end. We paid Mohammed ibn Achmed his fee and said a quick good-bye.

"God curse his black soul!" the geologist said feelingly as we boarded the boat.

I turned for one last look. All appeared to be peaceful and calm and happy in the early morning. There was no sight of the caravan, no indication of those tragic slaves. The black men and women were still somewhere among the palm trees, sleeping off the effects of their feast. The mules and horses had been pastured out of sight. Then we rounded the island, and the Gubbet was lost to view.

CHAPTER 20

THE YOUNG PRETENDER OF ETHIOPIA

Across the heat-shimmering bay Djibuti's few, unpretentious buildings showed as harsh excrescences above flat, arid desert. The three salt pyramids built by the convicts glittered and reflected the vicious glare of the sun. The Governor's white, stucco palace stood out, surrounded by dust-laden palms; the tall, steel radio masts topped everything. Squat and lifeless, the town appeared to be unchanged and unchanging – the same, hot, French colonial outpost of civilization I'd always known.

But when I landed and began to move about, I realized that I was mistaken in my first impression. The people were new, different, and feverishly excited. Djibuti had become a hotbed of international political intrigue. The suffocating rooms of the Continental, Arcade, and Grand Hotels were filled with newspaper correspondents drawn there by that irresistible magnet – war.

Less easy to recognize were the secret service agents from interested nations. The news that seeped in over the age-old caravan routes was expedited over official wires and wireless. Both whites and natives manned the intelligence service network from Addis Ababa, Eritrea, British Somaliland, and the Sudan.

Arms and munitions salesmen, salesmen from meat-packing companies, and adventurers rubbed shoulders with Greek and Levantine gun-runners, Ethiopian exiles, and the bearded and burnoused emissaries of independent and semi-independent kingdoms. Accommodations in the dingy hotels were as costly as if they had been first-class rooms in London or New York. Djibuti merchants were charging many times the value of their wares; to the rich visitors price was no object. Dhows and the other boats were in demand and were constantly moving across the bay to and from the ancient capital of Somaliland, Tajurrah.

When I tried to question the French officers about the seething excitement, they replied evasively. When I talked to Arab dock workers, they looked at me suspiciously. Apparently the military authorities had instilled a fear of talking or giving out any information to strangers. In the native quarter I saw an Arab whom I knew, Mohammed Abrahim, a slave- and gun-runner.

He looked at me as though he had never seen me before; I signaled him to follow me and turned into a waterfront café, The Palmier Zinc. A few minutes later he joined me at a table in the rear; he was not a true believer, for the Koran forbids the use of alcohol. He looked comical as he came in, rubbing his hands together, wearing a dirty turban, baggy trousers with red and yellow stripes along the seams, and a tight-fitting, soldier's tunic. But beneath that oily, obsequious exterior he was one of the most unmitigated scoundrels on that lawless coast.

When I brought up the subject of war and the excitement in Djibuti, he pretended that he did not know its cause. He said that the movements of the troops might mean nothing, but he did suggest in his broken French and water-front Arabic that there was some veiled mystery behind Tajurrah's mud and straw huts. After hours of talking and arguing, many drinks, and protestations of undying friendship, he leaned across the table and whispered, "You know who is over there in Tajurrah? The Emperor's son. He's a prisoner of the French."

I looked at him, disbelieving. "The French would never dare to imprison a son of the Emperor."

"That's not who I mean. Lidj Yassou was imprisoned by Haile Selassie in the Iron Cage; it's Yassou's son who is being held in Tajurrah."

"You mean young Menelik?"

"Yes. It is he. Being a son of Islam, he will be our legitimate Emperor after his father dies. And don't forget that he is the great-grandson of Menelik the Great."

The implications here were tremendous. There might be a Holy War; or one of the European nations might try to use young Menelik as means of gaining control of Abyssinia. This could involve a war of invasion, a civil war, or even a world conflict. For an invading nation the costs would be fantastic. A long drawn-out campaign would endanger popularity and leadership at home – I thought of Mussolini in Italy, Laval in France. An internal revolution in Ethiopia, led by Menelik the Third, could be manipulated and financed with far less risk.

"Three attempts have been made to kidnap Menelik the Third," Abrahim explained. "Haile Selassie's representative tried to lure him back into Ethiopia with promises of wealth and imperial privileges. His advisors refused to consider the offer; they feared it was a trick and that he might be imprisoned for life, as his father was. Also his returning would have killed any chance of ever ascending his father's throne.

"When one nation tried to get Menelik to go to Harrar, crown him king, and start a civil war, their plans were frustrated by the French. Today Menelik the Third is guarded against all visitors; his advisors fear there may be an attempt made on his life. That simplifies things for the French. Tajurrah has been made a closed, military area. When Haile Selassie tried to get him to come back he promised him slaves, concubines, and a general's rank in the army. The British tried to kidnap him and send him to their protectorate in Aden."

A Mohammedan uprising in Ethiopia might have serious repercussions in Algeria, Morocco, and Tunisia as well as in Arabia. Abrahim knew the gossip of the bazaars and trading posts all up and down the coast; and he knew how to do things or get them done, legally or extra-legally. Menelik the Third had become an outstanding figure possibly of world importance.

"I may want to talk to Menelik," I told Abrahim. "Now I must say good-night."

When I had returned to the English yacht where I was staying, I asked my host to invite the Military Port Superintendent and the Governor to dinner the following night. At that dinner we discussed Paris, London, and America. Around ten, when coffee and liqueurs were served on deck, I turned the conversation to archeology and got a very unenthusiastic response. When I mentioned Tajurrah, there was a moment of tense silence. Then the Governor asked, "What interest could an archeologist possibly have in Tajurrah?" He seemed at this moment to be genuinely interested. "Archeology involves an interest in history; and I have been tracing ancient caravan trails. Many of the oldest trails used to end in Tajurrah; that city may even have been the port the Queen of Sheba used. I could hope to find traces of the far past there, Your Excellency."

In answer to his questions I told him some of the things I had learned in my Ethiopian wanderings. Just before he left, the Governor said to me quietly, "Come to my office tomorrow morning."

After I had visited the Military Governor and obtained the required special permit to visit Tajurrah and the closed area, I sent for Mohammed Abrahim. At the end of hours of bargaining and explaining, he agreed to bring his boat alongside the yacht at dawn the following morning, take me to Tajurrah, and arrange for me to see and talk to Menelik the Third. My permit allowed me, a captain, and six men to visit the port and closed area of French Somaliland.

When Abrahim arrived, the sun was just showing red on the horizon. His crew of dirty ex-slavers tried to climb up on deck, but they were ordered back by the uniformed sailors on gangway duty. I took with me equipment and clothes for several days, not knowing how long the arrangements to see Menelik might take. Crossing the bay, Abrahim regaled me with stories of his past, of gun-running, slave and hashish trading. Twice he had been "officially" accused of murder by the French authorities. On both occasions he had been freed on the grounds of self-defense; tears came to his eyes when he told me how much it had cost him "to pay his witnesses." Of the murders for which he had not been tried, he seemed extremely proud.

When we reached a becalmed dhow, its sail hanging motionless, we drew alongside and Abrahim jumped aboard. I could see him gesticulating wildly and talking to the captain. At last, the captain handed Abrahim a package which he put under his tight tunic. He returned to us, followed by an unsavory-looking Arab.

"You can't do this," I stated as he cast off. "My permit clearly states that only the captain, six men, and myself may travel on this boat. You will get me into serious trouble, and you yourself will be arrested."

Abrahim smiled easily. "The man merely wishes to land along the coast before we get to Tajurrah. I am indebted to him, and could not refuse to grant him this favor."

"What did you hide under your tunic?" I demanded. Abrahim looked at me guilelessly and spoke as if he were assuring a small child, "That does not go to Tajurrah, nor does that." He pointed to a tarpaulin that covered some cases.

He was using my permit to leave the harbor and visit Tajurrah to carry contraband. Though I was paying him handsomely, he was using me as cover, and there was nothing I could do about it. If we were caught, I was bound to be accused of being his accomplice.

We left our illicit cargo and the Arab in a tiny cove along the coast, and turned the boat out to sea to create the impression of having come straight from Djibuti. Abrahim looked immensely ' pleased with himself. When we sighted the fortress above Tajurrah, he took out a bedraggled, tricolored flag, spat on it, and ran it up the mast. Back of the fortress hung the high, black, menacing Danakil Mountains; in front of it were the rows of mud and straw touculs. Six mosques raised white minarets over the town.

As we neared the shore, I could see people running out of their touculs like black ants. Naked children splashed into the calm water and swam toward us; the sand along the beach glittered in the sunlight. Abrahim pointed out to me a white house at the end of the beach; around it there were Senegalese soldiers with machine–guns mounted and ready for action.

"Menelik lives there," he explained.

Three uniformed figures came out of the gate of the fortress nearest us and were on the shore to meet us. One asked for my permit and studied it carefully; the other two looked suspiciously at Abrahim and his scurvy crew.

"Report to the Civil Commissioner at the Fortress," the man ordered, and handed me back the permit. We marched off under the guard of four Senegalese soldiers. Half way up the hill, Abrahim nudged me and indicated several Danakil chiefs who had stopped to watch our procession. Later he whispered that one of them was Menelik, but which one I had no way of knowing.

At his office the Commissioner looked at my permit and bellowed, "Are you a journalist?"

"Just an archeologist, Monsieur."

"Where did you pick him up?" He gestured toward Abrahim.

"I hired him to bring me here in his boat."

"What leads you to think that there are prehistoric ruins in this God-forsaken hole? I've never heard of any."

"This used to be the end of many caravan trails." For a moment the Commissioner looked as if he were going to send me back to Djibuti, so I hurried to add, "It is reasonable to suppose that there must be ruins near. Are you by any chance from Normandy?"

"But how could you guess that! I come from Le Havre."

"I've lived in Normandy so long – I thought I recognized your accent."

When he learned that the Chateau de Tancarville was mine, he told me that he had played there when he was a little boy. He dismissed Abrahim and his crew, and the guard, and offered me some of the hottest beer I've ever tasted.

"Perhaps I misinformed you about the ruins here. I did see some drawings on the rocks in a ravine six kilometers from here. Warriors, birds, and elephants. I myself should like to know what they mean. Give me a report and I'll send it on to the Governor."

He rang and ordered a guide to meet me at the boat in half an hour to help with my camera and other equipment. On the way back to the boat I was stopped by one of Abrahim's crew, who led me into an Arab house. A moment later two Danakil chiefs entered, followed by Abrahim. Over the mint tea – tea, boiling water, a large amount of rock sugar and mint – I learned that I was talking to Menelik's uncle, the Danakil Sultan of Tajurrah.

He wanted to know whom I represented – Italy or Britain, and how much money were my superiors prepared to contribute to Menelik's cause. I replied that I wanted to get the story of His Majesty, Menelik the Third. Was he popular with the rich Mohammedans? Would the Ethiopians come to his support in large numbers? Could I meet and talk to him?

We were interrupted by a guard who announced, "The Ferengi's guide is coming down from the fortress."

The bearded Sultan arose and said solemnly, "So be it. You cannot get to see His Majesty in his own house, but he can slip out and come here concealed in a shamma. Menelik will meet you here tonight as it grows dark."

The afternoon was a long one. The heat had that dead, breathless quality which saps strength and energy; most of the time I had to be directly in the sun, between oven-like, volcanic rocks. But it was worth it; till then there had been no known, recorded traces of Paleolithic man in Somaliland. The photographs were easy to take, but the perspiration ran off me so fast that the drawings I made were smudged and wet.

On our way back to the fortress I saw why the touculs were laid out in such straight rows. In the center of the main square of the town machine-guns were pointed down the narrow lanes, covering every avenue of approach to the town and fortress. With sundown I heard the Mohammedan call to prayer. Soon after came the boom of the curfew gun. No one was supposed to be out-of-doors after that signal without a pass, but I managed to get to the appointed house without being challenged.

When I entered, the pungent odor of incense greeted me. Several men were seated in the room, their thin, bronzed faces dimly lighted by one hanging, kerosene lamp.

"The blessings of Allah be upon you," was their greeting. I was given a cushion beside the Sultan.

Since they understood no French, Abrahim was there to translate their Danakil dialect for me. He was even able to tell me some of the things they were thinking and not saying. I learned that emissaries had been there recently from Lidj Yassou, the Italians, and the Yemen Arabs. Impatient at the length of the negotiations, the Italians had tried to kidnap Meneik. A Fascist had been stabbed to death, and the affair had been hushed.

The Sultan told me the tale of Menelik Third as if he had been a professional story-teller seated in the market place. The nobles of Tajurrah sat cross-legged, silent and respectful, listening. The only other sound was the bubbling of the narghile pipe as it was passed around.

"May Allah hear my words, so that the heart of the Ferengi may be touched by this story of injustice and woe. The history of the illustrious exile here in Tajurrah is sad. But not so tragic as that of his mother, the Empress Fatumata Aby Beker; not so terrible as that of his father, Lidj Yassou." He paused while Abrahim translated.

"Many reasons have been circulated," the Sultan continued, "many lies about the dethronement of His Majesty Lidj Yassou by Haile Selassie. The real reason was his marriage to our daughter, The Princess of the Danakils, who was then fourteen – a true believer in the Prophet. Lidj Yassou, may the blessings of Allah be upon him this night, also became a true believer.

"The Coptic priests were afraid of losing their hold over the Ethiopian people. They conspired for His Majesty's downfall, and to place the Dowager Empress Zavoita on the throne with Ras Tafari – now Haile Selassie – as regent.

"Lidj Yassou's wife, Menelik's mother, was born in 1902. Her grandfather was the Sultan of Zeila, a Mussulman of the ancient Assoba race. Her uncle was the richest slave-owner in all East Africa. Her father, Abu Beker, was created Nagradas by the Great Menelik. Later he became Belabatt, which means the great chief of the Danakils and the Adoimaras.

"When our daughter married Lidj Yassou amidst magnificent feasting at Addis Ababa, a period of glory began for her and for our people. She commanded thousands of slaves and untold riches. She was widely loved for her sympathy and kindness. But after months of splendor came the usurpation of the throne by Zavoita and the Ras Tafari. Lidj Yassou was exiled and imprisoned in Harrar. The Empress fled with six hundred Askari, more than a thousand slaves and a hundred thousand thalers. She went to Assoba in her native land, and the Ras Tafari did not try to stop her. He feared her righteous wrath. Lidj Yassou's reign ended in disaster in 1916, after he had ruled for eight years.

"The Empress, coming home, was hailed by all the Danakil tribes with great joy. They flocked to see her and to pay her homage. Four months later Menelik was born, and that spread more joy throughout the land. Many chiefs came to her with plans to regain the throne."

One of the noblemen interrupted the Sultan's recital, "By the beard of the Prophet, that is the living truth."

The Sultan continued, "Many moons were passed in considering what it was best to do. Our numerous allies pledged their wealth and their soldiers to our cause. Because of this the Empress marched across the desert to join her husband in Harrar. Along the way the people received her as the legitimate Empress; and for one hundred moons they ruled again, while the news spread among the villages throughout the land.

"On hearing of this, that dog of a Christian, Haile Selassie, became mightily alarmed. Secretly he gathered together a great army and descended on Harrar. Our Mohammedan warriors rose to defend their lawful rulers. For three days a bloody battle raged on the plain outside the city. The banner of the Prophet was trampled in the dust."

As he uttered these words in a solemn tone, the nobles bowed their heads as if they were praying. Abrahim listened like one entranced. He and I both knew a different version of that story. The Sultan shifted uneasily on his cushion, and then went on.

"That was a sad day for all Mohammedans. The Empress' father, Abu Beker, was slain on the field of battle. Lidj Yassou escaped, but was later taken prisoner by Ethiopian warriors who recognized him as he wielded his well-known sword. Our daughter, the Empress, fled with her son and a few faithful warriors who brought her here to Tajurrah. Her fortune — all our fortunes — were lost. We were utterly ruined.

"Haile Selassie wanted to kill Lidj Yassou, but the Dowager Empress liked this generous nephew of Menelik the Great; so he was sent in abject humility to Mount Garamoulta to be imprisoned in an Iron Cage, manacled with golden chains. The guards never left him; he was ever in sight of any who might choose to look; his wife and son were far away and never permitted to visit him."

"The blessings of Allah be upon his soul this night," chanted the nobles in unison.

The Sultan continued. "After many moons the Empress, poor and heart-broken, went with her son to see the Governor of Djibuti to ask for aid. She was granted a small pension, just enough to maintain a modest household. By the Beard of the Prophet, that was an insult to our whole race."

The Sultan concluded by spitting on the floor. Later I learned more of Menelik's earlier years. Growing up, he had spent much of his time with the wild, young Danakils in Tajurrah. He was educated as a Bedouin, though he learned to read and write in the little Koranic school in the village. An old wiseman, a friend of his mother, taught him the folklore of his people, but he lived like a beachcomber, wild and free. Haile Selassie in the meantime was crowned Emperor with great pomp, before the Ministers of many nations. The boy became an almost forgotten exile, living from day to day on slender means.

The Sultan began to speak again, telling me about the political importance of Menelik the Third and his significant place in the international situation, when suddenly the door swung open with a loud squeak. Captain Louis Jacquemin and another officer marched into the room.

The nobles of Tajurrah salaamed with excessive politeness. The Captain looked at me and smiled. "My compliments. My brother officers and myself want you to dine with us on the beach."

It was a thinly veiled order.

"Thank you." I stood up. It was obvious that my interest in seeing Menelik had leaked out and that the news had reached the fortress. I apologized to the Sultan and the nobles for leaving, thanked them for their courtesy, and followed Jacquemin and his friend down to the beach. For the moment there were two prisoners of the French in Tajurrah, Menelik the Third and "a strange archeologist."

The late dinner on the beach with the officers was pleasant enough, but I could not get my mind off some of the things the Sultan had been telling me. How much did these suave Frenchmen know about the people among whom they lived and worked and whom they governed; did they recognize their pride, their history, their hopes, and their ambitions?

Drinking our warm wine, the officers wanted to know about the new restaurants and cabarets in Paris. They were willing to discuss the possibilities of war or any other subject except the one in which I was most interested. Every time I mentioned Menelik, they stopped talking, or spoke of some entirely different matter. As a subject for conversation, he was taboo. Abrahim arrived, under the influence of too much tedj, and asked one of the officers for permission to go aboard his boat for the night.

"Not unless you want a bullet through your dirty hide," the man replied. "Just try to leave this shore!"

I got up and went over to Abrahim. "Remember that our agreement includes my talking to Menelik," I reminded him.

Abrahim shook his head as if to clear it.

The officer said to Abrahim so that he could be heard by the others, "Any ship that comes to Tajurrah with the idea of playing monkey tricks will be blown into Mohammed's paradise." He moved over to a light iron trestle on the beach. There he struck a match and lighted a rocket which went soaring into the sky and illuminated the whole bay. There was no ship in sight, not even a row boat, but it was evident that the French were taking no chances on their prisoner slipping away in the night.

Set out in a neat row on the beach were the camp cots, one of which was assigned to me. Soon after we retired, I saw twenty Senegalese march by, their bayonets shining in the moonlight. They marched up to the house where Menelik lived. Twenty other figures emerged from the shadows and returned – the guard was being changed.

Unable to sleep, I saw a native runner arrive an hour or two later. I heard him ask for the Captain. When he was taken over to the Captain's cot, he fell and dropped his flashlight. I heard him apologize for waking the Captain and saw several other officers go over to the cot. The Captain was reading a message.

He must have read it several times before he turned, and said to the others, "It's a wireless from Djibuti. Lidj Yassou is dead."

"Then Menelik is the Mohammedan Emperor of Ethiopia," another voice stated.

"Not so loud," a voice cautioned.

The official report of Lidj Yassou's death was not made until two months later, because of the many dangers involved, especially of an uprising and Holy War. But watching a sentry march up and down in front of me for hours lulled me to sleep in spite of all the implications I could see in the ex-Emperor's death. When I awakened, it was getting light and Abrahim was coming to my cot.

"We must get away from this accursed place," he said in a loud voice. "The French are angry, and there is some new excitement in the village. Ethiopian soldiers are arriving in great numbers. Now there may be war."

I got up and walked down to the edge of the water with him. "I have important news to give to Menelik. I must see him. While these French officers are busy with the arriving Ethiopians – – "

"Abrahim will arrange it – will be back soon." He moved off toward the fortress.

Just after breakfast, while we were smoking our pipes, there was a great hubbub in the village. Down through the canyon from above the town marched a long line of Ethiopian chiefs and their warriors. With them were hundreds of refugees. The French officers hurried off, followed by the Senegalese soldiers. Later I learned that they were coming from the Eritrean Aussa oasis near Moussi Ali, some forty miles to the north. The chiefs had come to arrange for the protection of their cattle and their other possessions – these included their women – while they went to fight against the Italians

Abrahim came hurrying back to me. "Quick!" he said. "Menelik is going to the well beyond his house to meet his chiefs – just outside the village. You are to meet him there."

I took a small camera and started down the beach behind Abrahim, stopping now and then to take a picture. That was an attempt to deceive any guard who might be watching from Menelik's house. For the French garrison this was a great occasion; for many of the officers this was their first contact with real war. Trying not to appear to hurry, I made my way as fast as I dared toward the well. When I arrived, the Danakil chiefs and the Sultan were seated in a semicircle some distance beyond. Danakil warriors were leaning on long spears, and were talking with the young women who came to draw water.

The old Sultan got up and came to meet me. "Here you may speak openly, for the desert has no ears," he said when he had greeted me.

"I have come with important news for His Imperial Highness," I told him. "I cannot stay long – the soldiers may return and come looking for me. Abrahim, send someone back along the beach to warn me if the soldiers come."

Menelik was as unlike Haile Selassie as black is unlike white. Brought up among the savage Danakils, he considered that anyone who was not a True Believer was a natural born enemy. His voice was sharp and domineering. He had a magnificently formed head, like that of a Greek statue. His eyes possessed the depths of mystery one finds in people who have lived for generations in the desert. When he spoke, they flashed with quick intelligence. His face was typical of the fanatical Danakils, proud and fearless. When he listened, he looked directly at the speaker – or gazed into the distance with no indication that he heard.

He knew that the French had supported Haile Selassie's rise to power and his usurpation of the Ethiopian throne; that his father's forced abdication and imprisonment had been hastened by their attitude. His Danakil mother had taught him to blame them for his exile, and to hate them. Danakils neither forgive nor forget; nor have they any slightest conception of, or word for, mercy. If ever he should lead Ethiopia's Mohammedan hordes into war, it would be a battle which could end only in death and complete annihilation.

When I had been presented and invited to join the men on the ground, I said: "I am sorry to come as a messenger with bad tidings, Your Majesty."

Menelik and his chiefs stared at me. "Continue," Menelik said.

"I have just learned that your father, His Majesty the Emperor Lidj Yassou, is dead." I looked from one to the other to see how it would affect them. After several minutes of silence and complete immobility of expression, the Sultan spoke.

"All souls must taste of death." He quoted the old Arab proverb solemnly. "Tell us how you know."

"Last night a runner came to the officers' camp when it was very late. He brought a wireless message from the radio station in Djibuti. I heard an officer repeat the message: 'Lidj Yassou is dead!'" Again there was a lengthy silence.

Suddenly the men arose as a group, salaamed to the ground and swore life-long allegiance to the startled Menelik. That is a moment I shall never forget. The hereditary Emperor stood, and threw back his shoulders. An enormous ring on his left hand reflected the rays of the sun. He towered over his chiefs, and I noticed that his long white shamma was lined with blue silk. He acknowledged his chiefs' pledge and accepted their allegiance before he turned to me.

"I thank you, Ferengi, for bringing me this news. Long have we waited for this day. By the sword of Allah, now my hour has struck. No longer will my people remain in ignorance of what happens in our land." He stopped, and considered for a moment before he continued. "This news shall be heralded from all the roof tops when our people go there in the cool of the evening. All shall know that the great-grandson of Menelik the Great is preparing. Soon I shall come among them in my wrath with my chiefs and tribesmen around me.

"When you return to your superiors, tell them that soon I shall be ready to fight for the throne of my ancestors. My orders will go out to all the villages where True Believers live, and to the places where our warriors have been forced to fight for the impostor. Their spears will shine and their guns be ready for my coming.

"There has never been unity in my land since the Great Menelik died. Haile Selassie has tried to force Ferengi civilization upon us, but our people are old and settled in their ways. They will not willingly accept these strange new customs. Ferengi soldiers will try to tear my kingdom apart like a ravenous dog crunching bones. We heard that when we joined the Great White Council – the League – great riches and plenty would flow throughout our land. Where are they?

"Now there is nothing save poverty and cruelty in our villages. When the warriors and their chiefs could not pay the enormous war-taxes, the tax collectors came and stole the children, so their mothers will never see them again. Born to freedom, they are sold like cattle to satisfy the ruthless demands of this unjust and cruel usurper." Menelik's voice was rising with anger.

"The Emperor lives in splendor at the Palace. He does not care for humble chiefs who have been ruined by bad crops, the pillage of the tax collectors, and the raids of slave traders and others. When I come into my own, all this shall end. Even the poorest chief may come to me for aid. The Great Menelik made his laws respected even in the farthest provinces. I also shall rule my people justly and impartially. The Great Menelik's laws were just laws. So shall my laws be – for the benefit of all. Tell your masters that, Ferengi."

A warning whistle sounded. I arose, bowed, and moved hurriedly away. My audience was over.

CHAPTER 21

A SOCIETY WEDDING IN TAJURRAH

When next I saw the Sultan he invited me to a "society wedding" in Tajurrah – I was to wear Arab costume. The whole event from the betrothal to the wedding ceremony, most of which took place in public, occurred in less than one day. The ceremonies were a blend of primitive African rites and Mohammedanism.

The bridegroom was a magnificent young Danakil sheik with an exceptionally fine military record. More than six feet of brawn and muscle, Moussa was typical of the fiercest fighting race of Eastern Africa. Inky black hair, shining with rancid butter, hung down to his shoulders.

The bride elect was the fifteen-year-old daughter of an important branch of a leading Somali family. Her parents had lost most of their wealth through backing the ill-fated cause of Lidj Yassou, though they were still so well-to-do that she had a handsome dowry to take to her husband.

With an escort of thirty nobles and warriors, twenty of his own soldiers, and many slaves, Moussa arrived at the house which had been taken for him in Tajurrah. This *toucul* was one of the largest in the town; complete with stockade, courtyard, compound, and small outbuildings. The main room was furnished with carpets, cushions, and narghiles – the same equipment is rented to different families when they celebrate weddings, births, circumcisions, and deaths.

Though the groom was only twenty-one, he had already won great military honors. Around his head he wore a broad band from which rose five long, deep-red ostrich plumes. The color indicated that they had been won in war, and their number showed that he had fought in five battles. Over his right shoulder hung a leopard skin; his broad shield of tough, antelope hide was studded with gold and silver, and hung down his back. In his right hand he carried a seven-foot spear with a razor-sharp point; and he moved with the assurance of a born leader.

Around his neck he wore a necklace of "relics," and two more of the same were fastened to his spear head. These objects which had been slashed from his victims and dried, had the same value for him that medals do for distinguished military men. Danakils were probably the original totalitarians, for no youth can be admitted to warrior rank until he shows that he has killed three enemies in hand-to-hand fighting.

In my Arabian disguise, I accompanied Moussa and his escort when they went to make the first call on the father of his fiancée. We arrived at the *toucul* with four donkeys loaded with *khat* – the herbaceous drug which is used as a stimulant by all classes in the countries along the Red Sea. It comes from a low shrub which grows at high altitudes, and a "shot" consists of chewing a few leaves. It has a powerful effect; and though it is not harmful, it creates a feeling of well-being and excitement.

In response to Moussa's knock, the girl's father came to the door, looked at the lavish supply of *khat,* and invited the suitor and his escort to enter. The offering of *khat* showed wealth; the grisly necklace proved courage, valor, and accomplishment.

All the men sat down and began to chew *khat;* not a word was spoken of the object of our visit until every one felt the effect of the drug. Then the question was asked, and the girl's father readily assented. Moussa returned to his own house, sending his escort to get in touch with the future bridesmaids. I went with them.

Around that section of the *toucul* in which the women lived, including the bride, was a high, thick, thorn-bush stockade. Its only entrance was barred. The men of Moussa's escort made a mock attack on the gate. Obscene demands and threats were shouted over the stockade; both the besiegers and the besieged laughed uproariously. The gate was kicked and banged to the tune of a chant.

Eventually the barrier was forced, and there was a mad scramble for the drinks and foods which had been arranged inside the stockade for the men. When they had gorged themselves on figs, honey, dates, stuffed intestines, and quantities of *tedj*, the men shouted for the bridesmaids to come out. Their demand met with silence; etiquette requires the girls to be coy and shy. Again the men shouted for the girls, and, when they refused to come out, the men forced their way into the women's quarters.

The first man to come out carried a black, fighting, biting, scratching, Somali girl. Others followed, each of them bringing a girl out with him. The bridesmaids wore bright-colored dresses of cheap, imitation, Japanese silk. The man who acted as master of ceremonies organized the dancing. With clapping, chanting, cymbals, tom-toms, and clouds of incense, the couples began their individual wiggling, their bodies never in contact. It was both grotesque and infectious.

The body was kept motionless, the feet shuffled forward and back, the torso going through strange contortions. The women danced away from the men, luring them on, yet always keeping a step or two in advance. A woman would move swiftly away as if she were going to run; then she would move slowly back toward the man, as though she could not resist his magnetism. Again she would pretend to run away.

According to etiquette, the Somali call to the bridesmaids to come out of the women's quarters must have the appearance of a forced attack and rape; and the girl must appear to be unwilling and to fight. When it was discovered that I was "a Christian dog," the Danakils passed me off as a holy madman, and roared with laughter. Meantime everyone continued to drink and dance. Up to this point the many bridesmaids had appeared, but not the bride.

Two hours after sunset the engagement dance ended, and we formed a procession to march to the home of the waiting bridegroom. Then the bride appeared. Yashminah was a blaze of beaten gold and beads – she wore her own necklaces and bracelets, those of her bridesmaids, and all those belonging to her immediate family. Naked to the waist, she was a tall, willowy girl like a sculptured Tanagra figure in ebony. With lighted torches we marched toward the bridegroom's house to the tinkle of cymbals and the chant: *"Mohammeda, Mohammeda, Mohammeda, zotcheine zabada."* (Mohammed has perfumed us like civet cats.)

It was like a carnival parade. The men carried baskets of gifts on their shoulders, and everyone of the more-than-a-hundred individuals was laughing and singing. A bridal procession must sing its way into the bridegroom's house. Without singing, they would not be admitted.

When we arrived, a man came out of the groom's house and named the song the bridegroom wished to hear. He complained that the instruments were out of tune, that the singers did not keep time, and that they were off pitch. This, too, is demanded by convention. We were asked to sing a song the nearest equivalent of which is "For he's a jolly good fellow."

As the song ended, the outer door of the house was thrown open, a sheep was slaughtered on the threshold, and we were invited to step over it and enter a large courtyard. In the center a large bamboo cage, ten or twelve feet in diameter, had been erected, covered with so much tinsel, ribbon, and flowers that it was almost impossible to look inside.

Beside the door of the cage stood the groom. He wore a white *shamma,* and in his hand he had a whip with a red and silver handle made from a hippo's tail. The bride-to-be was shoved into the cage, and forced to her knees by her bridesmaids. Moussa followed her in, and the bridesmaids came out; he beat her over the hips, and thighs and back, and he used strength in his blows, while he repeated: *"Shaitan kotcha. Shaitan kotcha."* (Get out, Satan!)

While he did this, several of the men entered the cage and gave Yashminah resounding slaps. This is their conventional way of preparing a bride for married life! When the men came out of the cage, three old women went in to perform a necessary operation, an ancient Abyssinian custom which is said to be increasing under the growing influence of Mohammedanism. Moussa, Yashminah, and the three old women were left alone in the cage while the rest of us sang and danced outside, for only the bridegroom remains with his intended while the old women operate.

"If you want to know all about it, I can get you a young Somali girl cheap," my interpreter, Yesu, suggested. His plan for making a quick profit and a deal was obvious. When I refused his offer, he sighed, and went on to explain what was happening in the cage.

"In our country virgin female slaves have a high value. The Ethiopians and Arabians have eunuchs, but they are so expensive that most of our people cannot afford them as guards for their daughters. The girls are sewed up instead. Slave girls undergo this operation when they are eleven or twelve years old, when they near the age of puberty; this keeps them from losing their market value.

"Free families who want their daughters to make good marriages have the same thing done. That is how it is with Yashminah: the women are removing the protective stitches now – they were put in four or five years ago. In the rich families silk sutures are used; for the poorer girls thin strips of gazelle hide have to serve. The old women who perform this operation use steel needles, but away from the sea a thorn suffices. They use no anesthetics. The natives in Ethiopia used to steal the telegraph wires along the railroad, and use the copper to make needles; this continued until Haile Selassie issued a decree that anyone stealing the wire would be hanged.

"Infibulation had its origin in the Sudan centuries ago, in an attempt to raise the price of female slaves whose virginity could be guaranteed. The free women of the Harraris, Gallas, Danakils, and Somalis persuade their daughters to undergo this operation. It is sometimes performed on the wives to insure their remaining faithful while their husbands are away for long periods; and I have never heard of any woman objecting. Sometimes infibulation is used to restore virginity, and to raise the price of a slave."

"One old woman in there," Yesu pointed to the cage, "stitches and uses herbs so skillfully that no one could ever tell that a girl was not a virgin. A slave can then be sold again as a virgin in some far-off place. Djibuti and Tajurrah women make an art of their surgery."

"But the operation without anesthetics is painful – dangerous too – "

"Yes – there are sometimes infections," Yesu said.

At that moment a piercing scream overrode the noise of the music and the boisterous laughter and talking.

"*Inschallah! Khalass!* The stitches have been removed, Kebir," Yesu remarked. There was a moment of utter silence;

dancing, talking, laughing, music – everything was stopped. "Yashminah's ready now for the second operation."

Some girl giggled hysterically. Everyone turned to stare at her resentfully, without a sound.

"What happens now?" I asked.

"We wait for Yashminah to scream – when she does the marriage has been consummated."

After several seconds the silence was broken by a sharp cry – a woman's stifled scream of pain. Pandemonium followed. Men and women shouted and banged on empty gasoline tins; they stomped on the earth with their feet and made as much noise as if they had clapped their hands. It was like a charivari. When Yashminah appeared, the whole crowd cheered and roared their approval. Tear-stained but smiling, she walked into the center of the compound. Moussa followed her proudly, wearing his leopard skin, carrying his whip in one hand (he would continue to carry the whip for the forty days of celebration, so Yesu said) his spear in the other. Attached to his spear was a piece of damask that looked like the flag of Japan – the center of the cloth was stained with blood.

These evidential, bloodstained cloths are referred to in the Bible – Deuteronomy ch. 22, v. 17 – and have both importance and value in polygamous countries. They become a family heirloom and are used as pillow covers. The women embroider these pieces of damask with arabesques or verses from the Koran. They represent a family's most treasured possession. In the time of great need they are sometimes sold, but always they are the last asset to be disposed of.

"Moussa will carry his spear, with its new emblem, at the head of the caravan on the long trek with his wife to their home in Abyssinia," Yesu said.

Moussa waved the spear, making a complete circle, thrust it a foot into the ground with one stroke, then turned and walked with great dignity to join his wife in the midst of her family. This was the end of the wedding ceremony – no priest or civil servant was present.

Then the feast began. Sheep and oxen had been barbecued over pits; they were carved and served to the guests with *tedj* –

tedj is frequently called *goboi* in Tajurrah. Everyone had to take one more drink, drunk or sober, and the young bride wiped the guests' lips with the tips of her breasts. With morning the whole assembly went to the sea and bathed.

"That is the end of the wedding officially, but the feasting and drinking go on for days and weeks," Yesu explained as we were leaving.

The eunuch market was something people whispered about, even in Tajurrah, though it was an annual event. The yearly sale was one of the most important in all Africa. Buyers came from all over the east – Arabia, Yemen, Ethiopia – from everywhere that eunuchs were used legally or illegally.

The French tried to enforce a law against it, but it went on just the same. Either the Government did not know about it, or they pretended that they did not. Whether or no, the eunuch market was the town's important annual occasion. No Europeans were permitted to see it, but my disguise as an Arab had been so successful and the natives so friendly that I determined to see the market, and with a camera-man if possible.

The only camera-man I could find was over six feet tall and spoke no Arabic, but he agreed to risk going in a hooded burnous, to keep silent, and to get what pictures he could. In our disguises we conversed with Arabs; or rather I did, and they took me for the tailor I pretended to be. That first encounter gave us confidence.

With a good supply of cognac for the Sultan, and gifts of beads and mirrors for the women of his household, we went to his house to call. The Sultan was not cordial. The *Ferengi* are never welcomed in Tajurrah; during the eunuch sale and Fair week the native quarter is closed to them.

That I had brought the first news of Lidj Yassou's death to Menelik the Third, the Sultan's nephew, and that I had made friends at Moussa's wedding had some effect. Finally the Sultan agreed, under protest, to lodge the camera-man and me on the top floor of his house. There we were taking the minimum of risk, but if we were caught – "Worse than death?" the camera-man questioned, and he really worried all the time that we were there.

Asiatic and African buyers and the slave dealers crowded the lower floors of the Sultan's house; by avoiding them as much as we could, we stood a better chance of getting out and taking the pictures when the time came. But that meant being confined to our room for long hours.

The houses and *touculs* in that part of the world are infested with vermin and fleas. In spite of insecticides and prepared tobacco juice, we were itchingly uncomfortable every moment we had to spend in that room. Our own cots with their mosquito nets were no protection, even though we kept our lamps burning through the night.

But Tajurrah has practically a monopoly in the eunuch market; the Arabian demand for them is high, and this annual Fair and special sale is the most important in this awful business. The ordinary slave traffic has been decimated by the efforts which have been made to suppress it, but Tajurrah's income from the eunuch monopoly remains substantial. Slave boats, with from forty to sixty slaves, are frequently captured by the British and other patrol boats in the Red Sea and the Gulf of Aden, but for every one captured there are others that escape. The slavers have learned to use speedy and shallow-draft boats. They can run away from the patrol-boats, or can find safety in the coastal waters where the heavier boats dare not go.

Since the Koran recognizes slavery as a legitimate institution, the traffic is bound to continue. Ibn Saud, for all practical purposes, is a dictator in Arabia, and he is personally anxious to see this trade suppressed; but he is helpless in the face of religious sanction. Fortunately, Mohammedans, as a rule, treat their slaves kindly – in many cases, as members of the family.

The castration of boys for sale as guards for the harems has been practiced for centuries. The Bagirmese in central Africa are of mixed blood, Arabian and Negroid. They are said to make raids regularly on the villages of the Sarras, whose men are noted for their stature. The little boys are kidnapped, castrated, treated, and trained for eventual sale to Arabian buyers. So many of the boys die as the result of this operation, cruelly performed without anesthetics, that the eunuch brings more than twice the price of an unaltered male slave.

While we were fighting fleas and vermin on the top floor of the Sultan's house and waiting for the Eunuch market to open, we were considered potential buyers, and several of these pathetic, altered men and boys were brought to us for our approval. The Sultan said that he hoped I could arrange some European contacts and sales for eunuchs. When I told him what I thought of the practice, he shook his head sorrowfully, and looked at me as though he couldn't believe such stupidity existed. "Mohammed permits it," he stated as though that should make it right.

The eunuchs were fat, black, and effeminate. One of them saw through my disguise, and for a moment in his eyes there was a gleam of hope, but it died as soon as it was born. The others giggled girlishly. The position of the eunuch in the Red Sea countries is a very difficult one. They are socially ostracized by both men and women; and they are laughed at and scorned. Until they become members of some household, they are outcasts. The women and girls have an antagonism toward them that amounts to hate; the eunuchs' worst ill-treatment comes from them, and is probably best accounted for in psychological terms.

While the eight eunuchs were being exhibited to me in the Sultan's house, before the market opened, a mob of screeching women waited outside the front door to throw stones and filth at them when they came out to be taken back to the market place – in front of the mosque on the waterfront.

I can still remember their sad, frightened, haunted eyes. Some of them were mature, but two of them were little more than children. They all had hairless, feminine faces; deep-bronzed, well-oiled skins; and long wavy hair. They were exhibited as if they had been horses which must be shown as sound in wind and limb. The women outside yelled and threatened so that I was afraid these helpless creatures would be mobbed and stoned. To guard them, we took them out by the back entrance, and the camera-man and I followed in our Arab disguises.

On one side of the market place was the emerald sea; on the beach, leading up the hillside were the orderly rows of *touculs* with their thatched roofs. Above the towering, volcanic mountains, the sky was so blue as to be almost painful to the eye. The wretched eunuchs were standing or lying on the ground in front of the mosque like a herd of sheep. There were nearly two hundred of them. The buyers moved about, looked at the "merchandise," and felt their flesh as a woman would test fruit for firmness or a chicken for tenderness. The noise of talk and laughter was added to by the eunuchs who shouted and yelled and pleaded to attract attention and possible purchasers. Some of them exhibited their best points – feminine breasts, their soft shoulders, their strong, white teeth. If a buyer were interested, he put a eunuch through revolting postures and disgusting physical examinations. While they were stripped, the eunuchs were made to perform suggestive dances, and to sing to show off their soprano voices for sweetness of quality and clarity of tone.

The better looking, younger boys were sold first, then the bigger ones who were to be used as harem guards, and lastly the less-attractive ones. From the roof of the mosque the camera-man took several reels of film which are unique.

As soon as a few slaves were sold, they were hurried down to the boats in groups to preserve them from injuries by the fanatical women. When I asked where the French Civil Governor was, I was informed that he usually absented himself during the "Fair," and left the Senegalese troops to keep order. The Resident had urgent business which was keeping him in Djibuti.

When the eunuch sale was over, those few who had not been sold were beaten by their disappointed owners, and maltreated by the women. After that, if they had not been killed or too seriously injured, they were taken back into the interior to await the next year's sale.

One of the most prominent buyers at the Fair was an *Agha* from Mecca who had come in a very large *dhow*. Whether he was a priest or merely an important harem warder, I could not learn. *Agha* or *Aga* may be used to denote a priest, a lord, a landowner, or even the chief eunuch of an important harem. Many of the eunuch harem-Aghas become wealthy. Some of them prefer to buy pregnant women slaves so that they may have "children of their own."

CHAPTER 22

LAST STORIES FROM THE TOMBS

Haile Selassie's permission to do archeological work in Ethiopia for five years now lost all value. War was in the air – inevitable. The joy of living luxuriously on a yacht anchored off Djibuti was a complete and happy change, after months of trekking and camping in deserts, jungles, and mountains; but the newspapers printed all sorts of fantastic stories both about the boat and my explorations. One story inferred that we were connected with the Imperial Court of Addis Ababa; another stated that I had talked oil with Haile Selassie, and had located the "liquid gold."

The yacht "Triona" belonged to some English friends of mine who had just come out from London. Our radio was constantly being bombarded for all kinds of information. The trip through the Mediterranean and down through the Suez Canal to Djibuti had provoked interest from the time the "Triona" left Gibraltar, so I was told. One paper referred to it as a boat under United States registry, carrying secret dispatches from the British and French Governments. The American Embassy in Paris jumped to make an official announcement: The "Triona" was under British registry – the neutrality of the United States was not in jeopardy.

The Italian papers referred to the yacht as "suspect," and watched its movements carefully. At Malta the rumors of an Anglo-Italian War were substantiated to some extent by the concentration of British warships in the harbor. Near Port Said the "Triona" had passed the British "Resolute" and later the "Conte Biancomo," jammed with Italian soldiers. The people on the yacht could hear thousands of voices singing; and then *Il Duce's* voice had come in over the radio from Rome:

"Nothing will stop us. We have decided to see this through to the bitter end. Victory or death. It is better to be a lion for a single day than a lamb forever. Are you with me?"

This provoked a tremendous ovation; cheers led to the singing of the Italian national anthem. Both Mussolini's voice and the singing carried to every part of the port. As the "Triona" passed the Italian liner, the soldiers jeered at the British flag floating gaily on the mast. It appeared that throngs on the shore at Port Said represented Italian patriotic societies, and that their cheering had been organized.

When the "Triona" passed the "Umbria" loaded with more Italian soldiers, they also howled and yelled. At Suez there were two large tugs at the entrance to the canal, with a supply of buoys and chains which made it look as if that waterway were going to be closed; the Captain feared that he might have to return to England around Africa. The Italian "Belvedere" carried two thousand men and two thousand mules, and smelled like a slaughter-house.

Port Sudan is the only port of a colonial empire nearly as large as India. It proved to be another madhouse. The Levantines, Greeks, and Armenians had collected all the camels, mules, horses, trucks, cotton, sheep, and cattle within miles. They were doing business with the Italians; and every available tin of sardines and bully beef was sold to them. Sanctions had not yet been declared, so Fascist ships were coaling, oiling, and provisioning frantically, before the port was closed to them. The British laughed, for the bully beef was years old – "hard enough and dry enough to pave the roads."

A corpulent, perspiring German was pacing up and down – he had a large amount of oil stored and could not deliver it to the Italians because of official red tape. When the British bought it from him, he was as happy as a child. In the harbor at Massua there were dozens of transports. A ship load of tar was unloaded on top of food supplies at night; when the morning sun hit it, it melted, ran, and ruined the food. A tropical storm washed supplies valued at hundred of thousands of *lire* into the sea. The largest army ever to invade the Dark Continent, two hundred and fifty thousand troops, were being landed. For the fifth time in history a great attack was to be made from there.

Massua first came into prominence three thousand years ago in the time of the Queen of Sheba. Nearby are the ruins of Adulis. Once this city stood on the shores of the Red Sea, at the mouth of the River Saba. Then the river carried a great amount of silt. Before the Saba dried and stopped flowing, it had formed a long delta which left Adulis seven miles from the sea.

Using this harbor, the Queen of Sheba opened up trade with Arabia and even Asia. Like Hannibal, she crossed the mountains of Ethiopia between Axum and Adulis with elephants, bringing with her a vast number of slaves, soldiers, and nobles. With a fabulous treasure of gold and precious stones, she probably embarked from this port to make her conquest of Solomon's imagination and heart.

This queen combined the fascination of Cleopatra with the commercial instincts of a modern business tycoon. Ethiopians have never been good traders; and for centuries they have left commerce to Greeks and Levantines. There is one theory that the Queen was of Phoenician and Semitic blood; in any event she conversed fluently and got on well with Solomon. The Emperor, Haile Selassie, a direct descendant of that Queen, has great powers of fascination.

Adulis and the caravan trail that led from there to "The Mountains of the Moon" where the legendary gold mines were located seems not to have appeared in history again until the days of two other African Queens, Candace and Berenice. One seduced the General of the Roman Army and persuaded him not to invade her country; the other was sufficiently wealthy to buy off the Persians. And each of these incidents saved Ethiopia from being conquered.

Ethiopia is next heard about through the activities of another strange woman, Judith, who was a very astute Jewess. Oddly, she possessed an enormous harem comprised of many nationalities – a harem full of men. Next came the semi-legendary empire in Ethiopia of Prester John. He ruled in the Middle Ages, and even sent a delegation to the Vatican in Rome, but, without ever promising allegiance and obedience to the Pope.

From Massua the yacht had gone to Assab, "The Forbidden." This is a place few people have ever heard of; it is the ancient Assoba and I believe that some day it may be an important center for petroleum. Once it was an outstanding port of embarkation for slaves going to Persia and Arabia. Caravan trails many centuries old lead from the cluster of white, Arab houses and tin-roofed Italian military barracks. One goes to the rich Aussa Sultanate, and the other crosses the Danakil desert and goes on to the highlands of African Tibet. There were found those mysterious Hebrew tablets which may someday substantiate the legend of the Jewish Falasha people – the Lost Tribe of Israel.

Almost two million people of Hebrew descent live isolated in the Ethiopian mountains of Southern God-jam. Noses, skulls, customs, and traditions are typically Jewish, and the people follow the old Mosaic Law to the letter. Their Rabbis dress, and carry out the sacred rites of the calendar, just as they did in the days of Moses and Solomon. They have had no slightest contact with the outside world for centuries. They are the only manufacturing people in Ethiopia. Though their methods are primitive, they make fine jewelry, pottery, and cloth. Coming among them is like going back, magically, three thousand years into that time in the history of Palestine when Solomon reigned.

The Falasha Jews are said to be very wealthy, but their riches are never apparent; when a stranger appears, everything of value, indicative of their accumulated wealth, is concealed. Persecuted through the ages, they have learned that displaying their riches is the surest way to attract invaders. The Ethiopians look down on these people, and the Falasha Jews in turn consider the Ethiopians as far inferior to themselves. My own belief, and it is borne out by many Ethiopian legends, is that they are descendants of a lost tribe of Israel.

During the Exodus, when Moses fled with his people from the persecution of the Egyptians, The Red Sea opened to let them pass. Scientists believe that a strong, sustained wind did open a path through the sea, but the wind changed before all of Moses' followers were able to cross. Finding themselves trapped on the Egyptian side, a large group turned south and followed the shores of the Red Sea until they came to a land of "Milk and Honey" –

Ethiopia. South of Assab there is no trace of the migration, so it is logical to deduce that they turned inland from there, and located in the far interior where they still live today.

In Assab the Italians had come aboard the yacht, so I was told, to make a search for contraband. When they found everything in order, they accepted an invitation for luncheon on board. They then explained how dreadful the life was for them in Assab. The troops had been ordered to Moussi Au in the south, and these officers cursed their luck at having to remain behind. The railway which was to follow the winding road up into the hills was their only interest, though plans were being considered for flooding the Danakil desert which would cover an area of many hundreds of square miles. A large part of this desert is a depression which is many feet below the level of the Red Sea; with the moisture and humidity which would result from flooding so many square miles, an additional large area, which has lain fallow for centuries, could be converted into a flowering garden.

The Fascists were so certain of victory that they were already calmly starting to unite Italian Somaliland with Eritrea. In 1906, and again in 1928, the Italian Government negotiated with the Ethiopians for a railroad from Assab to Addis Ababa, but the Abyssinians refused. The Italian plan offered the Ethiopians a free port at Assab, but would have compelled all trade to come through Eritrea and Fascist hands.

Oil had already been discovered, with promises of great further deposits in the Danakil and Aussa sultanates. Potentially this district appears to be as valuable as the Mosul oil field in the Persian Gulf. Assab is the logical port and location for the end of the pipe lines, storage depot, and the refineries. Later it was reported on the radio that the Italians believed the "Triona" to be the floating home of a gang of desperate oil concessionaires en route to the scene of hostilities.

With war and the danger of the Suez Canal being closed, we determined to return to the Mediterranean. In the course of the war the Italians captured, but never conquered Ethiopia. They treated the natives worse than ever the slave-owners did – even more harshly than a cruel and indifferent Abyssinian could treat his beasts of burden. They kept Ethiopia in their power for several years, only to lose it again in 1941. Haile Selassie returned to Addis Ababa on a white horse, on the anniversary of the day on which the Italian Commander entered the capital in the same manner. Ethiopia's great riches and natural wealth are bound to incite envy and desire for possession. Her primitive, uneducated peoples would be easy to exploit. The country's future may be the focal point for a religious war between the Christians and the Mohammedans, a European war, or even the World War. On that day as we steamed away from Djibuti, I re-pictured my long trek from the Blue Nile to the Red Sea, and visualized many of the things that could happen to this untouched, savage, wealthy country. Some of them have occurred, some of them may, and some of them never will, but for archeologists Ethiopia remains one of the great, unexplored, treasure lands. For people everywhere it is potentially one of the most important and promising countries on the globe.

Before I left Africa for an indefinite period, I had one further chance to explore – this time in French Somaliland. In the Spring of 1939, the Governor gave me the first and only permission to travel into the interior; until then those volcanic mountains had been unexplored. Even Abbé Bruel, one of the world's greatest archeologists, had been refused permission to visit this bleak land of dead volcanoes.

The French themselves had traveled along the coast; the vast interior they had surveyed by airplane, but aside from that, there had been no exploring. Because of the savagery of the bandits, the Governor insisted on sending a military escort with me, but that suited me very well, for native soldiers are willing to work with a pick and shovel for extra pay.

At dawn on April 1, 1939, the expedition started with Lieutenant de Lahaye, and Sergeant Le Grand, a camera-man, a surveyor, and myself. It had not been difficult to assemble the caravan of mules, men, and supplies, for I had been in Tajurrah before.

We followed the canyons which led north by northeast where the tall Somali guides had promised to lead us to the valley of the Devil Stones. The thrill of visiting a land that has never before been explored by white men is hard to explain. It is like the thrill of coasting or skiing down a perfect unmarked slope, like the feeling of satisfaction that goes with accomplishment. The Governor of French Somaliland and I had become friends shooting quail and partridge. That and the fact that he had come from Normandy near where I lived, and that we had drunk an occasional bottle of Normandy calvados together, accounted for my permit. But that did not lessen the thrill of going into new country, and I joyfully prepared to set out at once.

To the north lay sun-blasted, volcanic peaks – starved, naked, barren pillars of polished jet. They were sharp, unreal, nightmarish – dead volcanoes watching over ruined cities of long ago. To the south lay the Straits of Tears – so named because of the countless slaves who have come from the interior of Africa to be shipped like sheep across to Arabia, Persia, and the Near East.

Deep bays along the Straits made ideal hidden ports. It was from here that different, ancient civilizations had entered Africa. Here were black volcanic peaks, green waters, and shores bordered with black sand. The land was desolate. Scrub acacia and thorn bushes, on which the camels feed, were the only vegetation.

As the caravan moved along with heat eddying off the rocks, I thought of the questions that are always asked when I lecture on archeology. How do you find dead cities? When you find one do you dig a hole in the ground or what?

There are two kinds of archeological research: exploring and looking for sites, and the dry-as-dust, pick-and-shovel method where you settle down for months, or perhaps years, and excavate in one place. Exploring is more thrilling, for you are finding new places every week or two.

By following a line midway between two lost cities or two lost civilizations, you are likely to find an interesting place. It has been my good luck to make several such discoveries which other archeologists have said were unusual. That was the way I had found the Tomb of Queen Hanan with its traces of a new and different primitive civilization. That was the way I had found the Lost City of Garama – a rare Paleolithic town belonging to the Stone Age of perhaps 25000 BC

Here in French Somaliland I was looking for facts about the Queen of Sheba's lost empire in the land between Arabia and

Ethiopia. That empire was at its greatest in 950 BC. Then, because of changes in weather, rain, or earthquakes that smashed irrigation dams, this part of the empire had become a dead world. By the sixth century AD its civilization had been obliterated.

We had been en route less than a day when we came to rock drawings on the sides of the cliffs; some of them were ancient, others were modern. Here was proof that man had occupied this land which now was stark, bleak wastes between depressing, precipitous walls. When we reached a plateau, we could look back and see the Straits and beyond, across the ocean dotted with sail boats so far away that they looked like swallows on the wing.

To the north lay the volcanic peaks. On the plateau were quaternary Paleoliths – stones of the most primitive times. Here, too, were the remains of artifacts – the first weapons and tools made by human hands.

To make them one flint was heated in the coals; then it was chipped by means of striking it with a cold flint of harder grain; thus, slowly, a blade was formed, similar in shape to our hatchets of today. But those original ones were massive – made to be swung by both hands – to crash through the thick skulls of prehistoric beasts. In imagination one can see them in effective action.

Apparently this plateau had served as a factory for artifacts, for the ground was deeply covered with flint chips. Nodules of flints had probably been dug from dried-up river beds and brought up here to be chipped and fashioned into weapons and tools.

Here in this gateway to Asia were relics of the Stone Age of many thousands of years before. One of the men blew his whistle to attract attention. He had come upon artifacts of a very superior type; they showed indications of a later civilization and Paleolithic culture. Here were links with the best type of North and South Africans, South Arabian, Egyptian, and Palestinian cultures.

They seemed to indicate that there had been a bridge of land here at some early time linking Asia with Africa. They went far to prove that man in the very earliest times had had direct contact with peoples from the Atlantic, across the Sahara, to the shores of the Persian Gulf.

With the temperature at 110 in the shade, we traveled on through deep canyons until we came to a valley which showed the remains of an irrigation system. Groups of mounds and accumulated rubble made a line across the abandoned valley. A series of dunes that most people would not notice will catch the eye of the trained archeologist. These obstructions have led to many real "finds." We made camp on the plateau above, a site of about four acres which was rich in pre-Islamic pottery shards and flaked flints. From here the irrigation project was clear; and when we surveyed the valley later, we found that the ditches ran due north and south across the Oelian-silted, barren flats.

All over the world these once-fertile spots have become barren. Cutting of the forests is one cause, and changes in the rainfall is another. The United States has its own dust bowl of recent years; in parts of Texas there are other older wastes that were once fertile. These changes are responsible for some of the dead civilizations in the Sahara and in Libya.

La Kahina, the great Berber Queen – Africa's Joan of Arc – burned vast forests and despoiled her lands in ancient times. Today Russia is repeating history with her "scorched earth" policy. By burning her forests, La Kahina succeeded in keeping the Arabs from overrunning her country. But she created a waste of land with nothing for man or beast to eat. It kept the Arabs out for twenty years.

This once fertile valley, in which we were, shows stone boundary lines such as one sees in the Connecticut countryside; and there were just as many stones. On the plateau where we were camped, we discovered the vague outline of houses and buildings, so we began to dig an exploratory trench.

Everywhere there were microlithic obsidian flakes, geometric in form. There were triangles, rectangles, trapezoids, and crescents with beautifully worked toothed edges which placed them as to date between 4000 and 3000 BC. These were used for arrow tips and spear points. We found others of a chalcedony which was like a very hard carnelian; also there were others of chert and flint. Some of them were similar to those of Mesopotamia and predynastic Egypt.

In archeological research it is necessary to locate and excavate the burial sites and tombs, for "dead men do tell tales." Earthquakes, sandstorms, tidal waves, cloud bursts, and warfare destroy everything above ground. Only in the deeply buried tombs can one find the true historical details intact; and only the dead can tell you many truths.

Between the sites of two ruined cities, from the bottom of the deep canyon we looked up to see four well-cut apertures in the perpendicular face of the rock. It was about seven hundred feet to the top of the cliff; and these square cut holes were more than three-quarters of the way up.

When we started up the arret, it soon became clear that the only way to reach those holes in the face of the rock would be to descend on ropes from the top. The towns had been leveled through the years; the terrific heat of day and the icy air of night had caused even layers of the volcanic rock to slough off. That was the reason we could see those four square-cut holes; from a distance they looked like the gaping, socket eyes of skulls.

With alpine axes and ropes we succeeded in climbing, but with some difficulty; the stone was so old and so weathered that it would crumble when you tried to get a firm hand or foothold. The loosened stone and dust would start a small landslide that hit and bruised the men just behind. Gathering momentum and accumulating rocks and dust as it fell, it would hit the bottom of the canyon with a roar.

There could be little question that the apertures led to tombs; and we were all excited, for tombs as old as these appeared to be sometimes contain treasure. Halfway up the arret we found the debris of other tombs which had sheared off and fallen. In the debris we found carnelian beads, crudely painted pottery, and corroded bronze; and they were different from any I had found or seen, either in exploring or in museums. Here seemed to be traces of a new civilization of ancient times.

When we reached the top, we had to stop and rest. The heat was stifling, but on the top of the cliff there was at least a little air moving in from the Indian Ocean. Our field glasses showed nothing but the brittle, bleak, naked peaks on the land side. They were ugly black and brown with tawny purple shadows in the crevasses. There was nothing green in sight, no trees, no grass, no flowers.

While we ate dry biscuits with sardines and drank luke-warm distilled water, Lieutenant de Lahaye talked of iced champagne and the gourmet foods of London, Paris, and New York. Always on every expedition there is one person who harps on rare wines and viands till it irks each member of the party. To escape his visions, we got up and moved around the little plateau.

We saw weathered remnants of stairs cut into the black, basaltic rock; they led to an elevation on the edge of the precipice. There stood a crude altar; in the center of the stone there was a hollow from which a groove led to the side of the sheer rock. Here pagan priests had made sacrifices to their gods after burials in the necropolis below.

We photographed the altar and the site. I believe that the civilization of this place belonged to the Sabean, Himyarite Empires which had existed in Arabia and Ethiopia. Possibly this valley had been used as an emporia in trading with the interior of Africa. It was a natural gateway for the Phoenicians and Arabians who traded with the people around King Solomon's Mines, the Mountains of the Moon, and the far off ruins of Rhodesian Zimbabwe – the greatest ruins of all Africa.

We found a boulder to which we could safely tie our rope – which was over one-hundred feet long – and then let it down over the cliff. It reached the apertures. I started down, hand over hand. With a camera, flashlight, and alpine axe tied to my belt I swung out over the seven-hundred-foot drop. In such a trip with feet and knees around the rope one kicks out and swings away from the cliff and slides; knuckles are bruised and skinned, so are knees and elbows, swinging back against the rock. It is a technique known to Alpine climbers and to archeologists.

I kept swinging out and sliding down the rope till I came to the openings into the tombs. I looked in. There lay the ancient dead and the objects which had been placed beside them centuries before. Lieutenant de Lahaye followed me down the rope; and when he entered the tomb, he took off his sun helmet out of respect for the dead.

We could see sand-covered skeletons and amphorae. First we carved the date and our names on the walls of the tomb – archeologists always do this when they find an important site. It was an easy date to remember, May 5th, 1939 for Napoleon had died on that day in the year 1821.

We found that the light was fading and that it had gotten too dark to take any photographs that day; so there was nothing we could do but make the ascent up the rope, hand over hand, to the plateau. There the men had dug an exploratory trench, thirty feet long and six feet deep, which exposed the foundations of a pre-Islamic, pagan temple. The tombs in their state of preservation and this pagan temple were unusual finds; discovering both of them on one day called for a celebration.

After dinner at camp we sang the ribald songs of the Foreign Legion. The natives staged a weird concert and performed their tribal dances. In the light of the bonfire their semi-savage prancing, and the shadows of their gyrating bodies against the rocks, was like the centuries-old pictures we had found on the walls of the canyon. Probably no one had danced here since the days of the Sabean priests of twenty centuries before.

The nights were cold, but the days were so hot that our distilled water took on an odd taste; the only way we could make it drinkable was to add vinegar. We had had to transport a large part of our water supply in *guerbas* – animal skins coated on the inside with tar. In the valley, below the cliff where we had made our "finds," we discovered two low spots which would furnish water for our live stock, once we had cleared them out. We decided to move our camp there.

Rubble kept falling down from the cliff, and one landslide the photographer started in getting an unusual picture almost wiped out our camp. But in spite of the intense heat we kept on working, photographing, mapping the positions of the towns, tombs, and irrigation ditches, and making scale drawings of the tombs with their strange collection of objects.

In the tombs we had to remove the sand and dust with trowels and brushes, then sift it for beads and jewels. On the benches which had been carved in the rock lay the mummies. We sprayed the decorated wooden coffins, the bodies, and the objects to keep the outside air from disintegrating them. The mummies had a strange yellow color, different from any others I had ever found, and there was a strong aromatic odor in the tombs. The objects included amulets, beads, and seals depicting animal gods. The skulls were uniformly long and similar to those of the Phoenicians in that anthropological, Biblical period of the Old Testament. The first four tombs, whose apertures we had seen from the ground, were roughly twenty by twenty-four feet. Behind these we broke through walls to find round tombs hollowed from the rock. In all the tombs we found well-defined marks of chisels; and all entrances were sealed with closely fitted slabs of rock. This careful workmanship must have taken long periods of time and considerable expense. In Egypt many of the tombs had been emptied and re-sold through the years, but that was not true here.

Sifting the sand for small beads and jewels with the temperature at 110 degrees was only one of the trying things we had to do. Archeology always demands careful, exact work, frequently under trying conditions.

Large objects such as amphorae, spears, daggers and shields are easy to handle; so were the bronze stoves and amulets. But each object has to be treated, sterilized, catalogued, and placed in cotton-wool-lined boxes for shipping after it has been photographed and labeled.

In the sand we found small beads of purest gold, some of them no larger than a pinhead. Since they were hollow, they belonged to the classification known as King Solomon's Beads. Here was a further link with his justly famous gold mines. The amulets showed so great a variety of symbols that it was clear that these people had traded with Phoenicia and Persia as well as Egypt. We studied them with intense interest.

Day after day we slid down the ropes to the tomb openings and climbed back again at night. While we were doing this, other men were digging on the plateau. Two alabaster slabs which were unearthed near the ruins of the pagan temple had a ram and a gazelle carved on them, with Himyaritic inscriptions below. These were so rare and the writing so ancient that there were only two men in the world who could translate them – the Abbé J. B. Chabet of the French Academy in Paris and Professor D. S. Margoliouth of the British Academy in London.

Spengler in his *Decline of the West* regrets the lack of research that has been done on the civilizations of Southern Arabia and Ethiopia. There he believed lay the clues to the origin of earliest religions and their vast and potent influence on the affairs of the whole world, both past and present. Certainly it offers an almost untouched and very rich field for research.

The cold nights were made hideous with the howls of the jackals. We had to kill a sheep or a goat for food nearly every day; and the smell of blood seemed to attract howling animals for miles around.

One morning the photographer who had slid down the rope to the tombs asked to be first to enter a new tomb. When we broke through the wall there was a rush of acrid, pungent, fetid air. When that had cleared, he stepped through. I heard a crunch and a yell; he came out choking. But it proved to be nothing very serious; he had stepped on a skull and crushed it. We had to wait for the dust to settle before we could enter again.

Strange names were attached to these people. These cave-dwelling troglodytes had significant indicative names: translated they meant eaters of meat, of tortoise, of elephant, of ostrich, and of serpents.

In the round tombs we found seals of agate, carnelian, and lapis lazuli engraved with symbols which indicated that these were the mummies of priests. A bronze vase contained a collection of these seals. Around the neck of one mummy was a collar engraved with the figures of the ibex, the lion, and the falcon. Some of the pictures on the walls showed the priests in attitudes of worship.

One skeleton had an amethyst ring on the finger. It was formed in the shape of two twining serpents and was made of pure gold. All of the fabrics in these tombs had disintegrated into dust, so that the mummies and skeletons lay exposed. The leather, too, had disappeared, but there were quantities of bronze tacks. I was still puzzled by the strange yellow color of the mummies. A crystal bowl in one of the priests' tombs contained a collection of ivory buttons which were inscribed with the Lion of Judah. The bronze statues were such as to indicate Phallic worship; and the Baetyls or sacred stones confirmed it.

In all our days in this wilderness we had seen no signs of human beings who were still alive. One night we were awakened by a rock slide whose echoes made it sound alarming. Until then we had seen no reason to guard the tombs at night. The next morning we found footprints in the sand; and several of the more valuable seals were missing.

Unable to find any entrance from the tombs to the top of the plateau, we still had to climb up and down the rope, hand over hand. Then in the ceiling of one of the tombs deep in the rock we found a hole. It led upward and there were stone steps carved in it. When we climbed up, we found that there was a large slab of stone over the top. By measuring we were able to locate the spot and entrance on the top of the plateau; there was a large boulder over the slab, and the stone cover was so carefully fitted and so heavy that it took several men with levers to move it.

In the tombs we found mummies and relics of a civilization so old they had been all but forgotten by the historians. These tombs had gone untouched for at least three thousand years. The trinkets and relics showed signs of long, personal wear.

Sometimes one feels a vague, almost mystic reproof when one handles objects that have been buried for so long. You get a feeling of depression, a shiver will run down your spine, an oppressed feeling will permeate every member of the expedition.

It was one of those days on which our first mail came through by runner. This was our first news from the outside world, for we had no radio with us. The news from Europe was ominous, and Czechoslovakia had been taken. The two French officers with us thought that Hitler was only bluffing.

Mail and newspapers always cheer up an expedition in the wilderness. Then, too, we found that the walls and paved walks the men had uncovered on the top of the plateau covered an edifice of an even earlier date. The inscriptions led me to believe that this had been one center of the Cult of the Astral Triad – The Moon God, Sin; The Solar Goddess, Shems; and the mighty Isthar or Venus. Steps led to vestibules and passageways, and there was an "offering table" which bore a lunar design.

There was one oblong ruin showing a wide variety of styles and epochs which would have justified a long and detailed excavation. It was roughly forty by sixty feet; and the mortar that had been used in the masonry was so unusual that we collected a number of samples for analysis.

A laboratory and embalming room for the priests had just been uncovered when a runner arrived with orders from the Governor. We were to return at once. We had no choice. We had found bodies buried in the sand which contained different salts – these may have accounted for the strange yellow color of the mummies. This was the first time in my experience that I had discovered such a laboratory. There were amphorae which had contained chemicals of various kinds, and different spices and herbs. But we had no choice but to obey orders.

We closed up the tombs, collected as many specimens as we could carry, and trekked back to Djibuti. When we arrived, we learned that Europe was at war and that a state of emergency had been declared in French Somaliland.

Some day I hope to be able to return and complete the research in those ruins which promised so much in the way of ancient history, but that must be, if ever, when the War of the World has been won.

End

THE LIFE AND DEATH OF BYRON KHUN DE PROROK

by Michael Tarabulski

They say all lovers swear more performance than they are able, and yet reserve an ability that they never perform: vowing more than the perfection of ten; and discharging less than the tenth part of one. They that have the voice of lions, and the act of hares: are they not monsters?

Shakespeare,
Troylus and Cressida, III: ii

Dear beloved Byron has gone," said James B. Pond, editor of *Program Magazine*, writing in the November-December issue about the death of Byron Khun de Prorok. "In late November he was found in a dying condition on a railway train in France. He was taken to a hospital in Paris where he passed away on November 21st"

He should have had a State funeral. He was picked up alone, in trouble, almost unknown. Obituaries, funeral orations, are things of little moment. Byron needed them not. Forever in the memories of those who knew him will be something that will endure as long as mortals endure. He was loved. Can one say more?

One can. I have been looking into the facts and the fictions of Byron's life for over two decades and I've learned that for every reaction to him there is an equal but opposite reaction. "Of the dead," goes Roman wisdom, "speak no ill." Were I to do that, I'd only tell you half of this tale. To those whom the whole of it brings pain—and there will be at least two such—I offer my apologies. Those who saw only his public face, as a travel lecturer or the author of books and articles on his adventures, often admired him. Those who knew him only professionally, for his archaeological work, often reviled him. Those who knew him well often shared the sentiments of both camps.

If ever you have loved someone but could not bear to be around that person because his or her irresponsible, unreliable, and undependable behavior threatened your mental health and physical safety, then you can stop reading right now. If you've had that experience, then you have known Byron and reading what follows will be redundant if not painful. On the other hand, if you have not had that experience, or if you have had it and you believe that every unhappy story is unhappy in its own way, read on.

We begin at the end of *this* unhappy story on a train, not under one, with de Prorok dead in Paris in November, 1954, at age 58. The Foreign Service "Report on the Death of an American Citizen" gives the cause of death as "intoxication following absorption of an overdose of Nembutal." He was just concluding a travel lecture tour.

Here's more from his *Program Magazine* obituary:

> *One might use the word flamboyant in connection with him. Byron de Prorok was one of the rare personages of our times: handsome, highly intelligent, possessed of great platform ability. Everyone who knew him loved him. [Original emphasis.]*

> *On the lecture platform he was a supreme favourite. Year after year he went back to the same places. Each year he turned up some new subject. At his beginning, he lectured with old 35mm black and white movies. At the end he was using 16mm color movies. Throughout his career he never learned the slightest thing about motion pictures. He never knew whether they were good or bad (they were often atrocious), upside down, or hind side to. It made no difference.*

Audiences loved the man who, regardless of the film, poured out fascinating information that made other ages come to life, that instilled vitality into the places and people who passed on his screen. People forgot the pictures, in the man. His knowledge of almost everything was near to superhuman.

Comments from the fictional funeral of another desert adventurer, also dead through carelessness, come to mind. "Yes, it was my privilege to know him...and to make him known to the world," says the Lowell Thomas character, Jackson Bentley (Arthur Kennedy), in bombastic reply to a reporter's question at the State funeral of the eponymous hero of Lawrence of Arabia, "He was a poet, a scholar, and a mighty warrior." But, when the reporter moves away, Bentley speaks to a companion in cynical sotto voce: "He was also the most shameless exhibitionist since Barnum and Bailey."

I first heard about Byron in April of 1982. I was in my final semester at Beloit College and had traveled to northern Wisconsin to meet with Alonzo Pond (no relation to James B.), then 89 years-old. Beloit's Logan Museum of Anthropology had a collection of ethnological materials, and accompanying documentation in the form of reports, photographs, and film, relating to a 1925 expedition into the Sahara. Alonzo Pond and another Beloit alumnus, Bradley Tyrrell, had been on that expedition, in Byron's company, and had assembled the collection. These materials interested me and I jumped at the chance to meet with Pond.

So it was that I found myself with him, asking about the other members of the expedition. Along with Tyrrell and de Prorok were Maurice Reygasse, an Algerian government functionary and amateur archaeologist; Hal Denny, from the New York Times; Louis Chapuis, a guide; Caid Belaid, an interpreter; Henri Barth, a cameraman; and three drivers. De Prorok had definitely made an impression: "He was the most charming man I ever met," Pond told me, "but I don't think he himself knew what part of what he said was true and what part false."

De Prorok was given to making up answers on the spot, Pond said, in matters simple and complex. Serious omissions in camping supplies had already alerted Pond that de Prorok was weak on details, so before leaving Constantine for Batna, Pond asked him if the three cars had been properly fueled. De Prorok replied that they had been. Late in the day, two cars ran out of gas. During and after the six week trip, when issuing progress reports, Byron greatly exaggerated the hardships endured and the discoveries made by the expedition. Moreover, he left Algeria with archaeological materials he was not supposed to take. When I laughed at Pond's stories, out of sheer astonishment at de Prorok's chutzpah, he upbraided me. "It's not funny," he said, "we could've died! As it was, he got us into a lot of trouble. But he could say *anything* and, if you didn't know better, you'd believe him. Good God, even if you *did* know better you'd half believe him until you thought about it for a while. That was the wonder of the man."L. Sprague de Camp, in *Lost Continents: The Atlantean Theme in History, Science, and Literature* (1954), summarizes Byron's career. "De Prorok started out as a competent archaeologist who did sound work on the site of Carthage. Later he seems to have gone in for a type of exploration that, if it produced less substantial scientific returns, provided him with adventure and furnished lively copy for his books."

Others characterize him less generously. Anthropologist L. Cabot Briggs said this of de Prorok in a 1973 letter to Andrew Whiteford at the Logan Museum:

> *He was a distinctly dubious character, and pulled the wool over the eyes of Reygasse very effectively (and of quite a lot of other people too....). When I was a boy, I was taken to a lecture he gave at the Fogg Art Museum at Harvard (on the subject of his excavations at Carthage). I remember that he used as a pointer a very long ebony cane with an elaborate silver knob, the kind the dandies at the court of Louis XIV used to strut around with.*
>
> *He was that kind of guy.*

Or take this *Boston Transcript*, January 4, 1936, review of *In Quest of Lost Worlds*:

The author speaks with kindly condescension of the well founded camps of the more pedestrian scientists who spend years in excavating a single site and in making painstaking reports. The reader gets the general impression that anybody can do that. This blasé attitude is doubly unfortunate because so much of his material, especially that dealing with Ethiopia and Central America, is of such fascinating interest that the reader would be held spellbound if he weren't continually irritated by Prorok's literary gaucheries.

But the *New York Times* review of January 19, 1936, praises the same book:

Vividly told, this record of strange adventure and stranger discoveries is positively breath-taking, and the reader who has followed with tense absorption every word of the extraordinary narrative closes it feeling that the thing more amazing than any other is the fact that the count survived to write of his experiences.

Bradley Tyrrell, fresh from the Sahara expedition, equivocates in a diary entry written in Paris on December 8, 1925:

Prorok is a charming fellow - but flighty - he is an adventurer with a rich smattering of history & language - a title - a love of decorations and I think a sincere desire to add something to science, but without the guts to dig through the details necessary. He has brilliant ideas - enormous conceptions - at times- but is apt to go on to something 'new' before the old is even well started. Science is classified knowledge - but he will always need people willing to do his 'classifying.' He needs a balance wheel - more than that perhaps - a boss - a manager who can keep his feet on the ground. With that there is no end to the delightful dips he may take into the fringes of history and science - and the world will give him a hearing!

Back in Beloit, Logan Museum Director George Collie was less sanguine. De Prorok had been presenting himself as working for the museum. This from a letter of December 10, 1925:

Personally I have no use for de Prorok and I know that a good many of the American archeologists feel the same way. He is an advertiser and exploits the things he finds and tries to make money off of them apparently. He is in no way connected with the college and must not be so regarded....

The National Geographic Society had the same problem with de Prorok much later, in 1948. He appeared in Morocco and claimed to be making a film for them. L. Cabot Briggs, cited above, reported this news to the NGS and the society notified Moroccan authorities that de Prorok was not in their employ. However, an Internal Memo from Gilbert Grosvenor to J.O.L., dated 14 July 1925, shows that the Society did give him a chance:

Regarding Prorok: I agree with you that he is an unusually clever "personal press agent," social and otherwise, etc. But he is also a good organizer and has stirred up so much interest in Carthage and North African ruins that he has gathered into his project [the] ablest archaeologists of the United States and France.

But Byron would promise more than he could carry out, or go back on his promises. Grosvenor continues:

The last time he came to Washington the date was made six months in advance, with the understanding that it would be his only lecture, but, to my surprise, Mitchell Carroll arranged for Prorok to address the Archaeological Society the day before the National Geographic Society. Prorok should have known better. When I called him to task for doing this, he stated that he did not accept Carroll's invitation until he was assured by Carroll that the National Geographic Society had no objection.

Sorting out the Sahara expedition mess, Sheldon Whitehouse, Chargée d'Affaires at the American Embassy in Paris, in a June 4,

1926, letter back to the Department of State, wrote: "Prorok is a scatter-brained jackass and ought to have a nurse...."

[He] left a trail of unpaid bill behind him in Algeria, but these have now been settled and the Governor General of Algeria has withdrawn any complaint against him. He has, however, tangled matters up frightfully by enlisting the aid of Madame Rouvier, the widow of the former Premier, in obtaining the permit he now desires for the galley at Carthage. Madame Rouvier, who is not in the slightest degree interested in archaeology, naturally wanted a quid pro quo and asked Prorok to sell some antique furniture for her in America, which he said he would do. Madame Rouvier then got very busy, made various trips to the Foreign Office and apparently has got the permit, or the assurance of a permit, in her pocket. As Prorok did nothing about her furniture and apparently considered it a matter of no importance, she is very angry....

Yet, in a page two item of February 17, 1926, the *New York Times* said:

Count Byron Khun de Prorok, explorer of the buried cities of Northern Africa, lectured at Carnegie Hall last night on his recent discoveries on the sites of ancient civilizations. Introduced by George Palmer Putnam as "a man who has taken archaeology out of the hands of the graybeards," the count looked hardly older than a boy as he stood on the Carnegie Hall stage and told the dramatic story of his adventures.

More vivid even than his own descriptions was the showing of six thousand feet of motion picture film, illustrating the progress of the expedition on the plains where Hannibal fought Scipio, over the once flourishing submarine city of Djerba, and then inland to the sand wastes of the Sahara and Atlas Mountains....

Count de Prorok complained of a real estate boom which was developing on the site of modern Carthage, and which, he said, was making archaeological research there more and more expensive. Real Estate speculators, he said, were buying land under which priceless treasures lie buried and then extorted high prices when the archaeologists began their excavations....

That apparent concern for the archaeological enterprise, however, didn't translate abroad. Here's an excerpt from an exchange of U.S. Department of State correspondence dated January 26, 1927. Archaeologist Alfred Kidder, then with the National Research Council, had written to Assistant Secretary of State Robert Olds to ask for help in getting his older brother, Homer, permission to do some archaeological work in Algeria. Olds' office wrote this to a Mr. LeClercq in the Division of Western European Affairs:

I have written [Alfred] Kidder that we will notify the French Government that his brother, Homer Kidder, is all right. I think this should be done as a matter of routine through the Embassy. We do not, of course have to ask for any special facilities, but with Prorok, and people of his sort, making trouble in North Africa, I am afraid that without a word from the Embassy the French Government will not be friendly toward anything Homer Kidder may want to do.... [Emphasis added.]

Scatter-brained jackass" in need of a nurse seems a bit harsh but it is clear enough that Byron, shall we say, "had issues." It is true that in correspondence, official and personal, in newspaper accounts, and in his own writings, one sees that behind many of the negative things said about him there might be a more favorable explanation. His financial problems in Tunisia and Algeria might have been due to corrupt officials asking for bribes. The accusation that he stole things from Algeria might have been groundless. Madame Rouvier might have been exploiting him for her own ends. What some considered his scientific failings might more charitably be seen as a desire to make science appealing to a wide audience. And so on. However, taken all in all, and reflecting as they do a constant theme of deceit, the words of his detractors build a case against him. When we add to those the comments of supporters who praise him with faint damns, we may be comfortable in the assumption that the man was not completely misunderstood.

Complete understanding of him is a different matter. How are we to even partially understand the mind and motives of anyone, much less a man now half a century dead? Some clues are offered in what little autobiography he provides in his four books; but which details, in which of his four books, are true and which are false I cannot say.

Nor can I for certain even if he wrote the books himself or had editorial help that amounted almost to ghostwriting, or at least to clandestine co-authorship as in the more recent case of the late Jerzy Kosinski. (An apt analogy, for Kosinski had many versions of his own life story. So, for that matter, did T.E. Lawrence.) Regarding the 1925 "Tin-Hinan" expedition, for example, the writings of Alonzo Pond and Bradley Tyrrell tell a tale different from Byron's, and his own accounts differ from his first rendition of it in *Digging for Lost African Gods* (1926), through *Mysterious Sahara* (1929), to *In Quest of Lost Worlds* (1935). Readers should be on guard: Byron is a delightful but overly-imaginative guide.

Other clues to Byron's life are in the biographical details given in newspapers. Still others exist only as oral testimony (in this case family history) passed along from those who knew him to those who didn't. These varied clues are all we have to work with. Upon them I build the following biography. The conclusion I leap to is my own.

According to a statement in the New York Times of December 28, 1925, Byron was born in Mexico City on 6 October 1896. At birth he was named Francis Byron Khun (or Kuhn). His father was Leonard Khun (or Kuhn), a naturalized American citizen and owner of a large vinegar distillery. His mother was Therese de Prorok. Both were from well-to-do Austro-Hungarian families.

From his daughters I learned that Byron was the oldest of four children, with two brothers and a sister. When he was a boy, Byron's parent separated or divorced. His siblings stayed with their father. Byron lived with his mother and her brother and their mother, an Englishwoman. They lived in France, with one home near Paris and another at the Château de Tancarville, in Normandy, near Le Havre. His uncle, Theophile Konerski de Prorok, adopted him. At about the age of ten, Byron was packed off to boarding school in England. He attended several schools. His most revealing autobiographical sketch, in *Dead Men Do Tell Tales* (1942), deals with this period of his life. The archaeology and exploration bugs bit him early, and one bright spot in these otherwise miserable years, was a meeting with Ernest Shackleton who came to his school to lecture. Because Byron had done some digging at Roman ruins near the school, he says in all of his four books, he got to meet with Shackleton. He boldly promised money enough for a sled for Shackleton's next attempt to reach the South Pole, and managed to raise it.

In secondary school Byron moved from England to Switzerland, attending first a preparatory school and then the University of Geneva, where he studied archaeology. This led to work in Italy and then in Tunisia. He admits to having little interest in his education until prep school and college but he was an able polyglot. At least bilingual, in French and English, he had some German, Italian, and Spanish in addition to his boarding school Latin and Greek. (His ability to tell the truth in any of these languages is another matter.) Among his hobbies and talents was watercoloring. He illustrated the jacket covers of his first two books and the title cards for his travel lecture films. Around 1908 summer, his painting hobby, and his family wealth, brought him into contact with Robert Lansing, Woodrow Wilson's Secretary of State (1915-1920), on the French Riviera.

Although a U.S. Citizen from birth, Byron may only have visited the U.S. briefly, if at all, before arriving in New York in 1919. In April of 1920, a small display of his watercolors was mounted in the foyer of Washington's Corcoran Gallery under the name F. Byron-Khun. He soon dropped the "Francis" and added "de Prorok." (Late in life he dropped the Khun altogether.) He prefixed the whole with "Count," a title—also dropped later—from Polish nobility, he said, inherited from his adoptive father.

Now began a yearly cycle of excavation in Carthage through the summer and lectures in Europe and North America through the winter. Returning to America for the 1923-24 season, Byron met Alice Kenny, eldest daughter of William F. Kenny, a wealthy New York City contractor. They married in February of 1923, in St. Patrick's Cathedral, with Governors Al Smith, of New York, and Channing Cox, of Massachusetts (friends of the bride's father) in attendance. New York's Archbishop Hayes conducted the ceremony. The Pope sent blessings. Byron had a rich, well-educated, and musically-talented wife. Alice had a titled husband. They made their home in Paris. In short order, they had two daughters, Marie-Thérèse, born in 1924, and Aliska, born in 1925.

Byron continued his archaeological excavations in Carthage, mostly in connection with Francis Kelsey of the University of Michigan. W.F. Kenny provided some of the funding for this work through 1923 and 1924. By the spring of 1925, though, de Prorok and Kelsey had run afoul of the Tunisian Ministry of Antiquities and further work at Carthage was curtailed. In the disagreement with the Tunisian government, Kenny defended the integrity of his new son-in-law, calling on political contacts in Washington in an effort to secure permission to get Byron back to Carthage later in 1925.

These efforts came to naught and Byron decided to try some exploration in Algeria. This brought him into contact with Alonzo Pond and the Logan Museum and led to troubles already cited. Kenny defended his son-in-law again, in the debacle that arose from the Saharan trip. His letters to Washington, still in Department of State records at the National Archives, show whole-hearted support of Byron. Nonetheless, W.F. Kenny was an intelligent man and apparently saw a disturbing pattern in Byron's behavior.

As Kenny family lore has it, W.F. hired a detective agency to check into Byron's background. The agency, so goes the story, found something unpleasant. Perhaps it was infidelity. Perhaps Byron was not the rightful heir to the Polish title and had just made that up. Perhaps it was that Byron's father, Leonard Khun/Kuhn, was "Jewish" (though just as secular as Byron's "Christian" mother). Or perhaps it was that Khun was not his father at all. Again according to family lore, Byron's biological father was not Khun but a man named Oscar Straus.

And who was this Oscar Straus? There were two men of note with that name around 1895, and surviving Kenny family members thought it was the diplomat who was later Theodore Roosevelt's second term Secretary of Commerce. That Oscar Straus lived from 1854 to 1926. Looking into his life I found him an unlikely paternal candidate. Most importantly, I could find no way to connect his social crowd with that of Therese de Prorok. Less meaningful, given the way these things work, he was much older than she and, by the evidence, happily married.

The second Oscar Straus, the Viennese composer who lived from 1870 to 1954, and was just on the cusp of fame in 1895, is a good bet. First, Oscar and Therese moved in the same social circle. And a famously promiscuous circle it was: Think Arthur Schnitzler's bed hopping play, *Riegen* (1896), made into the film *La Ronde* (1950), with music by...Oscar Straus. Second, the Kenny family story has it that Therese left Europe, for Mexico, already pregnant, and married there. Third, Oscar Straus had just married, in 1895, to his first wife, Helene Neumann, also already pregnant. Finally, photographs of Straus and de Prorok show a startling resemblance: Both have the same tall, lanky build, high forehead, dark, curly hair, and prominent nose.

This is far from conclusive proof, I realize, and there are no rumors of Straus having fathered an illegitimate child. But it is unclear whether or not Therese ever made any claim on Straus. All we do know is that Leonard Khun, for some reason, separated from his wife and that she took this one child, of four, back to Europe. There, her brother adopted him. Among the Tuareg of the Sahara it is the rule that the mother's brother play social father to his sister's children. In our culture it is exceptional.

Returning to the realm of fact, we find that, in the fall of 1926, Alice de Prorok took the two little girls and returned to her parents' home in New York. She never went back to Byron. They were divorced the following July. Byron wrote her during the separation period. These letters make it clear that Byron's heavy drinking contributed to the break-up but also hint at something deeper. Writing on December 5, 1926, he says:

Am leaving this evening , & am thinking of last year when I left with Brad [Tyrrell] full of hope & and ambition, and the joy of adventure—and this year, alone, broken, ill & feeling like an old man. Mother last night said that she would swear or sign a document to the effect that I never knew those certain things that it was said this summer I did know. But what is past is past & I hope that those that would not believe me are content. They would be if they saw me now. [Original emphasis.]

Taking this to mean that the detectives uncovered the secret of Byron's birth and made it known to Kenny, and that word of it then came to Byron, one can imagine the shock. He might have suspected something because of his separation from his father and siblings and his adoption by his maternal uncle, but by evidence of this letter—if we are to believe it—he did not know he was illegitimate until he was 29 years-old.

After their daughter's divorce, William Kenny and his wife, Mary, adopted her two daughters and changed their surnames to Kenny and their given names to Maureen and Denise. Later, when Alice remarried, her new husband adopted the girls. Though Byron and Alice met at least once, years later, he and his two daughters never had direct contact again. He dedicated his *In Quest of Lost Worlds* to them—as Maureen and Denise de Prorok. Alice always spoke well of Byron, and of her time with him. The girls, growing up, had some limited contact with Byron's brothers and sister and others who knew him.

Byron remarried shortly after the divorce. The "companion on my recent expedition," of the introduction to *Mysterious Sahara*, is this second wife. They had a son together. He died at about age ten. This marriage broke up and Byron married again, around 1940, to a woman named Muriel Ivy. She survived him and died in Lausanne, Switzerland, in 1990, a fact I only learned of in 2002.

The question of Byron's parentage is important here, even as it was important for his close contemporary in so many things, T. E. Lawrence. In response to his troubles and his critics, he might have turned totally legitimate—such was within his grasp—but the revelation of "those certain things" and the loss of his wife and children in 1926 may have destroyed any pretensions he had of being "legitimate" in any sense. Or maybe he was just a big jerk. I don't know. What is clear is that after 1926 his work never had even the marginal credibility of the Tunisian and Algerian projects. (Some sources, none official, say he was a Colonel in a special desert unit of the U.S. Army in World War II.) By his post-1926 work he lost what respect he'd had in the archaeological community, but his wild stories sold in bookstores and on the lecture circuit. What happened to Byron Khun de Prorok? I think it was a mixture of personal loss and popular approval.

The issue of living within the stereotype of the archaeologist, and attracting fame and (relative) fortune, or taking arms against it and being considered irrelevant, is not so very different in our day than it was in Byron's. Modern archaeological museums and magazines rely upon ancient glitz and glamour to attract funding and subscribers. To paraphrase what has been said of university presidents: Many a museum director has entered that post a scholar and left it a showman; some do not suffer the original burden. The romance of archaeology catches the student's eye and mind and is mother to the amateur and the professional alike; only the wisest know who their father is. Perhaps, feeling no real identity of his own, Byron became what the public saw him as: a drawing room explorer and matinee idol archaeologist. Society made him, as much as it makes any of us. If not really a count, he was surely an heir of Baron Munchausen and, as Irving Howe said of T.E. Lawrence, a prince of our disorder. He was loved. He still is. Can one say more?

Acknowledgements and Sources

Contemplating the life of Byron makes a person appreciate family. I thank my wife, Sheila O'Brien, and our daughter, Lillian, for their patience when I was lost in the lives of another man and wife and their girls.

I would not have written this brief summary of de Prorok's life if it had not been for William Urschel and The Narrative Press so thoughtfully resurrecting Byron's books. I could not have written it without the help of the following people and institutions:

First and foremost, his daughters, Maureen and Denise, shared with me the information, and documents, that their mother, Alice, had passed along to them. Their cousin, Peter, supplied his memories, admittedly hazy, of old family stories. I hope I have done justice to all and betrayed no trusts.

John Tyrrell helped me to transcribe his father's 1925 trip diary. Thanks, John.

Thanks to Jane Ketcham and Nicolette Meister, former and current Collections Managers of the Logan Museum, and to Fred Burwell, Beloit College Archivist. Renee Braden, National Geographic Society; Sarah Demb, formerly of Harvard's Peabody Museum; Milt Gustafson, NARA-Archives II; Kathryn Hodson, University of Iowa; Don Lennon, East Carolina University; Robin Meador-Woodruff, Kelsey Museum of Archaeology; and Irena Murray, McGill University, each sent me a piece of this Osiris. Ann Owen Wearmouth and Jeanine Miedzwiecki, nature goddesses, gave me the suture to sew him back together. As always, parts are still missing.

The New York Times covered de Prorok's activities throughout the 1920s. The Times sent reporter Harold "Hal" Denny with de Prorok to cover the 1925 expedition. There are many articles about that trip and the subsequent scandal. A reference librarian at any major library can help you find these articles on microfilm or in electronic form. That same librarian can help you find his numerous magazine articles from his North African years, 1920-1930. Most of these are in Art and Archaeology Magazine. The fine librarians at the University of Idaho Library helped me find these and more occult Byronia. Standout help came from Jennifer O'Laughlin, Interlibrary Loan; and Donna Hansen (Ret.), Maria Jankowska, and Diane Prorak, Reference. Diane's family surname used to be Prorok; we could prove no family tie. Incidentally, Prorok, in Polish, means "prophet," as in "A prophet without honor."

Byron's own papers, films, and artifacts from his pre-World War II career were lost in France during that war. The loss of these materials compounds the tragedy of his life. If extant, they would show places and peoples that few but Byron saw fit to record.

Alonzo Pond's personal papers are in the State Historical Society of Wisconsin, in Madison. Records relating to his work for the Logan Museum are in the archives of the Logan Museum and the College Archives at Beloit College, as are Bradley Tyrrell's diary, scrap book, and "home movie" of the 1925 expedition. Additional materials, and copies of some of the materials mentioned above, are at the Human Studies Film Archives of the Smithsonian Institution, Suitland, Maryland, and in the Archives of the American Museum of Natural History in New York City.

THE NARRATIVE PRESS
HISTORICAL ADVENTURE & EXPLORATION

The Narrative Press publishes only true, first-person accounts of historical adventure and exploration. These books are first-hand journals, diaries, and memoirs, written by the explorers, mountain men, prospectors, scientists, spies, pioneers, lawmen, and fortune hunters themselves.

Most of these adventures are classics, about people and places now long gone. They take place all over the world – in Africa, South America, the Arctic and Antarctic, in America (in the Old West and before), on islands everywhere, and on the open seas.

Some of our authors are famous – Ernest Shackleton, Kit Carson, Henry Stanley, David Livingston, William Bligh, John Muir, Richard Burton, Elizabeth Custer, Teddy Roosevelt, Charles Darwin, Osborne Russell, John Fremont, Joshua Slocum, William Manley, Tom Horn, Philip St. George Cooke, Apsley Cherry-Garrard, Richard Henry Dana, Jack London, and Buffalo Bill, to name a few.

One thread binds all of our books: every one is historically important, and every one of them is fascinating.

Visit our website today. You can also call or write to us for a free copy of our printed catalogue.

THE NARRATIVE PRESS
P.O.BOX 2487
SANTA BARBARA, CALIFORNIA 93120 U.S.A.
(800) 315-9005
www.narrativepress.com